I0528142

Septuagint:

Paralipomena

Septuagint, Volume 9

SCRIPTURAL RESEARCH INSTITUTE
Published by Digital Ink Productions, 2024

Copyright

While every precaution has been taken in the preparation of this book, the publisher assumes no responsibility for errors or omissions, or for damages resulting from the use of the information contained herein.

Septuagint: Paralipomena

Second edition. March 2, 2024

The Septuagint was translated into Greek at the Library of Alexandria between 250 and 132 BC.

This English translation was created by the Scriptural Research Institute in 2019 through 2024, primarily from the Codex Vaticanus. Additionally, the Leningrad Codex, Aleppo Codex, and Targum on Chronicles were used for comparative analysis.

The image used for the cover is 'David and Saul' by Julius Kronberg, painted circa 1885. The original painting is currently located at the National Museum of Fine Arts (NM 1381), in Stockholm.

Table of Contents

TABLE OF CONTENTS

TABLE OF CONTENTS

TABLE OF CONTENTS

TABLE OF CONTENTS

TABLE OF CONTENTS

Forward

In the mid 3rd century BC, King Ptolemy II Philadelphus of Egypt ordered a translation of the ancient Israelite scriptures for the Library of Alexandria, which resulted in the translation of the Septuagint. It is generally accepted that there were several versions of the ancient Aramaic and Canaanite scriptures before the translation of the Septuagint. The two books of the Paralipomena were translated into Greek and added to the Septuagint around 180 BC, after a large number of refugees fled from the war in Judea and settled in Egypt. The two books of the Paralipomena were one book in the Masoretic Text: the book of Divrei-hayyamim. Subsequent Latin translations were renamed 1st and 2nd Chronikon by Jerome in the 5th century AD. Subsequent English translations of the Old Testament labeled these books as 1st and 2nd Chronicles.

The term Paralipomena (Παραλειπομένα), which means 'things left out,' is a general translation of Divrei-hayyamim (דִּבְרֵי־הַיָּמִים), which means 'things in the days.' The books are a collection of texts from various eras of Israelite history, spanning the era of the old Israelite Kingdoms, circa 1000 BC, through the Persian conquest, of circa 539 BC. Scholars have debated the origin of the books throughout their history, and there is no consensus within Rabbinical literature, Christian literature, or modern scholarship.

1

The general Rabbinical view is that the two books of Paralipomena were written by one author, as Divrei-hayyamim, and then translated into Greek. The dominant early-Christian view was that the books were written by Ezra the Scribe, circa 350 BC, however, this view was generally abandoned in Western Europe during the Protestant Reformation. Modern scholarly analysis has no consensus, however, the books do themselves indicate the eras they were compiled, nevertheless, the authors remain unknown.

Based on the references within 1st Paralipomenon, sections of the book were compiled sometime after 732 BC, when Tiglath-Pileser III deported the Reubenites, Gadites, and the people of Manasseh to other regions of the Assyrian Empire. The surviving Hebrew text of Divrei-hayyamim does, however, contain a reference to the Temple in Jerusalem as the 'Temple of the Gods' (בֵּית הָאֱלֹהִים), which means an Aramaic translation was likely made shortly after the Assyrian conquest of Samaria, before King Josiah's reforms in Judah circa 625 BC. Josiah is recorded as removing the idols of the gods from the temple, which had by all accounts been in the temple since it was built by King Solomon, other than during the reign of Josiah's grandfather Hezekiah.

1st Paralipomenon begins with the generations of the princes of Edom, indicating the text was complied in

Edom. It largely repeats the genealogy of nations found in Cosmic Genesis (Masoretic Bereshít) chapter 10, however, skips the genealogical lines that were not ancestral to the princes of Edom, indicating it was copied from Cosmic Genesis, and not a source for Cosmic Genesis. Like Bereshít, the Masoretic version found in Divrei-hayyamim includes Aramaic terms, supporting it being an Edomite version of the genealogy, which had been written in Aramaic between 715 and 706 BC.

Based on the references within 2nd Paralipomenon, sections of the book had to have been written at three different points in time, before being compiled sometime after 539 BC, when Cyrus the Great conquered the Babylonian Empire. The oldest section is the first 15 chapters, which differ from the middle section, chapters 15 through 22, in their identification of the Libyans. Chapter 12, which describes Shoshenq I's invasion, mentions that there were Libyans (Λιβυες / לוּבִים) and Kushites (Αιθιοπες / כוּשִׁים) in his army, along with another group called the Sukkiyyim (סֻכִּיִּים) in the Masoretic text, however, translated as 'troglodytes' (τρωγλοδυται) in Greek. Shoshenq I, known as Sousacim (Σουσακιμ) in the Septuagint and Shishak (שִׁישַׁק) in the Masoretic text, was the king of Egypt between circa 943 and 922 BC. He was also the founder of the Libyan (22nd) dynasty, which ruled parts of Egypt from 943 to 716 BC.

3

During Shoshenq I's reign, Egypt was reunited, and he was able to appoint his eldest son, Osorkon I, as son and heir to the throne, his second eldest Iuput as the High Priest of Amen at Karnak, and his third eldest son Nimlot, as head of the army. Late in his reign, after reuniting Egypt, Shoshenq I launched a massive invasion of Canaan, as recorded at Karnak, where towns throughout Canaan are listed as being conquered, including Meggido and Shechem. Remains of steles he erected have been found in Byblos in Lebanon and Meggido in northern Israel, confirming he was able to capture a large amount of Canaan. Jerusalem is not among the cities captured by Shoshenq listed at Karnak, which seems to confirm that King Rehoboam's massive tribute to Shoshenq saved the city.

The mention of Sukkiyyim (סֻכִּיִּים) serving in Shoshenq's army seems fairly conclusive evidence for the text being composed earlier than 672 BC, when the Neo-Assyrian empire forged an alliance with the Scythians. The Greeks translated the name Sukkiyyim as 'troglodytes' (τρωγλοδυται) instead of Scythicê (Σκυθικη), confirming that they read this as a reference to the people the Egyptians called the Såg (⌂ ⌂), not the Scythians, who the Egyptians called the Sek (⌂ ⌂). Troglodyte was a Greek term that referred to any group of cave-dwelling people. Greek geographers recorded the existence of several groups of troglodytes, along in Red Sea coast of Africa, in the Balkans, and Sahara.

The Troglodytes in question were likely the Troglodytes that Aristotle mentioned living in the upper Nile, and believed to have been the then mythical Pygmies. The Egyptians called these people the Såg (𓉐𓇌). It is not clear where they lived, however, the Egyptian name for their homeland was the 'Såg marshes' (𓉐𓇌𓆓), suggesting they came from the Sudd swampland of South Sudan, which was the farthest south the Greeks and Romans were able to explore the White Nile. This location is supported by the fact that they must have been located somewhere south of Kush, as they disappeared from Egyptian records after the Assyrians defeated the Kushites.

During the Persian era, the name Såg (𓉐𓇌) was often conflated with the Sek (𓏤𓏤𓇌), however, that name was adopted from the Persian name Saka (𓏤𓏤𓏤𓏤), their name for all Iranian nations to the north of the Persian empire, today known as Scythians in historical texts from their Greek name Scythicê (Σκυθικη). The Scythians did maraud through Samaria and Judea between 623 and 616 BC, when the Assyrian Empire was collapsing, however, that Scythian force was the enemy of Egypt, not their ally. In the 10th century BC, the Scythians were north of the Caucasus Mountains, and there is no evidence the Egyptians knew of them. Clearly the Greek translators in the 3rd century BC did not believe the reference was to the Scythians, or they would have used that name.

The fact that Hebrew translation retains a transliteration of the older Egyptian name of the Sags supports the text regarding Shoshenq I's invasion as being written before the Scythian alliance with the Neo-Assyrian Empire in 672 BC. After, that the similarly named Scythians quickly became important enough that the Judahite scribes would have specified that this was a different group. This suggests that the section dealing with Shoshenq I's invasion was written before the Kushite occupation of Egypt in 712 BC, however, that conclusion can only be reached by comparing the terminology used in the subsequent section regarding Orsokon I's invasion.

Osorkon is called Zare (Ζαρε) in the Septuagint and Zerach (זֶרַח) in the Masoretic text. He is listed as a king who attacked Judah after the time of Shoshenq I, however, is called a Kushite, instead of a Libyan or Egyptian. Additionally, the term 'Libyan' is missing from chapters 15 through 22 entirely, indicating that the text was likely composed between 712 and 673 BC, when the Empire of Kush ruled Egypt. During the era, the terms 'Egyptian' and 'Kushite' became synonymous, and are used interchangeably in other literature from the time. Before the Kushites took control of Egypt in 712 BC, no one would have referred to an Egyptian as a Kushite, and after Neo-Assyrian empire occupied Egypt in 673 BC, Egypt's independent identity was reestablished.

While the section dealing with Osorkon's invasion is entirely missing any direct references to either Libyans or Sags, there is a deviation between the Greek and Hebrew translations, as the Greek text has two references to what appear to be the Libyans, under their native name of Amazigh. The terms used in the Septuagint are Amazonis (Αμαζονεις), found in chapter 14, and Alimazonis (Αλιμαζονεισ) found in chapter 22. The second version of the word is clearly a Greek transliteration of the same name with the Aramaic word 1 (ᒪ), meaning 'to,' nevertheless, there are no equivalent terms found in the Masoretic text.

The Greek term is a variation of the name A'mazones (Ἄμαζόνες) referred to several tribes the Greeks recorded around the edge of their known world, with tribes listed from Eastern Europe to North Africa. Several notable Greek and Roman historians claimed that the Amazons ruled Egypt at some point in the past, however, originated in northwest Africa. The Greek name was probably a corruption of the name Amazigh

7

(oⵦoⵝⵥⵀ), the name the Libyan (Berber) tribes call themselves.

In the ancient Libyco-Berber script, it was recorded as Mzyɣ (ⵝⵣⵥ), which gave rise to the Classical Greek name Masices (Μάσικες) and Latin Mazices. The older script had no vowels in it, although the å (o) and ô (ⵀ) were added to the modern Tifinagh script to clarify pronunciation. Based on the ancient spelling of Mzyɣ (ⵝⵣⵥ), and the modern spoken forms, it is certain that their name would have been pronounced as something like Amazygh at the time. The Greek legends of female warriors are at least partially correct, as the ancient Amazigh were a gender neutral society, with both male and female warriors and monarchs.

In chapter 14, the word is used immediately after the battle between the Judahites and Osorkon's forces, when the Judahites plundered the livestock after the battle. The latter use was in reference to Arabs and another people attacking the Judahites a few decades later. The fact that the term was transliterated as 'Amazons' in Greek, and dropped entirely from the Hebrew translation, suggests it was not recognized by either group of translators in the Classical era. This was likely caused by the common written form of the name being Masices (Μάσικες) at the time. The final section, which includes the conquest of Babylon by Cyrus the Great in 539 BC, clearly must date to the Persian era.

The books of Paralipomena differ slightly from the later Masoretic book of Divrei-hayyamim, although the three are generally similar. In 200 BC, the Greek Kingdom of Syria under the Seleucid Dynasty took Judea from Egypt, and began an effort to Hellenize the Judeans, and effectively banned traditional Judaism. This Hellenizing activity was partially successful, creating the Sadducee faction of Judaism, however, it also led to the Maccabean Revolt in 165 BC, which itself created the independent Kingdom of Judea. This kingdom had a tenuous alliance with the Roman Republic until General Pompey conquered Syria into the Roman Republic in 69 BC. Pompey's goal was to liberate Greek-speaking communities in the Middle East that had fallen under the rule of non-Greeks when the Seleucids Syrian Empire had collapsed, and he carved up Judea, and Edom to the east, placing Greek-speaking cities under the protection of the Roman province of Syria. He also liberated several smaller communities that that Judea had occupied, granting them self-government, including Ashdod, Yavne, Jaffa, Dora, Marissa, and Samaria.

A series of wars, including both Julius Caesar's campaigns and a Parthian invasion, led to the weakening of the Hasmonean dynasty, and in 37 AD, the Roman

Senate appointed Herod the Great as King of the Jews. Herod's rule wasn't particularly popular, as he allowed the Romans to establish themselves within Judea, however, he did expand Judea, reintegrating the Greek and Samaritan cities, and annexing Galilee and Edom. When he died, his kingdom was divided between four successors, a situation that ended in 66 AD when the Romans conquered the region. An uprising in 120 AD led to the Jews being exiled from Judea, and the region became a Greco-Roman colony. In the wake of the Jews, the Samaritans rose in numbers, along with the Christians, once Christianity was legalized. Between 529 and 555 AD, the Samaritans revolted and were effectively annihilated by the Byzantine Empire.

The ancient documents found in the Caves in Qumran, more commonly called the Dead Sea Scrolls, span all of Judean history. Fragments of 2nd Paralipomenon have been found in Hebrew, but not Greek, Samaritan (Paleo-Hebrew), or Aramaic, implying that this book was primarily used by the Pharisee sect of Judaism at the time. These fragments date to between 37 BC and 44 AD, meaning the Septuagint contains the oldest surviving version of Paralipomena.

Outside of Judea, the Septuagint was the dominant form of Jewish scriptures across the Greek-speaking world, which by the beginning of the Christian era, extended from the Roman Empire in the west, to the Indo-Greek Kingdom in the east. Jewish traders had established small colonies along the trade routes of the Red Sea and the Indian Ocean, reaching as far south as Yemen, and as far east as southern India, and these Jews spoke Greek and used the Septuagint.

The earliest Christian Bibles all used the Septuagint, however, by the 4th century some Christian scholars were debating whether they should retranslate the Old Testament from the Hebrew translation the Jews were using, and some even suggested using the Samaritan version. Both suggestions were generally dismissed as heretical, as Jesus and the Apostles had quoted from the Septuagint, even though they had access to the Hebrew version then in use. This argument held in the west until the Middle Ages, when Catholic Bibles switched to the Masoretic Text. In the east, Orthodox Bibles continued to use the Septuagint, as they do today. To the south, the Ethiopian Tewahedo Church continued to use the Septuagint, and across Asia, the Thomas Christians and Nestorians continued to use the Septuagint. Only in Western Europe were the later Masoretic Text adopted, abandoning the more ancient Septuagint, on the assumption that the Jews had copied their texts more faithfully than the Greeks had translated them. This assumption carried forward into the Protestant Churches that broke off from the Catholic Church, and therefore almost all Protestant Bibles use the Masoretic Text for the basis of the Old Testament.

Unfortunately, this means that the earliest Christian writing is generally confusing and ignored by Protestants and Catholics. The earliest Christians of the first and second centuries quoted books that are no longer in the Bible, and as such, their writings are not always understood. Septuagint: Paralipomena is a 21st century translation aimed at correcting this problem.

One of the problems with academic translations of the Septuagint, is the use of unfamiliar names or terms, as the Septuagint was in Greek, and therefore many names are unrecognizable to modern readers. This project uses the more commonly understood Hebrew-derived names instead of their Greek translations, such as Canaan instead of Chanaan, and Melchizedek instead of Melchisedec. Common modern names are also used instead of either Greek or Hebrew terms when geographical locations are known, such as the archaeological name Uruk instead of the Greek Orech, or the Hebrew Erech, and the archaeological term Sumer instead of Shinar or Senar. While this could be argued as not being a correct academic procedure, it does fulfill the goal of making the translation easy to read and understand.

1ˢᵗ Paralipomenon: Chapter 1

Adam,[1] Seth,[2] Enosh,[3] Kenan, Mahalalel, Jared, Enoch, Methuselah, Lamech, Noah, (the sons of Noah were)[4] Shem, Ham, and Japheth.[5]

The descendants of Japheth were Cimmerians,[6] Magi,[7] Medes,[8] Ionians, (Alashiya,)[10] Tubal,[11] Mushki,[12] and Tiras.[13]

The descendants of Cimmeria were Ashkenaz,[14] Riphath,[15] and Torgama.[16]

The descendants of Ionians were Alashiya,[17] Tartessians,[18] Cypriots,[19] and Rhodians.[20]

The descendants of Ham were Khuz,[21] Egypt,[22] Put,[23] and Canaan.

The descendants of Khuz were Sabaeans,[24] Havilah, Shabwat,[25] the Ramanites,[26] and Sabacatha.[27] The descendants of the Ramanites[28] were Sheba[29] and Dedan.[30]

Khuz produced the Eridu,[31] he began to be a mighty ruler on the Earth.[32]

The descendants of Shem were Elam, Assur,[33] Arphaxad, Salah, Eber,[34] Peleg, Ragan, Serug, Nachon, Terah, and Abraham.

The sons of Abraham were Isaac and Ishmael.

These are their generations, the firstborn of Ishmael were Nebaioth, Kedar, Adbeel, Mibsam, Mishma,

Dumah, Moza, Hadad, Tehinnah, Jetur, Naphish, and Kedemah, these are the sons of Ishmael.

The sons of Keturah, Abraham's concubine, which she carried for him were Zimran, Jokshan, Medan, Midian, Ishbak, and Shage.

The sons of Jokshan were Daedan and Sheba.

The sons of Medan were Ephah, Epher, Enoch, Abida, and Eldaah, all these were the sons of Keturah.

Abraham fathered Isaac, and the sons of Isaac were Jacob and Esau.

The sons of Esau were Eliphaz, Reuel, Ishuai, Jaalam, and Korah.

The sons of Eliphaz were Tehinnah, Onam, Zephi, Gatam, Kedesh, Timna, and Amalek.

The sons of Reuel were Nahath, Zerah, Shemaiah, and Mizzah.

The sons of Seir were Lotan, Zobah, Zibeon, Rinnah, Dishon, Jazer, and Dishan.

The sons of Lotan were Hori and Heman. The sister of Lotan was Timna.

The sons of Zobah were Allon, Manahath, Ebal, Shephi, and Onam.

The sons of Zibeon were Aiah and Rinnah.

The son of Rinnah was Dishon.

The sons of Dishon were Amram, Eshban, Ithran, and Harran.

The sons of Jazer were Bilhan, Zavan, and Jakan.

The sons of Dishan were Uz and Aran.

These are their kings were Bela the son of Beor, and the name of his city was Dinhabah.

Bela died, and Joab the son of Zerah of Bozrah reigned in his place.

Joab died, and Hushim of the land of the Temanites reigned in his place.

Hushim died, and Hadad the son of Bered reigned in his place, who attacked Midian in the plain of Moab, and the name of his city was Gethaim.

Hadad died, and Samlah of Masrekah reigned in his place.

Samlah died, and Saul of Rehoboth by the river reigned in his place.

Saul died, and Baalhanan the son of Achbor reigned in his place.

Baalhanan died, and Hadad son of Bered reigned in his place, and the name of his city was Peor.

The princes of Edom were prince Timna, prince Aliah, prince Jether, prince Aholibamah, prince Elah, prince Pinon, prince Kedeshh, prince Tehinnah, prince Babsar, prince Magdiel, prince Zaphoin.

These were the princes of Edom.

1ˢᵗ Paralipomenon: Chapter 1 Notes

1 Codex Vaticanus: Adam (ⲁⲇⲁⲙ)

• Aleppo Codex: Ådm (אדם). Translation: man (or earth, soil, light brown, red

• Leningrad Codex: Adam (אָדָם). Translation: man (or earth, soil, light brown, red)

• Targum of Chronicles: Adam (אָדָם). Translation: man (or earth, soil, light brown, red)

2 Codex Vaticanus: Sêth (ⲥⲏⲑ)

• Aleppo Codex: št (שת). Translation: compensation (or placed, appointed)

• Leningrad Codex: Shet (שֵׁת). Translation: compensation (or placed, appointed)

• Targum of Chronicles: Shet (שֵׁת). Translation: compensation (or placed, appointed)

The name may be derived from the older Egyptian god Setekh (𓊖𓏏), which was also transliterated as Sêth (Σηθ) in ancient Greek, and Sêt (ⲥⲏⲧ) in Coptic, resulting in the other two common English names: Seth and Set. The oldest archaeological reference to Setekh is currently dated to the Amratian culture of pre-dynastic Egypt, generally dated to between 3790 and 3500 BC. Setekh was widely worshiped by Canaanites during the rule of the Hyksos dynasty, which ended around 1550 BC. At the time, he was viewed as the Egyptian version of the Amorite god Rašaap (𒀭𒊏𒊓𒀊), later known as Resheph (𐎗𐎌𐎔) in Ugaritic Canaanite, and Shed

(𓂋𓈙𓀭) in the New Kingdom Egyptian dialect spoken in Canaan. In the Masoretic Book of Job, Eliphaz referred to humanity as the 'sons of Resheph' (בני-רשף) instead of the 'sons of Adam,' and then used Šdy (שדי) as the name of his god, indicating that Shaddai was the iron age name of Resheph among the Israelites.

In the Eblaite texts, generally dated to the 3rd millennium BC, Rašaap's wife was the Amorite earth goddess Adamma, who continued to be worshiped by Hurrians, and was mentioned as the name of the earth goddess of the Israelites in Masoretic Numbers. Resheph's Babylonian counterpart was the war god Nergal, who was also married to the earth goddess dietyEreshkigal (𒀭𒊩𒌆𒆠𒃲), and associated with sunset during the Old Babylonian era. This indicates that Resheph was the Amorite version of Baal Shalim, the Canaanite god of the sunset and great dragon (galactic Great Rift), who was also married to Asherah, a Canaanite goddess of the earth and fertility during the bronze age, whose sacred oak trees were used as important grave markers.

If the origin of the name 'Seth' in this verse was a Middle Egyptian translation of an older Akkadian text, it must have taken place before the fall of the Hyksos dynasty, or the name would have been updated to Shed, and then Shaddai. Nergal's father was generally viewed as being Ellil, however, in the Old Babylonian Myth of Nergal and Ereshkigal, he referred to Ia (𒄿𒀀) as his father. Ia was the Old Akkadian replacement of the older Sumerian god Enki, whose name meant 'Earth Lord,' suggesting that the origin of this genealogy was a

Sumerian text about Ān (God), Enki (Adam/land), and Nergal (Seth), before being updated Middle Egyptian.

Nevertheless, Setekh was nothing like Nergal or Resheph before the Hyksos dynasty, suggesting that Setekh was a Hyksos era replacement of Osiris, his brother, who was virtually identical to Nergal, as god of death and rebirth. Before the Hyksos occupied Egypt, and again afterward, Osiris was viewed as the husband of Isis, who was also viewed as an earth and fertility goddess, like Asherah. Under Hyksos rule, Osiris place was usurped by his brother Setekh, who was viewed as the husband of Isis, and therefore the substitution of Setekh would have made sense under Hyksos rule.

In the Middle Egyptian version of the story, the older Sumerian Debate Between Sheep and Grain appears to have been synchronized with the Old Egyptian conflict of Setekh and Heru-ur (Horus the Elder), in which Setekh killed Heru-ur, creating the story of Cain and Abel. Setekh and Heru-ur were the older siblings of Osiris, who, along with Isis, were all viewed as the creation of Atum. Again, this melding of Sumerian and Old Egyptian mythology could only have taken place earlier than the Hyksos dynasty, as during the Hyksos dynasty Setekh replaced Osiris, and by the new Kingdom Heru-ur had been forgotten.

3 Codex Vaticanus: Enôs (ЄΝѠϹ)

- Aleppo Codex: Ånwš (אנוש). Translation: mortal man

- Leningrad Codex: Enosh (אֱנֹושׁ). Translation: mortal man

- Targum of Chronicles: Enosh (אֱנֹושׁ). Translation: human

4 Codex Vaticanus: Nôe. Huioe Nôe (ΝѠЄ·ΥΙΟΙΝѠЄ). Translation: Noah. Sons of Noah

- Aleppo Codex: Nh (נֿנ). Translation: rest

- Leningrad Codex: Noach (נֹח). Translation: rest

- Targum of Chronicles: Nach (נֹח). Translation: peace

The Septuagint adds a pause in the list, specifying that Shem, Ham, and Japheth were the sons of Noah, while the Masoretic version of the list simply continues the list, treating Shem, Ham, and Japheth as successive generations. This name Noah may be derived from the Middle Egyptian name Nww (𓈖𓅱𓅱). Nww was a Middle Egyptian variant of the name of the god Nu, the personification of the primordial waters, as Noah is not a Mesopotamian name, yet the story appears to be based on the older story of Ziusudra, found in several ancient Sumerian texts, including the Eridu Genesis, the Death of Gilgamesh, and the Poem of Early Rulers, most of which are dated to the 3rd millennium BC. In the Instructions of Shuruppak, he was listed as Zin-Suddu, the last king of Shuruppak before the flood that drowned the city.

Sedimentary strata from Shuruppak, Uruk, Kish, and other sites, have been radiocarbon dated to circa 2900 BC, indicating that was the time frame of the flood in question. If the name Noah is based on the Egyptian name Nww, it suggests a Middle Egyptian book of Noah earlier than 1550 BC.

5 Codex Vaticanus: Iapheth (ιΑφεθ)

- Aleppo Codex: Ypt (יפת)

- Leningrad Codex: Yefet (יֶפֶת)

- Targum of Chronicles: Yafet (יָפֶת)

Iapheth / Yefet has been considered a Canaanite variant of Iapetus (Ιαπετος) since at least the Classical Era, as recorded by Josephus in the 1st century. Iapetus was the Titan who created humans in Greek mythology.

6 Codex Vaticanus: Gamer (ΓΑΜΕΡ)

- Aleppo Codex: Gmr (גמר)

- Leningrad Codex: Gomer (גֹּמֶר)

- Targum of Chronicles: Gmer ... {s"å ... Afrika...} afarkevayathon ... Afkikei {s"å Garmanaya ...} (... ס"א ... גְמֵר { אַפְרְכְוַיָתְהוֹן ... אַפְקִיקֵי {ס"א גֵּרְמַנְיָא ...} אַפְרִיקָא...}). Translation: Gmer ... {alternate: ... Africa ...} their province was ... Afkiki {alternate: Germany ...}

This term was widely debated for over 1500 years, until the deciphering of Akkadian cuneiform in the past century. In the 1ˢᵗ century, the Jewish historian Josephus claimed the Gomer were the Galatians, which would make them Gauls, as the Galatians were Gauls who emigrated to Anatolia in the 3ʳᵈ century BC. In the early 3ʳᵈ century, the Christian theologian Hippolytus of Rome reported that Gomer was the ancient Cappadocian civilization near where the Galatians settled. Near the end of the 4ᵗʰ century, the Christian scholar Jerome claimed that Gomer were the Celts, likely a reinterpretation of Josephus. Around the same time, the Jewish Bereshít Rabbah was composed, in which Rabbi Samuel ben Ammi claimed Gomer was Germania.

After cuneiform was deciphered, and the Assyrian annals were studied, it became clear that Gomer was a reference to the ᵏᵘʳGimirrāya (𒆳𒄖𒈪𒊏𒀀𒀀), who the Greeks knew as the Cimmerios (Κιμμεριος), and the Armenians knew as the Gamirkô (Գամիրք). The Cimmerians were an ancient Indo-Iranian tribe that lived north of the Black Sea in modern Ukraine and southern Russia. They were driven south out of Europe into Anatolia and settled in the region of Cappadocia.

7 Codex Vaticanus: Magôg (ＭＡＧＯＧ)

• Aleppo Codex: Mgwg (מגוג)

• Leningrad Codex: Magog (מָגֹוג)

• Targum of Chronicles: Magog ... {sʺå ... Garmaya ...} afarkevayathon ... Garmanaya {sʺå ... Gittayah ...} (... מָגֹוג

{גְּתִיָה} ... ס"א {גֶּרְמַנְיָא ... אַפַרְכְּוָיַתְהוֹן ... גֶּרְמָנְיָא ... ס"א} ... גֶּרְמַיָא ... ס"א}).
Translation: Magog ... {alternate: ... Garma ...} their province
was ... Germany ... {alternate: ... Gatae ...}

The meaning of Magog has been disputed since the Greco-Roman era, as the term is used in Israelite texts referring to both a tribe and a group of priests or sorcerers. This usage is identical to the use of the term Magos (Μαγος) in Greek literature from the era, which was both the name of a Medo-Persian tribe, and a priestly caste. The Greek term is based the name Mguš (⸗𐎶𐎦𐎢) used in Persian cuneiform during the Achaemenid Empire, however, the earlier Persian spelling in Elamite cuneiform was Makuuka (𐎶𐎠𐎣𐎢𐎢𐎣). The archaic pronunciation may have been maintained in the Israelite texts in order to avoid seeming rebellious during the Medo-Persian era when the Magi were the official priesthood of the Median and Persian monarchs.

8 Codex Vaticanus: Madae (ⲘⲀⲆⲀⲓ)

• Aleppo Codex: Mdy (מָדַי). Translation: Medes

• Leningrad Codex: Madai (מָדַי). Translation: Medes

• Targum of Chronicles: Madai ... {s"å ... Chemada'ei...} afarkevayathon ... Hamda'ei {s"å hamren} (... מָדַי {ס"א ... {...חֲמָדָאֵי). אַפַרְכְּוָיַתְהוֹן ... הַמְדָאֵי {ס"א הַמְרֶן}). Translation: Medes... {alternate: ...Hamadan...} their province was ... Hamadan ... {alternate: ... Hamran ...}

9 Codex Vaticanus: Iôyan (ⲓⲱⲨⲀⲚ)

- Aleppo Codex: Ywn (יון)

- Leningrad Codex: Yavan (יָוָן)

- Targum of Chronicles: Yavan ... {s"å ... Mokedoneya ...} afarkevayathon ... Mokedonaya ... {s"å ... Ovisus ...} (... יָוָן {ס"א ... מוֹקְדוֹנְיָא ...} {אַפַרְכְּוַיָתְהוֹן ... מוֹקְדוֹנַיָא ... {ס"א ... אוֹבִּיסוֹס ...}. Translation: Ionia ... {alternate: ... Macedonia ...} their province was ... Macedonia ... {alternate: ... Ephesus ...}

The Hebrew term is a transliteration of the early Aramaic name Yawna (יונ^), and Neo-Assyrian name Iauna (𒅀𒌑𒈾), both meaning 'Ion.' The Neo-Assyrian and Aramaic words are accepted as being transliterations of the archaic Greek Iawôn (Ιαϝων), the name of a Greek patriarch who the Ionian Greek tribes were believed to descend from. Ionian Greeks primarily lived in Ionia, a region of western Anatolia. The term was in common use during the era of the Neo-Assyrian empire for 'Greeks' when pluralized into Yawnayīn (יונ^י^), which was adopted into Late Egyptian as the word Wynn (𓍯𓏭𓈖𓈖𓂜) meaning 'Greek,' which continued to be used in Coptic in the Classical era as Ouainin (Oⲩⲁⲓⲛⲓⲛ) and Ouenin (Oⲩⲉⲓⲛⲓⲛ).

As both the Greek and Hebrew transliterations are ultimately derived from a term that has a more common spelling in English, the more common name Ionians is used.

10 Codex Vaticanus: Elisa (ⲉⲗⲓⲥⲁ)

- Aleppo Codex: name missing from verse

- Leningrad Codex: name missing from verse

- Targum of Chronicles: name missing from verse

Elisa / Ålyšh is not mentioned in the Masoretic text at this point, only in the following list of the sons of Iôyan / Ywn. This deviation is also found in the parallel verse in Cosmic Genesis Chapter 10, indicating that this genealogy was copied from Cosmic Genesis. As it ends with the princes of Edom, it likely originated in Edom, probably after the Babylonian conquest of Judah.

For information on Alashiya, please see note 17.

11 Codex Vaticanus: Thobel (ⲑⲟⲃⲉⲗ)

- Aleppo Codex: Tbl (תבל)

- Leningrad Codex: Tuval (תֻבָל)

- Targum of Chronicles: Tuval ... {s"å ... Yattinya ...} afarkevayathon ... Ytinaya ... {s"å ... Ytanayah ...} (ס"א) ... תוּבָל {... יְתַנְיָה ... ס"א} ... יָתִינְיָא ... אַפְרְכְּוָיַתְהוֹן {... יַתִּינְיָא ...}.
Translation: Tabal {alternate: ... Bithynia ...} their province was ... Bithynia ... {alternate: ... Bithynia ...}

Tabal was an early iron age kingdom in southeast Anatolia. It was conquered by the Neo-Assyrian Empire in 713 BC, around the time the genealogy of nations was added, after entering into an anti-Assyrian alliance with the Mushki and the city of Carchemish.

12 Codex Vaticanus: Mosoch (ᴍocoх)

• Aleppo Codex: Mšk (מֶשְׁךְ)

• Leningrad Codex: Meshech (מֶשֶׁךְ)

• Targum of Chronicles: Meshech ... {s"å ... Oseya ...} afarkevayathon ... Mosaya ... {s"å ... Mosayah ...} (... ס"א} ... מֶשֶׁךְ {... אוֹסְיָא). אַפַרְכְוָיַתְהוֹן ... מוֹסְיָא ... {ס"א ... מוֹסָיַה ...}
Translation: Meshech ... {alternate: ... Ossetia ...} their province was ... Mysia ... {alternate: ... Mysia ...}

The Muški (𒈟𒄧𒅗𒂊) were recorded in Neshite (Hittite) and Assyrian records as invading northeast Anatolia during the bronze age collapse, however, they were repulsed, and initially settled in the region of modern Georgia. Later the tribe divided into two tribes, and one migrated to Cilicia, settling around Tabal. In the era of the Neo-Assyrian Empire, they were recorded in the annals of Urartu as the Muškini (𒈟𒄧𒅗𒂖𒌅), while the Greeks later called them the Moschoi (Μοσχοι). Josephus identified the Mosoch as the Moschoi in the 1st century, which is generally accepted today, however, was heavily debated during the Medieval era, with European scholars identifying Mosoch with variety of locations, including France, Britain, and Moscow.

13 Codex Vaticanus: Thiras (ⲑⲓⲣⲁⲥ)

- Aleppo Codex: Tyrs (תִּירָס)

- Leningrad Codex: Tiras (תִּירָס)

- Targum of Chronicles: Tiras ... {s"å ... Turkeya ...} afarkevayathon ... Tarkei ... {s"å ... Tarkei ...} (... תִּירָס {ס"א ... אַפַרְכְּוַיָתְהוֹן ... תַּרְקֵי ... {ס"א ... תַּרְקֵי ...}). Translation: Tiras ... {alternate: ... Turkey ...} their province was ... Thrace ... {alternate: ... Thrace ...}

The location of Thiras/Tiras has been debated for millennia. In the Second Temple Era Book of Jubilees, the descendants of Tiras had four large lands in the sea, possibly a reference to the Etruscans, who controlled the Tyrrhenian (Etruscan) Sea before the rise of the Carthaginian, Greek, and Roman empires, as the Tyrrhenian Sea is surrounded by Sicily, Sardinia, Corsica, and the Italian peninsula.

In the first century AD, Josephus claimed Tiras was the ancestor of the Thracians in the Balkan Peninsula. In the Talmud's Yoma tractate Tiras is identified as the ancestors of the Persians, however, this may simply be a conflation with the early dynastic Persian king Teispes (𒌑𒅖𒁔𒅖𒉿𒅖). In the medieval Jewish Yosippon, Tiras was identified as the ancestor of the Kievan Rus. Since the deciphering of Egyptian hieroglyphs, the dominant theory turned to them being the Turshå (𓏏𓂋𓈙𓅱), generally anglicized as Teresh, one of the sea peoples who attacked Egypt during the bronze age collapse. The Teresh are often identified with the

'Tyrrhenians,' however, according to Strabo, Tyrrhenian was simply the Greek name of the Etruscans.

The Etruscans called themselves the Rassena (ᴠᴠᴠᴇsᴠᴘ), and the name 'Etruscan' was ultimately derived from the early Greek name for them Tyrsênoe (Τυρσηνοι), essentially meaning 'tower people,' as their cities were built on hills. This means that any identification of the Rassena and Turshå based on the later Greek term Tyrsênoe, is entirely anachronistic. If any of the sea peoples were the Rassena, they were likely the Wåshåshå (𓂧𓈖𓈖𓈖), generally anglicized as Weshesh, as the Egyptians had difficulty transliterating foreign words that involved the R sound. Since the deciphering of Akkadian cuneiform, and then the Neshite (Hittite) language in the past century, an alternate interpretation of the Turshå has emerged, as the Neshites referred to their neighbors to the northwest as Taruiša (𒋫𒊒𒄿𒊭).

A similar term for the people from the region has been found in Mycenaean Linear-B as Toroja (𐀵𐀫𐀊). As this is the same location as the later Greek legends about Troy (Τροία), and the names are clearly similar, Taruiša and Toroja are viewed as alternative ways of writing Troy. Given that the other locations in this list are mostly in Anatolia, the Aegean, or the Black Sea, and Tyrs (תירס) appears to be a transliteration of Taruiša (𒋫𒊒𒄿𒊭), the name Troy is used in this translation.

14 Codex Vaticanus: Aschanaz (ᴀᴄxᴀɴᴀz)

- Aleppo Codex: Åšknz (אשכנז)

- Leningrad Codex: Ashkanaz (אַשְׁכְּנַז)

- Targum of Chronicles: Ashkenaz ... {s"å ... Asya ...} afarkevayathon Asaya (אַשְׁכְּנַז ... {ס"א ... אָסְיָא ... אַפַרְכְּוָיַתְהוֹן} אָסְיָא). Translation: Ashkanaz ... {alternate: ... Asia} their province was Asia

The earliest records of the Aschanaz date to the Neo-Assyrian era, when the Cimmerians invaded the Urartu, and were repulsed by the Áškuzai (𒅖𒆪𒍝𒀀𒀝), which Armenian historians have accepted as the earliest reference their ancestors arriving in Urartu. As the Armenians were established in the region by the beginning of the Persian era, this interpretation does seem likely, however, the Urantians continued to be the dominant culture until the Neo-Babylonian era.

The report regarding the Cimmerian (𒁹𒄖𒈪𒊏𒀀𒀀) invasion of Urartu was from the reign of Sargon II, and along with other reports show a series of invasionary migrations of the Cimmerians as the Scythians pushed them south into the Armenian Highlands and northern Anatolia. These reports are dated to between 720 and 714 BC, during the early years of Sargon II, which, combined with the subsequent scribal note about Kalhu being the capital city, indicate that the genealogies of nations was likely added between 720 and 705 BC.

15 Codex Vaticanus: Eriphath (ЄΡЄΙΦΛΘ)

• Codex Alexandrinus: Riphath (ΡΙΦΛΘ)

• Aleppo Codex: Dyft (דִיפַת)

• Leningrad Codex: Difat (דִיפַֿת)

• Targum of Chronicles: Difat ... {s" ... Farkevi ...} afarkevayathon ... Farsavev ({... פַּרְכְּוִי ... ס"א} ... דִיפַת אַפַרְכְּוָיַתְהוֹן ... פַּרְסְוֵוִי). Translation: Difat ... {alternate: ... Hyrcania ...} their province was ... Farsavev (generally thought to represent the ancestral homeland of the Persians, somewhere in Central Asia)

The Greek name is not a transliteration of the Hebrew Dyft (דיפת), but the Aramaic Ryft (ריפת), meaning 'Iberia.'

16 Codex Vaticanus: Thorgama (ΘΟΡΓΛΜΛ)

• Aleppo Codex: Twgrmh (תוֹגַרמה)

• Leningrad Codex: Togarmah (תוֹגַרְמָה)

• Targum of Chronicles: Togarmah ... afarkevayathon ... Varberaya (תוֹגַרְמָה ... אַפַרְכְּוָיַתְהוֹן ... בַּרְבְּרִיָא). Translation: Togarmah ... their province was ... Barbary

The location is generally considered unknown. The author of the Targum of Chronicles interpreted Togarmah as Garama, an ancient Libyan city in southern modern Libya. Barbary was the ancient Roman name for North Africa west of Egypt, where the Amazigh (Berber) tribes lived. The Romans conquered Garama in 202 AD.

17 Codex Vaticanus: Elisa (ελιϲα)

- Aleppo Codex: Ålyšh (אלישה)

- Leningrad Codex: Elishah (אֱלִישָׁה)

- Targum of Chronicles: Alsu ... {s"å ... Elisha Alas ...} (אַלְסוּ ... {ס"א ... אֱלִישָׁא אֱלָס...}). Translation: Alsu ... {alternate: ... Elisha Alas ...}

The Kingdom of Alashiya was mentioned in many texts from the late bronze age. Based on chemical analysis of the clay tablets sent from Alashiya to other kingdoms during the bronze age, is believed to have been in southern Cyprus, spanning the region where the cities of Kalavasos (Καλαβασός) and Alassa (Άλασσα) are located today. The name of Alassa is probably descended from Alashiya. During the bronze age, the Egyptian court corresponded with the civilization using the Akkadian cuneiform script, in which it was known as Alašiia (𒀀𒆷𒅆𒅀), which is probably the closest to its native pronunciation. The Mycenaean Greeks of the era recorded the name as Arasijo (𐀀𐀨), while the Ugaritic Canaanites recorded the name as Ålṯy (𐎀𐎍𐎘𐎊).

18 Codex Vaticanus: Tharsis (θαρϲιϲ)

- Aleppo Codex: Tršyš (תרשישה)

- Leningrad Codex: Tarshishah (תַרְשִׁישָׁה)

- Targum of Chronicles: Tarsus ... {s"å ... Tarsas...} (טַרְסוּס ... {ס"א ... תַרְסַס...}). Translation: Tarsus ... {alternate: ... Tarsus ...}

1st PARALIPOMENON: CHAPTER 1 NOTES

This civilization was also recorded in the Neo-Assyrian records of Esarhaddon as Tarsisi (𒋻𒋙𒋛), where it was used as a metaphor for the most distant known land. It was also recorded as Tršš (𐤕𐤓𐤔𐤔), on the Phoenician language Nora Stone discovered in Sardinia, which is also believed to date to the era. It was later known as Tartêssos (Ταρτησσος) in Greek myths, however, was no longer viewed as being a known land that people sailed to. In the 4th century BC, Aristotle identified Tartêssos as being on the Atlantic coast of Iberia. Around the same time, the Greek geographer and explorer Pytheas reported that the civilization once existed on the Baetis River, the modern Guadalquivir River in southwest Spain.

While the location of the civilization has been debated for thousands of years, it is commonly accepted as being the 'Tartessian' culture of southwest Iberia. During the 1900s, extensive remains of a bronze age civilization were discovered by archaeologists working ins southwest Spain and southern Portugal. This civilization existed between approximately 1900 and 700 BC. It controlled extensive mines in southwest Iberia, which produced both metals and gemstones, and it also appears to have traded extensively with both the Phoenicians and Celts. The script used by the Tartessians was similar to the Greek script, which may have been why they were included in this list of nations.

19 Codex Vaticanus: Citioe (ΚΙΤΙΟΙ). Translation: Citians

- Aleppo Codex: Ktym (כתים). Translation: Cypriots

- Leningrad Codex: Kittim (כִּתִּים). Translation: Cypriots

- Targum of Chronicles: Italyon ... {s"å ... Achzavayah...} (אִיטַלְיוֹן ... {ס"א ... אַכְזַוְיָה...}). Translation: Italy ... {alternate: Achzabiah}

Kt (𐤊𐤕) and Kty (𐤊𐤕𐤉) were the Canaanite and Aramaic names of Cyprus during the Neo-Assyrian and Neo-Babylonian era, based on the name of the ancient Cypriot city-state, subsequently known as Cition (Κίτιον) in Greek. The name was recorded as Kåtjåy (𓎡𓍿𓇋𓅱) in Egyptian records from the New Kingdom Era in the late Bronze Age, and appears to have survived the bronze age collapse better than most states. Based on the Akkadian cuneiform correspondences between Egypt and Cyprus during the Amarna Period, it is assumed that they were Semitic, however, this list places them with the Greeks and other Mediterranean peoples, indicating that the list was composed after the Greeks had become dominant in Cition.

20 Codex Vaticanus: Rodioe (ΡΟΔΙΟΙ). Translation: Rhodians

- Aleppo Codex: Rwdnym (רודנים). Translation: Rhodians

- Leningrad Codex: Rodanim (רוֹדָנִים). Translation: Rhodians

- Targum of Chronicles: Dardenaya: {s"å ... Dardenaya Ridom vaChamein ve'Anteyuch} (דַּרְדְּנַיָּא ... {ס"א ... דַּרְדְּנַיָּא רְדוֹם)

(וְחֲמֵין וְאַנְטְיוּךְ). Note: Dardania {alternate: Dardania, Rhodes, and Chamein and Antioch

The Greek and Masoretic translations match in this verse, however, do not match in the parallel verse in Cosmic Genesis, where Dodanim (דֹּדָנִים) is used in the Masoretic Text. The Greek Rhodioe referred to people from the island of Rhodes (Ῥόδος), as did the Hebrew Rodanim (רוֹדָנִים), while the Hebrew Ddnym was a plural of Dodona (Δωδώνη). There were two Dodonas in Greece, one in Epirus, and the other in Thessaly near Mount Olympus. Both were oracle sites of Zeus.

The name Rwdnyn (𐤓𐤅𐤃𐤍𐤉𐤍) was almost certainly in the Aramaic text the Greek translated, as the letters representing D and R are almost identical in Phoenician (𐤃 and 𐤓), Aramaic (𐡃 and 𐡓), and Hebrew (ד and ר), meaning the error could have originated in several scripts, however, as the Greek translation uses the name Rhodians in both places, the error was likely made when the translation of the genealogy was translated into Hebrew.

21 Codex Vaticanus: Chous (ΧΟΥΣ)

- Aleppo Codex: Kwš (כוש)

- Leningrad Codex: Kush (כּוּשׁ)

- Targum of Chronicles: Arav (עֲרָב). Translation: Arab

The Septuagint generally uses the name 'Aethiopia' where the Masoretic Text uses 'Kush,' however, as it is interpreted here as the name of a patriarch, as transliterated directly, confirming that the Aramaic text did use the same name as the Hebrew.

In the context of the genealogy of nations, this 'Kush,' who is the father of the Southern Semites, well as Eridu, can only be interpreted as the Sumerians, who are otherwise conspicuously absent from the genealogy of nations. According to Assyriologists, the Elamites were the ethnolinguistic group most closely related to the Sumerians, and therefore, like the Southern Semites and Elamite, the Sumerians were probably dark skinned, which was called kusaaa (𒆪𒊍𒈨) in Assyrian. The translator of the Targum of Chronicles recognized that this could not have been a reference to the nation in Sudan, and therefore substituted 'Arab,' however, the Sumerians were not Arabs. The name Khuz used as a transliteration for 'Chous,' derived from the name Khuzistan, the modern Iranian region that derives its name from the ancient Assyrian word 'kusaaa.'

22 Codex Vaticanus: Mestraem (ΜΕϹΤΡΑΙΜ)

• Aleppo Codex: Mṣrym (מצרים). Translation: Egypt (or Egyptians)

• Leningrad Codex: Mitzrayim (מִצְרַיִם). Translation: Egypt (or Egyptians)

• Targum of Chronicles: Mitzrayei (מִצְרָיֵי). Translation: Egypt

The Canaanite form of the words meaning 'Egypt,' and 'Egyptian,' were both spelled as plural form of Mṣr, as there were two lands of Egypt, Upper and Lower Egypt. The plural form was used in Ugaritic as Mṣrm (𐎎𐎕𐎗𐎎), Phoenician as Mṣrm (𐤌𐤑𐤓𐤌), Aramaic as Mṣryn (𐡌𐡑𐡓𐡉𐡍), and Hebrew as Mṣrym (מצרים). The origin of the name 'Mṣr' isn't clear, however, it was used as a singular form in Akkadian as Muṣur (𒈬𒋩), and later East Semitic languages as Miesri (𒈫𒂖𒅖𒊒𒄿), and continues to be a singular form in Arabic as Miṣr (مِصر). In the names comprising the genealogy of nations, there are the names of mythical patriarchs, countries, and tribes, and therefore it is not clear if the original list referred 'Egypt,' or 'Egyptians,' or if a mythical patriarch was actually being referred to. It is possible the author was thinking of Menes (𒈨𒉌) the quasi-mythical founder of Egypt. The Egyptians had legends of Menes, however, to date no clear evidence has been found confirming his existence.

It is theorized the legends of Menes may have been based on early dynastic king Narmer, who is known from the archaeological record, but not the king lists, and if so, it is plausible that Muṣur is also a corruption of his name.

If so, it probably started as the Sumerians transliterating Nar-mer (𒊏) as Amar-mu (𒀫𒈬), and the Akkadians reversing the logograms to Mu-amar (𒈬𒀫), as they did with some other names. As the Sumerian AMAR (𒀫) logogram was commonly pronounced as ṢUR in Akkadian, it would have resulted in the name Mu-ṣur. While the Greeks may have interpreted the name as a literal patriarch, the genealogy of nations appears to be more figurative, attempting to explain which nations descended from which other nations, and so the name 'Egypt' is imported from the Masoretic Text.

23 Codex Vaticanus: Phoud (ϕογⲁ)

- Aleppo Codex: Pwt (פוט)

- Leningrad Codex: Put (פּוּט)

- Targum of Chronicles: Alyeyachrak (אַלְיְיַחְרַק)

The Pyt (𓂝𓏲𓏏𓏤𓏥) were a Libyan tribe recorded in Egyptian records of the 22ⁿᵈ dynasty, who appear to have lived in Cyrene before the Greeks colonized the region in 631 BC. The annals of Nebuchadnezzar II report that in 567 BC, the Greeks from Putu, called the Putu Iáaman (𒐊—𒆠𒂍 𒌋𒐉) in Neo-Babylonian, were fighting in the Egyptian army. The Canaanites appear to have been trading with the Pàdu for centuries before the Greeks established a colony in Cyrene, and so the name Pwt (𐤐𐤅𐤕) appears to have been applied to the entire Libyan (Berber) population of northern Africa. Cyrene was known as the the satrapy of Putāya (𒌋𒌋𒐕𒐊𒐉𒐊) when it was part of the Persian Empire.

24 Codex Vaticanus: Saba (cⲁⲃⲁ)

- Aleppo Codex: Sbå (סבא)

- Leningrad Codex: Seva (סְבָא)

- Targum of Chronicles: Sinida'ei (סִינִידָאֵי). Translation: Sind

This reference, along with the Sabatha / Savta / Savtah (Σαβαθα / סַבְתָּא / סַבְתָּה) and Sabacatha / Savtecha (Σαβακαθα / סַבְתְּכָא), appear to be references to Sabaean tribes of southern Arabia. Based on them all being descends of Kush, it appears the other Sabaean tribes were not viewed as being descendants of Saba at the time. Sbâ (ሐⵏሐ), generally anglicized as Saba, was a kingdom in modern western Yemen, based out of its capital of Mryb (ⵏⵦ)ⵝ). Based on the archaeological evidence, the Sabaeans formed a small kingdom around Mryb circa 1200 BC, and by 800 BC dominated western Yemen.

25 Codex Vaticanus: Sabatha (ⲤⲀⲂⲀⲐⲀ)

- Aleppo Codex: Sbtå (סבתא)

- Leningrad Codex: Savta (סַבְתָּא)

- Targum of Chronicles: Semada'ei (סְמָדָאֵי)

This is probably a reference to a kingdom based out of Šbwt (ⵝ) in central modern Yemen. The root terms Sb (ⵝ) and Šb (ⵏሐ) were used by most of the tribes of southern Arabia, making identification of the specific land difficult, however, the first century AD guide to the Indian Ocean known as the Periplus of the Erythraean Sea, a major trading center named Sabbatha (Σαββαθα) was recorded as being in the interior of modern Yemen. Pliny the Elder's Natural History, written at approximately the same time, called the city Sabota (Σαβοτα), and claimed it was the capital city of the Adramitae Sabaean tribes, which is considered to be the origin of the regional name Hadhramaut (حَضْرَمَوْث) for modern eastern Yemen.

The ruins of Šbwt, generally anglicized to Shabwat or Shabwa, have been studied by archaeologists in the past century, and were not inhabited by the similarly named Sabaeans to the west, but a different South Semitic people. Sabaean and Hadramitic writing have been found in the remains of the city, but mostly Hadramitic. Based on the archaeological evidence, the city of Shabwat existed from the 1300s BC until the 200s AD.

26 Codex Vaticanus: Regma (ρεϲμα)

- Aleppo Codex: Rômå (רֶעְמָא)

- Leningrad Codex: Ra'ma (רַעְמָא)

- Targum of Chronicles: Lova'ei (לוֹבָאֵי). Translation: Libya

This location is somewhat debated, however, generally accepted as a reference to the Ramanitês (Ραμανίτης) tribe, who Pliny the Elder later recorded in the first century AD as living in the region of modern UAE. Around the same time, Strabo referred to them as the Rammanites (Ραμμανίτες) in his *Geographica*.

27 Codex Vaticanus: Sabacatha (ϹΑΒΑΚΑΘΑ)

- Aleppo Codex: Sbtkå (סבתכא)

- Leningrad Codex: Savtecha (סַבְתְּכָא)

- Targum of Chronicles: Zinna'ei (זִינְנָא)

This may be the same location later recorded as Sachalitês (Σαχαλίτης), in the first century AD guide to the Indian Ocean known as the Periplus of the Erythraean Sea. The exact location of Sachalitês is debated as different Classical era authors placed it either east or west of Suagros, another trading port generally accepted as being in the region of Dhofar, Oman. In Claudius Ptolemaeus' 2nd century Geography, it was simply known as Sachlê (Σαχλη), and placed to the east of Suagros, in the bay where islands of Kurya Murya lay, which is also in Dhofar.

28 Codex Vaticanus: Regma (ΡΕΓΜΑ)

- Aleppo Codex: Rômå (רעמא)

- Leningrad Codex: Ra'ma (רְעְמָא)

- Targum of Chronicles: Mavreyatinos (s"a Zemarged) (מַוְרְיָאטִינוֹס {ס"א זְמַרְגֵד}). Translation: Mauritania {alternate: Zemarged}

The Targum of Chronicles includes two alternate readings, neither of which mirror the earlier mention of Lova'ei (לוֹבָאֵי). Mauritania was the name of an Amazigh (Berber) kingdom in the western Atlas mountains, known in Latin as

Mauretania, and Greek as Mauroúsii (Μαυρούσιοι). Zamarged was a country somewhere in the Indian Ocean, likely in Madagascar or the Zambezi-Kafubu region. Neither translation makes much sense geographically, as the child nations were both located in southern Arabia.

In 2nd Paralipomenon chapter nine, the Targum of Chronicles uses the similar name Zemargad (זְמַרְגַד) as a translation for the land that the queen of Saba (Σαβα) / Sheva (שְׁבָא) came from. As the Canaanites dominated the trade between the Mauretanians and the Mediterranean, and the Mauretanians were a gender neutral society, with both kings and queens ruling at different times, it is plausible that a Mauretanian queen visited Solomon, however, no other ancient sources list Mauretania as the land the queen came from.

Medieval Aramaic sources occasionally reference a land of Zemarged somewhere in the Indian Ocean, and are often assumed to be referring to region along the Zambezi-Kafubu river system of Mozambique and Zambia, as the Kafubu region is the largest sources for emeralds in the eastern hemisphere. Trade in the Kafubu region flowed along the Zambezi river into the Indian Ocean, as it later did for the Zimbabwe civilization to the south. However, if the Medival Arameans were referring to Kafubu as Zemarged, it indicates the Greeks had already established trade with the region by the Greco-Roman era, as the Arameans used the Greek name for the civilization. Alternative suggestions for the location of Zemarged include Madagascar, which fell under the control of the Indonesians during the Greco-Roman era, or other smaller emerald mining locations in Somalia, Tanzania, or Mozambique.

The name does not appear in the 1st century AD Periplus of the Erythraean Sea, a Greek description of the trade routes and ports in the Red Sea and Indian Ocean. The African ports listed only go as far south as Rhapta, believed to have been the Rufiji River region of modern Tanzania, where a Greoco-Roman era trade port has been excavated. The book does claim it is possible to sail south around the continent and return to the Mediterranean that way, indicating that there had been attempts to find more trading partners to the south. In the book, the name of East Africa is Azania, and therefore, if Smáragdos was applied to a region the Greeks later open trade with, it must have been south of Azania, in the region of Madagascar, or the Zambezi-Kafubu region. If the translator of Scroll A was using the name Zemarged in this context, it suggests that he viewed Sheba as a sub-Saharan African state along the east coast of Africa, however, the queen was described as traveling over land to Jerusalem, making this interpretation unlikely.

The medieval Arabs called the region south of Azania the Sea of Zinj, meaning 'sea of Blacks,' while the medieval Persians knew the regions collectively as Zangbâr, meaning 'Black land.' This suggests that the Aramaic term Zemarged was already antiquated by the medieval era, and implies that Scroll A was translated during the early Christian era.

29 Codex Vaticanus: Saba (ⲤⲀⲂⲀ)

- Aleppo Codex: Šbå (שְׁבָא)

- Leningrad Codex: Sheva (שְׁבָא)

- Targum of Chronicles: Demeregad (דִמְרְגַד)

This is a reference to the city that the queen who visited Solomon came from, however, it is not clear from the context where it was. Saba, and most of the southern coast of Arabia appears to have been established. The following reference to Dedan, along the incense roads from the southern coast to Canaan, suggests that this Sheba may likewise have been somewhere along the interior roads of Arabia, possibly in the Asir Mountains in the southwest, north of the kingdom of Saba, but south of Dedan.

30 Codex Vaticanus: Oydadan (ⲞⲨⲆⲀⲆⲀⲚ)

- Aleppo Codex: Ddn (דדן)

- Leningrad Codex: Dedan (דְדָן)

- Targum of Chronicles: Mezag (מְזָג). Translation: Amazigh (Berber)

The Greek and Hebrew texts deviate here, however, the parallel verse in Cosmic Genesis chapter 10 uses the name Dadan (Δαδαν), supporting the Masoretic name. Dedan was the name of a kingdom in the Hijaz mountains during the 7th and 8th centuries BC.

31 Codex Vaticanus: Chous egennêsen ton Nebrôd (ⲭⲟⲩⲥ ⲉⲅⲉⲛⲛⲏⲥⲉⲛ ⲧⲟⲛ ⲛⲉⲃⲣⲱⲁ). Translation: Chous generated (or produced) the Nebrod

- Aleppo Codex: Kwš yld åt Nmrwd (כוש ילד את נמרוד).
Translation: Kush carried (in Aramaic) the Nmrwd

- Leningrad Codex: Chush yalad et-Nimrovd (כּוּשׁ יָלַד אֶת־נִמְרוֹד). Translation: Kush boy the-Nimrovd

- Targum of Chronicles: Arav olid yat Nimrod (עֲרָב אוֹלִיד יַת נִמְרוֹד). Translation: Arab produced the Nimrod

The Masoretic version of this name deviates between Nimrod (נִמְרֹד) / Nmrd (נמרד) in Bereshít, and Nimrod (נִמְרוֹד) / Nmrwd (נמרוד) in Divrei-hayyamim, while the Septuagint uses Nebrôd (Νεβρωδ) in both Cosmic Genesis and 1ˢᵗ Paralipomena. Based on the description of this 'patriarch,' it has to be a reference to the original Sumerian city of Eridu, which was spelled as Nunᵏⁱ (𒉣𒆠) in Sumerian. Nunᵏⁱ can be variously interpreted as 'noble place,' or 'ruling place,' or, more relevantly 'first place.' The Akkadians pronounced Nunᵏⁱ as Eridu, which may have also been the latter Sumerian nickname of Nunᵏⁱ as the Sumerian word for 'copper' was urudu (𒊨), and the city's primary industry was working the copper from the trade on the Euphrates. The copper trade in Eridu was so important to the Sumerian civilization that the Sumerian name of the Euphrates was ⁱᵈBuranun (𒀀𒌓𒁺𒉿𒉣), believed to mean 'source of copper.'

In this section of text, it appears the author misunderstood a cuneiform text about Eridu, which had the name both written as Nun^{ki} (卌⟨⟩) and then spelled phonetically as Eriduᵏⁱ (⟩卌⟨⟩). This would have been necessary after the rise of the Old Babylonian Empire, as the name 'great place' (卌⟨⟩) was appropriated by Babylon. This also explains why Babylon (Βαβυλων / בָּבֶל) is listed as being in Sumer, as Nunᵏⁱ by itself meant 'Babylon' by the time the Aramaic translation was made. Transliterated directly into Aramaic, the name Nunᵏⁱ Eriduᵏⁱ (卌⟨⟩ ⟩卌⟨⟩) is Nnrd (נברד), which can itself by transliterated into Greek as Nebrôd by misreading the second Aramaic N (נ), as the similarly shaped Aramaic B (ב), or into Hebrew as Nmrd, by misreading the second N (𐤍) in the Phoenician script as a similarly shaped M (𐤌). As 1ˢᵗ Paralipomena appear to have originated in an Edomite text, the deviation in Divrei-hayyamim must have originated when a Judahite translation of the genealogy of nations in Bereshít was translated into Edomite, which interpreted the pronunciation of the difficult to pronounce Nmrd (𐤌𐤓𐤃𐤍) as Nmrwd (𐤃𐤅𐤓𐤌𐤍). As this 'patriarch' has to have originally been Eridu, the name 'Nimrod' is restored to 'Eridu.'

32 Codex Vaticanus: gigas cynêgos epi tês gês (ΓΙΓΑϹ ΚΥΝΗΓΟϹ ΕΠΙ ΤΗϹ ΓΗϹ). Translation: Gigas hunter (or seeker) on the earth (or land)

• Aleppo Codex: gbwr bårs (גבור בארץ). Translation: powerful (or strong) on earth (or land)

- Leningrad Codex: gibbovr ba'aretz (גִּבּוֹר בָּאָרֶץ).

Translation: powerful (or strong) on earth (or land)

- Targum of Chronicles: merod kodam Yya (מְרוֹד קֳדָם יְי).

Translation: rebel before Yahw

In Greek mythology, a Gigas was one of the Gigantes, an ancient tribe or demigods who challenged the rule of the gods. The Greek translators appear to have interpreted this story as being much the same, using the word gigas essentially as 'apostate.' This verse differs from the parallel verse in Cosmic Genesis, which labeled 'Nebrôd' as an 'apostate of the lord,' while this verse labels him as an 'apostate hunter.'

The Masoretic version is quite different, as it indicates the Aramaic term would have been gbrå (ܐܬܒܓ), meaning 'husband,' 'owner,' or 'ruler.' This means the term translated from the Akkadian cuneiform precursor text would have been lugal (𒈗), also meaning 'lord,' 'master,' or 'king.' As the Greek and Hebrew texts are different, however, both appear to be derived from an Akkadian version of the story, the Akkadian meaning is followed.

According to various king lists recovered from archaeological digs in Iraq, Eridu was the original 'capital city' of Sumer, before a great flood destroyed all the cities of Sumer. Based on the archaeological evidence uncovered to date, the city was founded around 5400 BC, and reached a peak around 3000 BC. After the massive flood of 2900 BC, it went into decline and was almost abandoned by 2000 BC, when King Amar-Sin of Ur began a massive reconstruction of the city, culminating in the unfinished Ziggurat of Amar-Sin. Therefore, the era when Eridu would have dominated Mesopotamia, would have probably been around 3000 BC. However, this verse is about the rebuilding of Eridu, which took place under Amar-Sin circa 2000 BC.

33 Codex Vaticanus: Assour (ᴀᴄᴄoϒᴘ)

• Aleppo Codex: Åšwr (אשׁור)

• Leningrad Codex: Ashur (אַשּׁוּר)

• Targum of Chronicles: Attura'ei (אַתּוּרָאֵי). Translation: Assyrians

ᵈⁱᵉᵗʸAššur (𒀭𒀸) was the national god of Assyria, normally anglicized as Ashur, while Aššurᵏⁱ (𒀸𒋗𒆠) was the original capital city of Assyria, normally anglicized as Assur. Assyrian historical records do not record the city of Assur being founded by someone called Ashur, instead recording that the ancestors of the Assyrians original lived in tents, and later settled in a Hurrian city called Baltil, which later became Assur after the Assyrians became dominant. This suggests the Aramaic author viewed the god Ashur as having been the patriarch of the Assyrians, who had later been deified.

34 Codex Vaticanus: Eber (ϵвϵρ)

- Aleppo Codex: Ôbr (עבר)

- Leningrad Codex: Ever (עֵבֶר)

- Targum of Chronicles: Ever (עֵבֶר)

If Eber was the name of a town or tribe like most of the names on the list, it was likely the city of Íabru (𐎹𐎀𐎁𐎗) that King Amar-Sin of Ur destroyed in the Syrian desert circa 2000 BC. In Israelite mytho-history, Eber was the ancestor of all of the Hebrews, also translated as Eberites. The word Ôbr (עבר) means 'crosser' suggesting the city was at an oasis one would stop at when crossing the desert.

1st Paralipomenon: Chapter 2

These are the names of the sons of Israel: Reuben, Simeon, Levi, Judah, Issachar, Zebulun, Dan, Joseph, Benjamin, Naphtali, Gad, and Jezer.

The sons of Judah were Er, Onam, and Shelah. These three were carried for him by the daughter of Shage the Canaanite woman.

Er, the firstborn of Judah, was wicked before the Lord,[1] and he killed him. Tamar his daughter-in-law carried for him Pharez and Zerah. All the sons of Judah were five.

The sons of Pharez were Hezron and Hamul. The sons of Zerah were Zabdi and Ethan, and Heman, and Calcol, and Dara, in all five.

The sons of Carmi were Sacar the troubler of Israel, who was disobedient in the cursed thing.

The son of Ethan was Azariah.

The sons of Hezron who were born to him were Jerahmeel, and Ram, and Caleb.

Ram fathered Amminadab, and Amminadab fathered Nahshon, chief of the house of Judah.

Nahshon fathered Salma, and Salma fathered Boaz, and Boaz fathered Obed, and Obed fathered Jesse.

Jesse fathered his firstborn were Elihu, Amminadab was the second, Shimma the third, Nethanel the fourth, Raddai the fifth, Ozem the sixth, and David the seventh. Their sister was Zeruiah, and another was Abigail.

The sons of Zeruiah were Abishai, Joab, Asahel, three in total.

Abigail carried Amasa, and the father of Amasa was Jethro the Ismaelite.

Caleb the son of Hezron took Azubah as a wife, and Jerioth and these were her sons were Jesher, Shobab, and Ardon.

Azubah died, and Caleb took for himself Ephratah, and she carried for him, Hur.

Hur fathered Iri, and Iri fathered Bezaleel.

After this Hezron went in to the daughter of Michri the father of Gilead, and he took her when he was sixty-five years old, and she carried for him Serug.

Serug fathered Jair, and he had twenty-three cities in Gilead. He captured Geshur and Aram, the towns of Jair from them, with Kenath and its towns, sixty cities. All these belonged to the sons of Michri the father of Gilead.

After the death of Hezron, Caleb traveled to Ephratah, and the wife of Hezron was Abihud, and she carried for him Ashur the father of Tekoa.

The sons of Jerahmeel the firstborn of Hezron were, the firstborn Ram, Bunah, Aram, Ashan his brother. Jerahmeel had another wife, and her name was Atarah, she is the mother of Ozom.

The sons of Ram were the firstborn of Jerahmeel were Maaz, Jamin, and Eker.

The sons of Ozom were Shemaiah and Jehoadah.

The sons of Shemaiah were Nadab and Abishur.

The name of the wife of Abishur was Abihail, and she carried him for Ahban and Molid.

The sons of Nadab were Seled and Appaim, and Seled died without children.

The son of Appaim was Ishi, and the son of Ishi was Sheshan, and the son of Sheshan was Dadaiah.

The sons of Dadaiah were Shemaiah, Jether, Jonathan, and Jether died childless.

The sons of Jonathan were Peleth and Zaza.

These were the sons of Jerahmeel.

Sheshan had no sons, but had daughters. Sheshan had an Egyptian slave whose name was Jarha. Sheshan gave his daughter to Jarha, his slave, as a wife, and she carried for him Attai.

Attai fathered Nathan, and Nathan fathered Zabad, and Zabad fathered Ephlal, and Ephlal fathered Obed.

Obed fathered Jehu, and Jehu fathered Azariah.

Azariah fathered Helez, and Helez fathered Eleasah, and Eleasah fathered Sisamai, and Sisamai fathered Shallum, and Shallum fathered Jekamiah, and Jekamiah fathered Elishua, and Elishua fathered Ishmael.

The son of Caleb the brother of Jerahmeel, was Mareshah his firstborn, who was the father of Ziph, and the son of Mareshah was the father of Hebron.

The sons of Hebron were Korah, Tappuah, Rekem, and Shammua.

Shammua fathered Raham, the father of Jorkoam, and Jorkoam fathered Shemaiah. His son was Maon, and Maon is the father of Bethzur.

Ephah the concubine of Caleb carried Haram, Moza, and Gazez. The sons of Jahdai were Regem, Jotham, Zuar, Pelet, Ephah, and Sagae.

Caleb's concubine Maachah carried Sheber and Tirhanah. She also carried Sagae the father of Madmannah, and Sheva the father of Machbenah, and the father of Gibea. The daughter of Caleb was Shuah.

These were the sons of Caleb, the son of Hur, the firstborn of Ephratah: Zobah the Abbot of the village of groves,[2] Solomon the Abbot of the temple of Lahem,[3] and Arim the Abbot of the fortified temple.[4]

The sons of Zobah, the Abbot of the village of groves, were Haroeh, Aesi, Ammanith, Umasphae, of the cities of Jair, Ithrites, Puhites, Shumathites, Mishraites. From these came the Zareathites and the sons of the Eshtaulites. The sons of Solomon[5] of the Temple of Lehem were Netophathi, Ataroth of the house of Joab and half of the family of Malathi and Esari. The families of the scribes living in Jabesh were the Tirathites, Shimeathites, and Suchathites, these are the Kenites that came from Hama, the father of the house of Rechah.

1ˢᵗ Paralipomenon: Chapter 2 Notes

1 Codex Vaticanus: cyriou (ⲕ**Ⲩ**ⲣⲓⲟⲨ). Translation: lord (or main, chief, dominant, master)

- Aleppo Codex: Yhwh (**יהוה**)

- Leningrad Codex: Yehvah (יְהֵוָה)

- Targum of Chronicles: Yya (יְיָ). Translation:Yahw

The differences between the Greek and Hebrew translations appears to be related to the Hasmonean Redaction of circa 140 BC, which replaced ådn (ⲁⲆⲚ), meaning lord in Aramaic, with Yhwh (יהוה).

2 Codex Vaticanus: patêr Cariathiarim (ⲡⲁⲧⲏⲣ ⲕⲁⲣⲓⲁⲑⲓⲁⲣⲓⲙ). Translation: father of Cariathiarim

- Aleppo Codex: åby qryt yôrym (**אבי קרית יערים**). Translation: father (or abbot) of village (in Aramaic) of groves (or forest, thicket)

- Leningrad Codex: avi kiryat ye'arim (אֲבִי קְרֵית יְעָרִים). Translation: father (or abbot) of village (in Aramaic) of groves (or forest, thicket)

- Targum of Chronicles: rabbehon dekiryat ye'arim (רַבְּהוֹן דְקִרְיַת יְעָרִים). Translation: rabbi (or great one) of village of groves (or forest, thicket)

According to various ancient texts, including the book of Joshua (chapter 15, and 1ˢᵗ Paralipomenon (chapter 13, this village was also known as Baalia / Baalah. The reference to the groves, is likely a reference to the oak trees that were planted by worshipers of Baal and Asherah. 'Village of Groves' appear to be a cryptic interpretation reference to Baalia, indicating that this section of 1st Paralipomenon was written after the reforms of King Josiah, who banned the worship of Baal, and tore down the Asherah trees, circa 625 BC.

3 Codex Vaticanus: Baethlaem (ΒΑΙΘΛΑΕΜ)

• Aleppo Codex: byt lhm (בית לחם). Translation: house (or temple, abode) of Lehem

• Leningrad Codex: veit-Lachem (בֵּית־לָחֶם). Translation: house (or temple, abode) of Lehem

• Targum of Chronicles: veit Lechem (בֵּית לֶחֶם). Translation: house (or temple, abode) of Lehem

4 Codex Vaticanus: Baethgedôr (ΒΑΙΘΓΕΔΩΡ)

• Aleppo Codex: byt gdr (בית גדר). Translation: house (or temple, abode) of Gader (or wall, compound)

• Leningrad Codex: veit-Gader (בֵּית־גָּדֵר). Translation: house (or temple, abode) of Gader (or wall, compound)

• Targum of Chronicles: veit Gader (בֵּית גָּדֵר). Translation: house (or temple, abode) of Gader (or wall, compound)

Gdr (𐤂𐤃𐤓) was the Phoenician word meaning 'walled enclosure.' Similar words with the same meaning were also used in Egyptian: imdjer (), Atlas Tamazight: agadir (oⲬoⲖⲤO), and Arabic: qādis (قَادِس), which confirm its meaning in this text. The fortified temple in question is likely the same fortified temple of the god of the covenant, mentioned in Judges.

5 Codex Vaticanus: Salômôn (ⲤⲀⲖⲰⲘⲰⲚ)

- Aleppo Codex: Šlmå (שלמא)

- Leningrad Codex: Salma (שַׂרְמָא)

- Targum of Chronicles: Shalma (שַׂלְמָא)

1st Paralipomenon: Chapter 3

These were the sons of David that were born to him in Hebron. The firstborn was Amnon who was carried by Ahinoam the Jezraelitess. The second was Daniel, by Abigail the Carmelitess. The third was Absalom, the son of Maachah, the daughter of King Talmai of Geshur. The fourth was Adonia the son of Haggith. The fifth was Shephatiah, the son of Abital. The sixth was Ithream, born of Eglah his wife. Six were born to him in Hebron, where he reigned seven years and six months, and then he reigned thirty-three years in Jerusalem.

These were born to him in Jerusalem: Shammua, Shobab, Nathan, and Solomon, all four of Bathshua the daughter of Ammiel. Also Ibhar, Elishua, Eliphalet, Nogah, Nepheg, Japhia, Elishua, Eliada, and Eliphalet, nine in all. All these were the sons of David, besides the sons of the concubines, and there was also Tamar their sister.

The descendants of Solomon were Rehoboam, Abihud his son, Asa his son, Jehoshaphat his son, Joram his son, Ahaziah his son, Jeush his son, Amaziah his son, Azariah his son, Jotham his son, Ahaz his son, Hezekiah his son, Manasseh his son, Amon his son, Jeshaiah his son.

The sons of Jeshaiah were Johanan the firstborn, Jokim the second, Zedekiah the third, Shallum the fourth.

The son of Jokim was Jeconiah his son, and Zedekiah his son.

The sons of Jeconiah were Assir, Salathiel his son, Melchiram, Pedaiah, Shenazar, Jecamiah, Hoshama, and Nedabiah.

The sons of Pedaiah were Zerubbabel and Shimei.

The sons of Zerubbabel were Meshullam and Hananiah, and Shelomith was their sister.

Hashubah, Ohel, Berechiah, Hasadiah, and Asobed, five in all.

The sons of Hananiah were Pelatiah, and Jesaiah his son, Rephaiah his son, Arnan his son, Obadiah his son, Shechaniah his son.

The son of Shechaniah was Shemaiah, and the sons of Shemaiah, were Hattush, Joel, Bariah, Noadia, and Shaphat, six in total.

The sons of Noadia were Eliehoenai, Hezekiah, and Azrikam, three in total.

The sons of Eliehoenai were Hodaiah, Eliashib, Pelaiah, Akkub, Johanan, Dalaiah, and Hanani, seven in total.

1st Paralipomenon: Chapter 4

The sons of Judah: Pharez, Hezron, Carmi, Hur, Zobah, Reaiah his son.

Zobah fathered Jahath.

Jahath fathered Ahumai and Lahad.

These are the generations of the Zorathites.

These are the sons of Etam: Jezreel, Ishma, and Idbash, and their sister's name was Hazelelponi, Penuel the father of Gedor, and Jazer the father of Osan. These are the sons of Hur, the firstborn of Ephratah, the fore-father of Bethlehem.

Asur the father of Tekoa had two wives, Aoda and Thoada. Aoda carried for him Ochaia, Ephal, Tehinnah, and Haahashtari, all these were the sons of Aoda. The sons of Thoada were Zereth, Jezoar, and Ethnan.

Coz fathered Anub, and Zobebah, and the progeny of the brother of Rechah, the son of Harum. Jabesh was more famous than his brothers, and his mother called his name Jabesh, saying, "I have born as a sorrowful one."

Jabesh called on the god in Israel, saying, "If only you would bless me, and enlarge my frontiers, and that your hand might be with me, and that you would make me know that you will not grieve me!" God granted him all that he asked.

Caleb the father of Shuah fathered Michri, he was the father of Eshton. He fathered Bethrapha, Paseah, and Tehinnah, the founder of the city of Irnahash, the brother of Eselom the Kenezite. These were the men of Rechah.

The sons of Kedesh were Othniel and Shiphi, and the sons of Othniel were Hathath.

Meonothai fathered Ophrah, and Shiphi fathered Joab, the father of Ageaddair, and they were artisans.

The sons of Caleb the son of Jephunneh were Iru, Elah, and Naam, and the son of Elah was Kedesh.

The sons of Aleel were Ziph, Ziphah, Tiria, and Asareel.

The sons of Ezra were Jether, Mered, Epher, and Jalon, and Jether fathered Madon and Shimei, and Jesba the father of Eshtemoa. His wife Adia carried Jared the father of Gedor, and Heber the father of Socho, and Jekuthiel the father of Zanoah.

These are the sons of Bithiah the daughter of Pharaoh, who Mered married. The sons of the wife of Hodiah, the sister of Naham, the father of Keilah, Garmite, and Eshtemoa the Nochathite.

The sons of Shimon were Amnon, Rinnah the son of Phana, and Inon, and the sons of Ishi, Zoan, and the sons of Zoab.

The sons of Shelah the son of Judah were Er the father of Lecah, and Laadah the father of Mareshah, and the descendants of the family of Ephrathabac belonged to the house of Ashbea, Jokim, and the men of Chozeba, and Jeush and Resheph, who lived in Moab, and he changed their names to Abederin and Athukiim. These are the potters who lived in Nataim and Gadira[1] with the king, and they grew strong in his kingdom and lived there.

The sons of Simeon were Nemuel, Jamin, Jarib, Zerah, and Saul, and his son Shallum, and his son Mibsam, and his son Mishma, and his son Hamuel, and his son Sabud, and his son Zakkur, and his son Shimei.

Shimei had sixteen sons, and six daughters, and his brothers did not have many sons, nor did all their families multiply like the sons of Judah. They lived in Beersheba, Moladah, Hazarshual, Bilhah, Ezem, Tolad, Bathuel, Hormah, Ziklag, Bethmarcaboth, and Hazarsusim, and the house of Baruseorim.

These were their cities until the time of King David. Their villages were Etam, Ain, Rimmon, Tochen, and Aesar, five cities. All their villages were around these cities, as far as Ba'al was their possession and their distribution.

Meshobab, Jamlech, Jeshaiah the son of Amaziah, Joel, Jehu the son of Hashabiah, the son of Shiphi, the son of Asiel, Eliehoenai, Jaakobah, Jeshohaiah, Asaiah, Jediael, Ishmael, Benaiah, Zina the son of Saphai, the son of Allon, the son of Jedaiah, the son of Shimri, the son of Shemaiah. These went by the names of princes in their families, and they increased abundantly in their fathers' households. They went to Gedor, to the east of the gorge,[2] looking for pasture for their livestock. They found abundant and good pastures, and the land before them was wide, and there was peace and quietness, for there were some of the children of Ham who lived there before.

These, who are written by name, came in the days of Hezekiah king of Judah, and they attacked the people's houses, and the Minaeans[3] whom they found there, and destroyed them until this day, and they lived in their place because there was pasture there for their livestock. Some of them, the sons of Simeon went to Mount Seir, in all five hundred men, and Pelatiah, Noadia, Rephaiah, and Uzziel the sons of Ishi, were their rulers. They slaughtered the remnant that was left of the Amalekites, on that day.

1st Paralipomenon: Chapter 4 Notes

1 Codex Vaticanus: Nataem cae Gadêra (ΝΑΤΑΙΜΚΑΙ ΓΑΔΗΡΑ). Translation: Nataem and Gadêra

- Aleppo Codex: Ntôym wGdrh (נטעים וגדרה). Translation: Ntôym and Gdrh

- Leningrad Codex: Neta'im uGederah (נְטָעִים וּגְדֵרָה). Translation: Neta'im and Gederah

The location is likely a reference to Khirbet Judraya and Beit Nattif west of Jerusalem.

2 Codex Vaticanus: Gae (ΓΑΙ)

- Aleppo Codex: gyå (גיא). Translation: valley (or gorge, ravine)

- Leningrad Codex: gaye (גָּיְא). Translation: valley (or gorge, ravine)

- Targum of Chronicles: cheilta (חֵילְתָא). Translation: hollow (or glen, ravine)

As the Greeks transliterated the word for gorge or valley, the Semitic word is restored in this translation.

3 Codex Vaticanus: Minaeous (ΜΙΝΑΙΟΥC). Translation: Minaeans

- Aleppo Codex: hmôynym [hmôwnym] (המעינים [המעונים]). Translation: the mayns (the mawns)

- Leningrad Codex: hamMe'inim K [hamMe'unim Q]
(הַמְּעִינִים כ וְהַמְּעוּנִים ק). Translation: the Meins (K) [the Meuns (Q)]

- Targum of Chronicles: merodei (מְרוֹדֵי). Translation: rebels

The Minaeans were an Arab tribe that settled in Yemen in the 9ᵗʰ century BC, and built the Ma'in civilization, which dominated Yemen until circa 150 BC. The Greek translation is clear, in that they interpreted the name in the text they translated as Minaean, however, the Hebrew term is generally debated as there are no records of conflict between Judah and Ma'in in the 7ᵗʰ century BC. The Targum of Chronicles interprets the word as 'rebels.'

1st Paralipomenon: Chapter 5

The sons of Reuben the firstborn of Israel (as he was the firstborn, but because of his going up to his father's couch, his father gave his blessing to his son Joseph, the son of Israel, and he was not considered as firstborn, as Judah was very mighty among his brothers, and was chosen to be a ruler out of them, but the blessing was Joseph's).

The sons of Reuben the firstborn of Israel were Enoch, Pallu, Hezron, and Carmi.

The sons of Joel were Shemaiah, and Benaiah his son, and the sons of Gog the son of Shimei. His son was Micah, and his son Recha, and his son Joel, and his son Baal, who King Tiglath-Pileser[1] of Assyria carried away captive. He was the chief of the Reubenites.

His brothers in his family, in their distribution according to their generations were, the chief Joel, and Zechariah, Bela the son of Azuz, the son of Shemaiah, the son of Joel. He lived in Aroer, and as far as to Nebo, and Baalmeon.

He lived eastward to the edge of the wilderness, from the river Euphrates, for they had a great deal of livestock in the land of Gilead. In the days of Saul, they made war on the travelers in the land, and they fell into their hands, all of them living in their tents east of Gilead.

1st PARALIPOMENON: CHAPTER 5

The Gadites lived near them in the land of Bashan near Salchah. Joel was the firstborn, and Shapham the second, and Jaanai the scribe, in Bashan.

Their brothers according to the houses of their fathers were Michael, Meshullam, Sheba, Jorai, Jachan, Zia, and Obed, seven in all. These are the sons of Abihail the son of Huri, the son of Idai, the son of Gilead, the son of Michael, the son of Jeshishai, the son of Jeddah, the son of Buz, who was the brother of the son of Abdiel, the son of Guni. He was chief of the house of their families. They lived in Gilead, in Bashan, and their villages, and in all the country around Sharon to the frontier. The counting of them all took place in the days of Jotham, king of Judah, and the days of Jeroham, king of Israel.

The sons of Reuben and Gad, and the half-tribe of Manasseh, mighty men carrying shields and sword and bending the bow, and skilled in war, were 44,760, going out to battle. They made war with the Hagarites, Jetur, Nephish, and Nodab, and they defeated them, and the Hagarites were given into their hands, they and all their tents, for they cried to God in the battle, and he listened to them because they trusted in him. They took captive their stores, five thousand camels, and two hundred and fifty thousand sheep, two thousand donkeys, and a hundred thousand men. Many fell dead because the war was from God.

They lived in their place until the captivity. The half-tribe of Manasseh lived from Bashan to Ba'al, Ermon, and Senir, and Mount Hermon, and they increased in Lebanon. These were the heads of the houses of their families, Epher, Ishi, Eliel, Jeremiah, Hodaviah, and Jediael, mighty men of valor, men of renown, heads of the houses of their families. But, they rebelled against the god of their fathers and went following the gods of the nations of the land, who God threw out from before them. The god in Israel stirred up the spirit of King Tiglath-Pileser[2] of Assyria, and the spirit of King Tiglath-Pileser of Assyria carried away Reuben and Gad, and the half-tribe of Manasseh, and brought them to Halah, Habor, and to the Khabur River, where they remain until today.[3]

1st Paralipomenon: Chapter 5 Notes

1 Codex Vaticanus: Thaglathphalnasar (ΘΑΓΛΑΘΦΑΛΝΑϹΑΡ)

- Aleppo Codex: Tlgt Plnåsr (תלגת פלנאסר)

- Leningrad Codex: Tillegat Pilne'eser (תִּלְגַת פִּלְנְאֶסֶר)

- Targum of Chronicles: Tilgat Pilne'eser (תִּלְגַת פִּלְנְאֶסֶר)

Tiglath-Pileser III was the ruler of the Assyrian Empire between 745 and 727 BC, who forged the Neo-Assyrian Empire.

2 Codex Vaticanus: Phalôch (ΦΑΛΩΧ)

- Aleppo Codex: Pwl (פול)

- Leningrad Codex: Pul (פּוּל)

- Targum of Chronicles: Pul (פּוּל)

Tiglath-Pileser III is the more common throne name of General Pulu, after he usurped the throne of Assyria in 745 BC.

3 This verse has to have been written after Tiglath-Pileser III deported the Reubenites, Gadites, and the people of Manasseh, circa 732 BC.

1st Paralipomenon: Chapter 6

The sons of Levi were Gershon, Kohath, and Merari.

The sons of Kohath were Amram, Izhar, Hebron, and Uzziel.

The sons of Amram were Aaron, Moses, Mariam.

The sons of Aaron were Nadab, Abihud, Eleazar, and Ithamar.

Eleazar fathered Phinehas.

Phinehas fathered Abishua.

Abishua fathered Bukki.

Bukki fathered Uzzi.

Uzzi fathered Zerahiah.

Zerahiah fathered Meraioth.

Meraioth fathered Omri.

Omri fathered Ahitub.

Ahitub fathered Zadok.

Zadok fathered Ahimaaz.

Ahimaaz fathered Azariah.

Azariah fathered Johanan.

Johanan fathered Azariah, who ministered as a priest in the temple that Solomon built in Jerusalem.

Azariah fathered Omri.

Omri fathered Ahitub.

Ahitub fathered Zadok.

Zadok fathered Shallum.

Shallum fathered Hilkiah.

Hilkiah fathered Azariah.

Azariah fathered Seraiah.

Seraiah fathered Jehozadak, and Jehozadak went into captivity along with Judah and Jerusalem under Nebuchadnezzar.

The sons of Levi were Gershon, Kohath, and Merari.

These are the names of the sons of Gershon: Libni and Shimei.

The sons of Kohath were Amram, Izhar, Hebron, and Uzziel.

The sons of Merari were Mahli and Mushi, and these are the families of Levi, according to their families.

To Gershon, to Libni his son was born Jahath his son, Zammath his son, Joab his son, Eri his son, Zerah his son, Jethri his son.

The sons of Kohath were Amminadab his son, Korah his son, Jezer his son, Elkanah his son, Ebiasaph his son,

Jezer his son, Tahath his son, Uriel his son, Uzziah his son, and Saul his son.

The sons of Elkanah were Amasai and Ahimoth.

Elkanah his son, Zophai his son, Cainaath his son, Elihu his son, Jeroham his son, Elkanah his son.

The sons of Samuel were Vashni the firstborn, and Abihud.

The sons of Merari were Mahli, Libni his son, Shimei his son, Uzza his son, Shammua his son, Angia his son, Asaiah his son. These were the men whom David set over the service of the singers in the Temple of the Lord when the box was at peace. They ministered in front of the tabernacle of witness playing on instruments until Solomon built the Temple of the Lord in Jerusalem, and they stood according to their order for their services.

These were the men that stood, and their sons, of the sons of Kohath. Heman the psalm singer, son of Joel, the son of Samuel, the son of Elkanah, the son of Jeroham, the son of Eliel, the son of Toah, the son of Zuph, the son of Elkanah, the son of Mahath, the son of Amasai, the son of Elkanah, the son of Joel, the son of Azariah, the son of Zephaniah, the son of Tahath, the son of Jezer, the son of Ebiasaph, the son of Korah, the son of Izhar, the son of Kohath, the son of Levi, the son of Israel.

His brother Asaph, who stood at his right hand, Asaph the son of Berechiah, the son of Shammua, the son of Michael, the son of Baaseiah, the son of Malchijah, the son of Ethni, the son of Zerah, the son of Adaiah, the son of Ethan, the son of Zimmah, the son of Shimei, the son of Jahath, the son of Gershon, the son of Levi.

The sons of Merari their brothers on the left hand. Ethan the son of Kishi, the son of Ibri, the son of Malluch, the son of Asebi, the son of Amaziah, the son of Bani, the son of Samaria, the son of Mahli, the son of Mushi, the son of Merari, the son of Levi.

Their brothers according to the houses of their fathers, were the Levites who were appointed to all the work of ministration of the tabernacle of the Temple of God. Aaron and his sons were to burn incense on the altar of whole burnt offerings, and the altar of incense, for all the ministry in the holy of holies, and to make atonement for Israel, according to all things that Moses the servant of God commanded.

These are the sons of Aaron were Eleazar his son, Phinehas his son, Abishua his son, Bukki his son, Uzzi his son, Shiphi his son, Meraioth his son, Omri his son, Ahitub his son, Zadok his son, Ahimaaz his son. These are their residences in their villages, in their coasts, to the sons of Aaron, to their family the Kohathites, for they had the lot. They gave them Hebron in the land of Judah, and its suburbs around it. But the fields of the city, and its villages, they gave to Caleb the son of Jephunneh. To the sons of Aaron, they gave the cities of refuge, including Hebron, and Libnah and her suburbs around it, and Selna, Eshtemoa, Jattir, Debir, Ashan, Bethshemesh, and their suburbs.

Of the tribe of Benjamin, were Geba, Alemeth, Anathoth, and their suburbs, and all their cities were thirteen, according to their families. To the sons of Kohath that were left of their families, there were given out of the tribe, namely, out of the half-tribe of Manasseh, by lot, ten cities. To the sons of Gershon according to their families, there were given thirteen cities of the tribe of Issachar, of the tribe of Jezer, of the tribe of Naphtali, of the tribe of Manasseh in Bashan. To the sons of Merari according to their families, there were given, by lot, twelve cities of the tribe of Reuben, of the tribe of Gad, and the tribe of Zebulun. So the Israelites gave to the Levites the cities and their suburbs.

They gave by lot out of the tribe of the children of Judah, and out of the tribe of the children of Simeon, and out of the tribe of the children of Benjamin, these cities which they call by name. To the members of the families of the sons of Kohath, there were also given the cities of their borders out of the tribe of Ephraim. They gave them the cities of refuge, Shechem and her suburbs in the Mountains of Ephraim, and Gezer, Jokmeam, Bethhoron, Ayalon, and Gathrimmon and her suburbs.

The half-tribe of Manasseh were Aner, Jemblaan, and their suburbs, to the sons of Kohath that were left, according to each family.

To the sons of Gershon from the families of the half-tribe of Manasseh, they gave Golan of Bashan, Hazeroth, and their suburbs.

Out of the tribe of Issachar: Kedesh, Daberath, Dabor, Ramoth, Anan, and their suburbs.

Of the tribe of Jezer: Mashal, Abdon, Hukok, and Rehob and their suburbs.

Of the tribe of Naphtali: Kedesh in Galilee, Hammon, Kirjathaim, and their suburbs.

To the sons of Merari that were left, they gave out of the tribe of Zebulun: Rimmon, Tabor, and their suburbs, out of the country beyond Jordan. Jericho west of the Jordan, out of the tribe of Reuben, Bezer in the wilderness, Jahzah, Kedemoth, Mephaath, and their suburbs.

Out of the tribe of Gad: Rammoth in Gilead, Mahanaim, Ezbon, Jazer, and their suburbs.

1st Paralipomenon: Chapter 7

In regards to the sons of Issachar, they were Tola, Puah, Jashub, and Shimron, four in all.

The sons of Tola were Uzzi, Rephaiah, Jeriel, Jahmai, Jemasan, and Samuel, chiefs of their fathers' houses belonging to Tola, men of might according to their generations. Their number in the days of David was twenty and two thousand and six hundred.

The sons of Uzzi were Izrahiah, and the sons of Izrahiah were Michael, Obadiah, Joel, and Ishiah, five in all, all rulers. With them, according to their generations, according to the houses of their families, were men mighty to set armies in a battle formation, thirty and six thousand, for they had multiplied their wives and children. Their brothers among all the families of Issachar, also mighty men, were eighty-seven thousand, this was the number of them all.

The Benjaminites were Bela, Becher, and Jediael, three in all. The sons of Bela were Ezbon, Uzzi, Uzziel, Jerimoth, and Iri, five in all, all heads of houses of families, mighty men, and their number was twenty and two thousand and thirty-four.

The sons of Becher were Zemira, Jeush, Eliezer, Eliehoenai, Omri, Jerimoth, Abihud, Anathoth, and Alameth. All these were the sons of Becher. Their number according to their generations, (they were chiefs of their fathers' houses, men of might), was 20,200.

The sons of Jediael were Bilhan, and the sons of Bilhan were Ishuai, Benjamin, Ehud, Chenaanah, Zethan, Tharshish, and Ahishahar. All these were the sons of Jediael, chiefs of their families, 17,200 warriors going out to war in strength, and Shuppim, Huppim, the sons of Ir, Hushim, whose son was Aher.

The sons of Naphtali were Jaasiel, Guni, Jezer, and Shallum, his sons, Bilhah his son. The sons of Manasseh and Azarel, who his Syrian concubine carried, and she carried to him also Michri the father of Gilead. Michri took a wife for Huppim and Shuppim, and his sister's name was Maachah, and the name of the second son was Zelophehad, and to Zelophehad were born daughters. Maachah the wife of Michri carried a son and called his name Pharez, and his brother's name was Sheresh, his sons were Ulam, and Rakem.

The son of Ulam was Badam. These were the sons of Gilead, the son of Michri, the son of Manasseh. His sister Hammoleketh carried Ishod, Abiezer, and Mahalah. The sons of Shemida were Ahian, Shechem, Likhi, and Anian.

The sons of Ephraim were Shuthelah, and Bered his son, and Tahath his son, Eladah his son, Tahath his son, and Zabad his son, Shuthelah his son, and Jazer, and Elead.

The men of Gath who were born in the land killed them because they went down to take their livestock. Their father Ephraim mourned many days, and his brothers came to comfort him. He went in to his wife, and she conceived and carried a son, and he called his name Beriah, because, he said, 'he was afflicted in my house.' His daughter was Zorah, and he was among those who were left, and he rebuilt Bethhoron the upper and the lower. The descendants of Uzzen were Sherah, and Rephah his son, Resheph and Telah his sons, Tahan his son. To Laadan his son was born his son Ammihud, his son Elishua, his son Nun, his son Jehoshua, these were his sons. Their possession and their homes were Bethel and her towns to the east of Naaran, west to Gezer, Shechem, as far as Gaza and her towns, as far as the borders of the sons of Manasseh, Bethshean, Taanach, Megiddo, Dor, and their towns. In this, the children of Joseph the son of Israel lived.

The sons of Jezer were Imnah, Isuah, Ishuai, Beriah, and Serah their sister.

The sons of Beriah were Heber and Malchiel, and he was the father of Birzavith.

Heber fathered Japhlet, Shamir, and Hotham, and Shage their sister.

The sons of Japhlet were Pasach, Bimhal, and Ashvath.

The sons of Shamed were Ahi, Rohgah, Jehubbah, and Aram.

The sons of Helem his brother were Zophah, Imna, Shelesh, and Amal.

The sons of Zophah were Suah, Harnepher, Suda, Beri, Imrah, Bashan, Oa, Shemaiah, Shilshah, Ithran, and Beera.

The sons of Jether were Jephunneh, Pispah, and Ara.

The sons of Ulla were Arah, Hanniel, and Rezia.

All these were the sons of Jezer, all heads of families, choice, mighty men, chief leaders. Their number for battle-formation was 26,000 men.

1st Paralipomenon: Chapter 8

Benjamin fathered Bela, his firstborn, and Ashbel his second son, Aharah the third, Nohah the fourth, and Rapha the fifth.

The sons of Bela were Addar, Gera, Abihud, Abishua, Naaman, Ahijah, Gera, Shephuphan, and Huram.

These were the sons of Ehud.

These are the heads of families of those that live in Geba, and they moved them to Manahath, Naaman, Ahiah, and Gera, he moved them, and he fathered Uzza and Jachicho.

Saarin fathered children in the plain of Moab after he had sent away Osin and Baara his wives. He fathered through his wife Elah, Jolab, Zibia, Mesha, Malcham, Jebus, Zabia, and Mirma. These were heads of families.

Through Osin he fathered Abitol and Elpaal.

The sons of Elpaal were Obed, Misham, and Shamed. He built Ono, and Lod, and its towns, and Beriah, and Shemaiah. These were heads of families among the residents in Helem, and they drove out the inhabitants of Gath.

His brothers were Shashak, Jeremoth, Zebadiah, Arad, Eder, Michael, Ispah, and Joha.

The sons of Beriah were Zebadiah, Meshullam, Hezeki, Heber, Ishmerai, Jezliah, and Joab.

The sons of Elhaal were Jakim, Zikri, Zabdi, Eliehoenai, Zilthai, Eliel, Adaiah, Beraiah, and Shimrath.

The sons of Shimhi were Ishpan, Heber, Eliel, Abdon, Zikri, Hanan, Hananiah, Omri, Eglon, Anathoth, Jathin, Iphedeiah, and Penuel.

The sons of Shashak were Shamsherai, Shehariah, Athaliah, Jaresiah, Eliah, and Zikri.

The son of Jeroham were heads of families, chiefs according to their generations, these lived in Jerusalem.

The father of Gibeon lived in Gibeon, and his wife's name was Maachah. Her firstborn son was Abdon, followed by Zur, Kish, Ba'al, Nadab, Ner, Gedor and his brother, Zakkur, and Mikloth.

Mikloth fathered Shammua, and these lived in Jerusalem with their brothers.

Ner fathered Kish, and Kish fathered Saul, and Saul fathered Jonathan, and Malchishua, and Amminadab, and Eshbaal.

The son of Jonathan was Meribbaal, and Meribbaal fathered Micah.

The sons of Micah were Pithon, Melech, Tahrea, and Ahaz.

Ahaz fathered Jehoadah, and Jehoadah fathered Alemeth, Azmaveth, and Zabdi.

Zabdi fathered Moza, and Moza fathered Binea, and Rapha was his son, Eleasah was his son, and Azel was his son. Azel had six sons, and these were their names: Azrikam his firstborn, and Ishmael, Sheariah, Obadiah, Hanan, and Asa. All these were the sons of Azel.

The sons of Azel his brother, Eglon his firstborn, and Jehush the second, and Eliphalet the third.

The sons of Eglon were mighty men, bending the bow, and multiplying in sons and grandsons, a hundred and fifty. All these were of the Benjaminites.

1st Paralipomenon: Chapter 9

This is all Israel in their enrollment, and these are written down in the book of the kings of Israel and Judah, with the names of them that were carried away to Babylon for their transgressions. They who previously lived in their possessions in the cities of Israel, the priests, the Levites, and the appointed ones.

Some of the children of Judah lived in Jerusalem, and of the children of Benjamin, and of the children of Ephraim and Manasseh. Uthai, the son of Ammihud, the son of Omri, the son of Imri, the son of Buni, son of the sons of Pharez, the son of Judah.

Of the Shilonites, Asaiah was his firstborn, and his sons.

Of the sons of Zerah, Jehiel, and their brothers, 690.

Of the Benjaminites, Sallu son of Meshullam, son of Hodaviah, son of Hasenuah, and Jemnaa son of Jeroham, and Elah, these are the sons of Uzzi the son of Michri, and Meshullam, son of Shephathiah, son of Reuel, son of Jemnai, and their brothers according to their generations, 956, all the men were heads of families according to the houses of their fathers.

Of the priests, Jehoiada, Jehoiarib, Jachin, Azariah the son of Hilkiah, the son of Meshullam, the son of Zadok, the son of Meraioth, the son of Ahitub, the ruler of the

Temple of God,[1] and Adaiah son of Jeroham, son of Pashur, son of Malchijah, and Maaseiah son of Jediael, son of Ezerah, son of Meshullam, son of Meshillemith, son of Immer, and their brothers, chiefs of their families, 1760, mighty men for the work of the ministration of the Temple of God.

Of the Levites: Shemaiah son of Hasshub, son of Azrikam, son of Hashabiah, of the sons of Merari, and Bakbakkar, Ares, Galal, Mattaniah the son of Micah, son of Zikri, son of Asaph, and Obadiah, son of Shemaiah, son of Galal, son of Jeduthun, and Berechiah son of Asa, son of Elkanah who lived in the villages of the Netophathites.

The doorkeepers were Shallum, Akkub, Telmon, Ahiman, and their brothers. Shallum was the chief, and he remains until now in the king's gate in the east, these are the gates of the companies of the sons of Levi.

Shallum the son of Korah, the son of Ebiasaph, the son of Korah, and his brothers belonging to the house of his father, the Korhites were over the works of the service, keeping the watches of the tabernacle, and their fathers over the Temple of the Lord, keeping the entrance.

Phinehas son of Eleazar was head over them before the Lord, and these were with him. Zachariah the son of Meshelemiah was the keeper of the door of the tabernacle of witness. All the chosen porters in the gates were 212, these were in their courts, and this was their distribution. These David, and Samuel the seer, established in their charge. These and their sons were over the gates in the Temple of the Lord, and in the house of the tabernacle, to keep watch. The gates were towards the four winds, eastward, westward, northward, southward. Their brothers were in their courts, to enter in weekly from time to time with these. For four strong men have the charge of the gates, and the Levites were over the chambers, and they kept watch over the treasures of the Temple of God. The charge was on them, and these were ordered to open the doors of the temple with the keys every morning.

Some of them were appointed over the vessels of service, that they should carry them in by number, and carry them out by number. Some of them were appointed over the furniture, and over all the holy vessels, and the fine flour, the wine, the oil, the frankincense, and the spices. Some of the priests were makers of the ointment and appointed to prepare the spices. Mattithiah of the Levites, (he was the firstborn of Shallum the Korahite,) was placed in charge over the sacrifices of meat-offering of the pan belonging to the high priest.

Benaiah the Caathite, from among their brothers, was set over the showbread, to prepare it every sabbath. These were the singers, heads of families of the Levites, to whom were established daily courses, for they were employed in the services day and night. These were the heads of the families of the Levites according to their generations, these chiefs lived in Jerusalem. Jehiel the father of Gibeon lived in Gibeon, and his wife's name was Maachah. His firstborn son was Abdon, and he had Zur, Kish, Ba'al, Ner, Nadab, and Gedor and his brother, and Zakkur, and Mikloth.

Mikloth fathered Shammua, and these lived among their brothers in Jerusalem. Ner fathered Kish, and Kish fathered Saul, and Saul fathered Jonathan, Malchishua, Amminadab, Eshbaal. The son of Jonathan was Meribbaal, and Meribbaal fathered Micah.

The sons of Micah were Pithon, Melech, and Tahrea.

Ahaz fathered Jehoadah, and Jehoadah fathered Alemeth, Azmaveth, and Zabdi, and Zabdi fathered Moza.

Moza fathered Binea, and Rephaiah was his son, Eleasah was his son, Azel was his son.

Azel had six sons, and these were their names. Azrikam, his firstborn, and Ishmael, Shiphi, Obadiah, Hanan, and Asa. These were the sons of Azel.

1st Paralipomenon: Chapter 9 Notes

1 Codex Vaticanus: oecou tou theou (ΟΙΚΟΥΤΟΥΘΕΟΥ).
Translation: house of the god

• Aleppo Codex: byt hålhym (בית האאלהים). Translations:
house (or temple, abode) of the gods

• Leningrad Codex: beit ha'elohim (בֵּית הָאֱלֹהִים).
Translations: house (or temple, abode) of the gods

• Targum of Chronicles: beit makdesha daYay (בֵּית מַקְדְּשָׁא
דַּיְיָ). Translations: house (or temple, abode) of sanctuary of
Yahw

As this is a reference to Solomon's Temple in Jerusalem, it
appears to be the older name, pre-dating King Josiah's
removal of the statues of the gods from the temple, circa 625
BC, meaning this book likely dates back to before Josiah's
reforms.

1st Paralipomenon: Chapter 10

The Pelesets[1] warred against Israel, and they fled from before the Pelesets and fell dead in Mount Gilboa. The Pelesets chased after Saul, and after his sons, and the Pelesets killed Jonathan, Amminadab, and Malchishua, the sons of Saul. The battle turned against Saul, and the archers attacked him with bows and arrows, and they were wounded by the bows. Saul said to his armor-bearer, "Draw your sword, and run me through with it, in case these uncircumcised come and mock me."

But his armor-bearer would not, as he was terribly afraid, so Saul took a sword, and fell on it. His armor-bearer saw that Saul was dead, and he also fell on his sword. So Saul died, along with his three sons on that day and all his family died at the same time. All the men of Israel that were in the valley, saw that Israel had fled, and that Saul and his sons were dead, and they left their cities and fled, and the Pelesets came and lived in them.

On the day after the Pelesets came to strip the slain, they found Saul and his sons fallen on Mount Gilboa. They stripped him, and took his head, and his armor, and sent them into the land of the Pelesets all around, to proclaim the good news to their idols, and the people. They put their armor in the temple of their god,[2] and they put his head in the Temple of Dagon. All the residents in Gilead heard what the Pelesets had done to Saul and Israel. All the mighty men rose up from Gilead, and they took the body of Saul, and the bodies of his sons, and brought them to Jabesh, and buried their bones under the oak in Jabesh, and fasted seven days. So Saul died for his actions, when he turned against God, against the commands of the Lord, in that as he did not follow them when Saul inquired of a wizard to seek counsel, and Samuel the prophet answered him, and he did not seek the counsel of the Lord, so he killed him, and turned the kingdom to David the son of Jesse.

1st Paralipomenon: Chapter 10 Notes

1 Codex Vaticanus: allophylôn (ΑΛΛΟΦΥΛΩΝ).
Translation: tribals (or nationals)

- Aleppo Codex: Plštym (פלשתים). Translation: Philistines (or Palestinians, Pelesets)

- Leningrad Codex: Felishtim (פְּרִשְׁתִּים). Translation: Philistines (or Palestinians, Pelesets)

- Targum of Chronicles: Felishta'ei (פְּלִשְׁתָּאֵי). Translation: Philistines (or Palestinians, Pelesets)

The Pelesets were an ancient people based in the region of the modern Gaza Strip of the Palestinian Territories. The earliest surviving mention of them is from the reliefs of the Temple of Ramses III at Medinet Habu in Egypt that dates back to some time between 1186 and 1155 BC, in which they were called Peleseti (𓊪𓇌𓂋𓄿𓊃𓏏𓏭). In Akkadian cuneiform texts they were called the ᵏᵘʳPalastu (𒆳𒉺𒆷𒊍𒌅). It is unclear where they came from, however, one theory is that they were the Pala, a Luwian people from the Black Sea coast of Anatolia. The region was an independent country called Palaa (𒉺𒆷𒀀) in the Neshite (Hittite) records from the 1600s BC, however, have become part of the Nesite Empire by the 1500s BC. Around the time the Pelesets invaded Canaan, the Pala were driven from their homeland by the neighboring Kaskians from northeast Anatolia, which supports the connection between the groups, however, it has yet to be proven conclusively.

They were later taken as captives by the Babylonians and resettled in Mesopotamia in 604 BC. After the Romans exiled the Jews from Judea, they renamed the province Palestine and recolonized the area with Greeks, Romans, Egyptians, and Syrians. Modern Palestinians descend from these colonists.

2 Codex Vaticanus: oecô theou autôn (ΟΙΚѠѲΕΟΥ ΑΥΤѠΝ). Translation: house of their god

- Aleppo Codex: byt ålhyhm (בית אלהיהם). Translation: house (or temple, abode) of their gods

- Leningrad Codex: beit eloheihem (בֵּית אֱלֹהֵיהֶם). Translation: house (or temple, abode) of their gods

- Targum of Chronicles: beit ta'avatehon (בֵּית טָעֲוָתְהוֹן). Translation: house (or temple) of idols (or mistakes)

1st Paralipomenon: Chapter 11

All Israel came to David in Hebron, saying, "Look, we are your bone and your flesh. When Saul was king, you were the one that led Israel, and Lord the god[1] said to you, 'You will feed my people Israel, and you will be a ruler over Israel.'"

All the elders of Israel came to the king in Hebron, and King David made a covenant with them in Hebron before the Lord, and they anointed David to be king over Israel, according to the word of the Lord by Samuel. The king and his men went to Jerusalem, (this was Jebus), where the Jebusites, the inhabitants of the land, said to David, "You will not enter in here."

He captured the castle of Zion (this is the City of David), and David said, "Whoever slaughters the Jebusites first, he will become chief and captain. Joab the son of Zeruiah went up first and became chief. David lived in the castle, and therefore he called it the City of David, and he fortified the city around it.

David continued to increase, and Lord Shaddai[2] was with him. These are the chiefs of the mighty men that David had, who strengthened themselves with him in his kingdom, with all Israel, to make him king, according to the word of the Lord concerning Israel.

This is the list of the mighty men of David: Jashobeam, son of Hachmon, first of the thirty, he drew his sword once against three hundred, who he killed at one time. After him Eleazar son of Dodo, the Ahohite, he was among the three mighty men. He was with David in Pasdammim, and the Pelesets were gathered there to battle, and there was a portion of the field full of barley, and the people fled before the Pelesets. He stood among the portion, and rescued it, and struck the Pelesets, and the Lord worked a great deliverance.

Three of the thirty chiefs went down to Petra[3] to David, to the cave stronghold,[4] and the camp of the Pelesets was in the valley of the Raphites.[5] David was then in the hold, and the garrison of the Pelesets were then in Bethlehem. David longed, and said, "Who will give me water to drink from the well in the gateway of the Temple of Lehem?"[6]

The three broke through the camp of the Pelesets, and they drew water out of the well that was in the gateway of the Temple of Lehem, and they took it, and came to David, but David would not drink it, and poured it out to the Lord, and said, "God forbids that I should do this thing! Will I drink the blood of these men, with their lives?"

Through the peril of their lives, they brought it, so he would not drink it. The three mighty men did these things. Abishai the brother of Joab was chief of three, and he drew his sword against three hundred killed at one time. He had a name among the second three. He was more famous than the two others of the three, and he was chief over them, yet he was not as famous as the first three. Benaiah the son of Jehoiada was the son of a mighty man, many were his acts for Kabzeel. He struck two Ariel of Moab, and he went down and struck a lion in a pit on a snowy day.

He struck an Egyptian, an awesome man five cubits[7] high, and in the hand of the Egyptian, there was a spear like a weavers' beam, and Benaiah went down to him with a wand, and took the spear out of the Egyptian's hand, and killed him with his spear. These things did Benaiah son of Jehoiada, and his name was among the three mightiest. He was distinguished beyond the thirty, but not before the first three, and David placed him over his family.

The mighty men of the forces were:

Asahel the brother of Joab, Elhanan the son of Dodo of Bethlehem, Shammoth the Harorite, Helez the Pelonite, Ira the son of Ikkesh the Tekoite, Abiezer the Anathothite, Sibbechai the Hushathite, Ilai the Ahohite, Maharai the Netophathite, Chthaod the son of Nooza the Netophathite, Airi the son of Ribai of the hill of Benjamin, Benaiah the Per-Atenite,[8] Uri of the wadi of

Gaash,[9] Abiel the Arbathite, Azmaveth the Baharumite, Eliahba the Shaalbonite, Bennaeas, Hashem the Gizonite, Jonathan the son of Shola the Aroerite, Ahiam the son of Sacar the Aroerite, Elphal the son of Ur, Ophar the Mecherathite, Achia the Pelonite, Hezro the Carmelite, Naarai the son of Ezbai, Joel the son of Nathan, Mibhar son of Haggeri, Zelek the Ammonite, Nachon the Berothite armor-bearer of Joab the son of Zeruiah, Ira the Ithrite, Gareb the Ithrite, Orion[10] the Cypriot,[11] Zabad the son of Ahlai, Adina the son of Shiza a Reubenite chief and thirty with him, Hanan the son of Maachah, Josaphat the Mitanni,[12] Uzia the Ashterathite, Shama and Jehiel, sons of Hothan the Ararite, Jediael the son of Shimri, and Joha his brother the Tizite, Eliel the Mahavite, Jeribai, and Jeshaiah his son, Elnaam, and Ithmah the Moabite, Eliel and Obed, and Jaasiel the Mezobaite.

1ˢᵗ Paralipomenon: Chapter 11 Notes

1 Codex Vaticanus: cyrios o theos (ⲔⲨⲢⲒⲞⳞⲞⲐⲈⲞⳞ).
Translation: Lord the god

- Aleppo Codex: Yhwh ȧlhyk (**יהוה אלהיך**). Translation:
Yhwh your god

- Leningrad Codex: Yehvah eloheicha (יְהֹוָה אֱלֹהֶיךָ).
Translation: Yehwah your god

- Targum of Chronicles: Yya elahach (יְיָ אֱלָהָךְ). Translation:
Yahw your god

The name Aramaic name Yhw (𐤉𐤄𐤅^) was transliterated as
Iaw (Ιαω) in the Septuagint, and as Yhwah (יְהוָה) in the
Masoretic text. This name was later transliterated as Iaw by
the Pre-Christian Romans from the Greek translation. The
name Iaw is found in fragments of the 3ʳᵈ century AD
Papyrus Oxyrhynchus 1007, however, is represented by a
double Yod (״), meaning it was copied from a later Hebrew
or Aramaic text from that era. After the sixth century AD the
occasional copy of the Septuagint is found which uses the
name, either written as Ιαω or a Greek approximation of יְהֹוָה
(ΠΙΠΙ), however, all of these can be traced back to the
Hexapla, Quinta, Sextus, and/or Septima, which attempted to
retranslate and harmonize the Old Testament in the 3ʳᵈ
through 6ᵗʰ centuries AD.

There are no early surviving copies of the Septuagint's
version of Paralipomena which have the name Iaw (Ιαω /
יְהֹוָה) in it, like some of the other books of the Septuagint, and
therefore it cannot be proven if the name was in the
Septuagint's Paralipomena or not, however, several other

books in the Septuagint appear to retain older versions of the Hebrew scriptures that pre-date the redaction during the Hasmonean dynasty, which replaced many older names of gods with Yahweh or Yahweh Sabaoth, the national god of Hasmonean Judea.

The Septuagint's version of 1st Paralipomenon was translated circa 200 BC, before the Hasmonean redaction, and contains the term Lord the god (Κύριος ὁ θεὸς). As Κύριος ὁ θεὸς translates directly as Lord the god, that term is used.

2 Codex Vaticanus: cyrios pantocratôr (ΚΥΡΙΟC ΠΑΝΤΟΚΡΑΤѠΡ). Translation: lord omnipotent (or almighty)

• Aleppo Codex: Yhwh ṣbåwt (יהוה צבאות). Translation: Yhwh forces (or armies)

• Leningrad Codex: Yhvah tzeva'ovt (יְהֹוָה צְבָאֹות). Translation: Yhvah forces (or armies)

• Targum of Chronicles: Yay tzeva'ot (יְּ צְבָאֹות). Translation: Yahw of desires

3 Codex Vaticanus: Petran (ΠΕΤΡΑΝ). Translation Petra (or rock)

• Aleppo Codex: ṣr (צר). Translation: narrow (in Hebrew) or rock (or Tyre if transliterated from the Phoenician 𐤑𐤓)

• Leningrad Codex: Tzur (צֹר). Translation: narrow (in Hebrew) or rock (or Tyre if transliterated from the Phoenician 𐤑𐤓)

• Targum of Chronicles: Tinara (טִנָרָא)

This is generally accepted as being a reference to Petra in southern Jordan, which has been inhabited since at least 7000 BC. During the era of David, the Edomites inhabited the area. Earlier Egyptian records from the New Kingdom called the region Sela, which appear to have been the Edomite name, Slô (𐤎𐤋𐤏), also meaning 'rock.' The Edomite name Sela was also used in Isaiah and Obadiah, suggesting that this book was translated from Judahite (Phoenician) into Aramaic before being translated into Greek and Hebrew.

4 Codex Vaticanus: spêlaeon Odollam (ϹΠΗΛΑΙΟΝ ΟΔΟΛΛΑΜ). Translation cave of Odollam

• Aleppo Codex: môrt ôdlm (**מערת עדלם**). Translation: cave stronghold

• Leningrad Codex: me'arat adullam (מְעָרַ֖ת עֲדֻלָּ֑ם). Translation: cave stronghold

• Targum of Chronicles: me'arat adulam (מְעָרַת עֲדֻלָם). Translation: cave stronghold

The location of the Cave of Odollam / Adullam has been debated for thousands of years. There was a Canaanite settlement called Adullam in the plains mentioned in Joshua, and a Persian era city named Adullam in the highlands south of Jerusalem that was occupied until the early Christian era. Neither of the mentioned cities were near Petra, and therefore this cave stronghold must have been a different location. Many of the famous ruins of Petra, such as the Al-Khazneh, are caves that have been hollowed out and expanded, however, most of the work on the surviving ruins dates to the Persian and Greek eras, hundreds of years after the time of David. Nevertheless, the caves were inhabited since at least 7000 BC according to archaeologists, and therefore the cave stronghold would have been a reference to one of the caves.

5 Codex Vaticanus: coeladi tôn gigantôn (ΚΟΙΛΑΔΙΤѠΝ ΓΙΓΑΝΤѠΝ). Translation: Valley of the Gigantes

- Aleppo Codex: bômq rpåym (בעמק רפאים). Translation: in the valley (or depths, hollows) of the Rephaim

- Leningrad Codex: be'emek Refa'im (בְּעֵמֶק רְפָאִים). Translation: in the valley (or depths, hollows) of the Rephaim

- Targum of Chronicles: bemeishar gibbaraya (בְּמֵישַׁר גִּבָּרַיָּא). Translation: in the plains of the husbands

The Canaanite Rpåm (𐤓𐤐𐤀𐤌 / 𐎗𐎔𐎀𐎎) were a semi-deified long-dead people by the 1300s BC, as the Ugaritic Texts include the so-called Rephaim Text. They appear to be an ancient people that had been deified and were believed to live in the underworld. The word's etymology implies they were healers. The fact that they were described as 'ruling from Mount Hermon' in Joshua implies they were the 'watchers' from the Enochian tradition. The similarities between the name Anak (Εναχ / עֲנָק) and Enoch (Ενωχ / חֲנוֹךְ) may have led to the confusion in the translation, resulting in both Anaks (𐤏𐤍𐤒𐤉𐤌 / עֲנָקִים) and Rephaites (𐤓𐤐𐤀𐤉𐤌 / רְפָאִים) as Gigantes in different places in the books of Numbers, Deuteronomy, Joshua, and 1st Paralipomenon.

A scribal note in Joshua chapter 18 identifies the Valley of the Raphites as being the 'northern' name of the Forest of Hinns, which was located near Jerusalem. The two terms translated as 'Hinns' and 'Raphites' are not generally found in the same ancient literature, with hinns being mostly found in Arabic literature, and Raphites being mostly found in Canaanite literature. The origin of the name Hnm (הנם) is likely a plural of hinn (حن), a reference to an ancient extinct type of being that once lived on the Earth in Semitic folklore. The hinns continue to be part of the Islamic and Druze religions, although their roles in the religions vary. It is agreed that they are extinct, however, it isn't clear what they were. Many sources describe the hinns and binns as powerful, gigantic primordial creatures, suggesting they were influenced by finding the bones of extinct animals.

Conversely, the Revelations of 'Abdullah Al-Sayid Muhammad Habib claims the hinns were air creatures, and the binns were water creatures, while the medieval Islamic historian al-Tabari claimed they were created from poisonous fire (سموم). In most versions of the stories, they fought in part of a series of wars for control of the earth before the creation of humanity, and most of the ancient species became extinct, including the hinns.

The combination of 'valley/abyss' and 'forest/woodland' suggests it is a reference to a gravesite, and not a physical valley. At the time, Canaanites marked gravesites by planting trees, usually oak, which was known as the 'Asherah' tree, because it could self-pollinate, and was therefore seen as a 'virgin' tree. In the context of a gravesite, it is likely that the term 'sons of hinns' did not refer to some known people, but an ancient gravesite of a by then unknown people. Oak trees are known to live over 1000 years, and reproduce, so the gravesite in question could have already been thousands of years old. Later during the reforms of King Josiah, ancient graves and Asherah groves near Jerusalem were destroyed, and he was specifically recorded as destroying a statue in the valley of the sons of Hinns, implying that this was the gravesite he destroyed.

6 Codex Vaticanus: Baethleem (ΒΑΙΘΛΕΕΜ)

- Aleppo Codex: Byt Lḥm (בית לחם). Translation: house (or temple, abode) of Lehem

- Leningrad Codex: beit-Lechem (בֵּית־לָ֑חֶם). Translation: house (or temple, abode) of Lehem

- Targum of Chronicles: veit Lachem (בֵּית לָחֶם). Translation: house (or temple, abode) of Lehem

The term refers to both the temple of Lehem, as well as the city of Bethlehem that was built around it. There are several mentions of the waters of life that flowed from the gate of the temple, indicating that this was the reference to the temple, not the city.

7 Codex Vaticanus: pentapêchyn (ΠΕΝΤΑΠΗΧΥΝ).
Translation: five cubits

- Aleppo Codex: ḥmš båmh (חמש באמה). Translation: five in cubits (or forearms, ells)

- Leningrad Codex: chamesh ba'ammah (חָמֵשׁ בָּאַמָּה).
Translation: five in cubits (or ells)

The length of the cubit changed from culture to culture and through time. Around the time the Septuagint was translated into Greek, the Greek cubit was approximately 46 cm (18 inches), while the Judahite cubit is believed to have been around 51 cm (21 inches). This measurement would make the Egyptian 230 to 255 cm (7'6" to 8'8") tall.

8 Codex Vaticanus: Pharathôni (ΦΑΡΑΘΩΝΙ)

- Aleppo Codex: Prôtny (פרעתני)

- Leningrad Codex: Pir'atoni (פִּרְעָתֹנִי)

- Targum of Chronicles: Pir'aton (פִּרְעָתוֹן)

9 Codex Vaticanus: Oyri ec Nachaligaas (ΟΥΡΙΕΚ ΝΑΧΑΛΙΓΑΑϹ). Translation: Oyri of the Nachaligaas

- Aleppo Codex: ḥwry [r] mnḥly gôš (חוּרי [ר] מנחלי געש). Translation: Hwry [R] from the stream (or river, gorge, valley, possession, inheritance) Gash

- Leningrad Codex: churai minnachalei Ga'ash (חוּרַי מִנַּחֲלֵי גָעַשׁ). Translation: Churay from the stream (or river, gorge, valley, possession, inheritance) Gaash

- Targum of Chronicles: Churayah demin nachalaya (חוּרַיָה דְּמִן נַחֲלַיָא). Translation: Churayah who was the stream (or river, wadi, valley, gorge)

As the Greek name is a transliteration of the Canaanite word nḥl (𐤍𐤇𐤋) meaning ravine or wadi, that was term is used in this translation.

10 Codex Vaticanus: Oyrias (ΟΥΡΙΑϹ)

- Aleppo Codex: Åwryh (אוּריה)

- Leningrad Codex: Uriyyah (אוּרִיָּה)

- Targum of Chronicles: Uriyah (אוּרִיָה)

The Greek name used in 1ˢᵗ Paralipomenon is a translation of the Masoretic Åwryh, however, this name is spelled as Oyrian (Ουριαν) in 2ⁿᵈ Kingdoms, indicates that the Aramaic name was Åwrôân (אורואן) before the Hebrew translation. This suggests that the Hebrew translators substituted 'Yah' (יה) for 'An' (אן), in this name, which is consistent with other changes made when the Hebrew translation was made. The Septuagint's Exodus includes Moses' god identifying himself as Ôn (Ὧν), a name later found in the Septuagint's Book of Hosea, which is mirrored in the Masoretic Text by the name Aven (אָוֶן) / Åwn (אוֹן). Therefore, the original name of this person was likely the Akkadian name úru An (𒌷𒀭), meaning 'Light of An,' which was imported to Greece in the early Iron Age as Orion (Ὠρίων). As Orion is more common than Uru-An, the name used in this translation is Orion.

11 Codex Vaticanus: Chetti (ΧΕΤΤΙ)

- Aleppo Codex: hty (חתי). Translation: Cypriot

- Leningrad Codex: Chitti (חִתִּי). Translation: Cypriot

- Targum of Chronicles: Chitta'ah (חִתָּאָה)

This term has created a great deal of confusion since the misidentification of the ruins of the Neshites as being 'Hittite' in the 1800s. The modern archaeological name 'Hittite,' is not derived from an ancient name for the culture applied by themselves, or anyone else, but rather adopted from the biblical reference to a then-unknown civilization somewhere in the region. There was an ancient culture in the region called the Hattians, however, they were conquered by the Nesites before 1700 BC, and subsequently disappeared from the historic records.

The name was applied to culture today referred to as 'Hittites,' before the 'Hittite' language had been translated, and is incorrect. Since 1906, excavations at Boğazköy, the ancient 'Hittite' capital Hattusa have uncovered more than 10,000 'Hittite' texts, including the royal achieve. The actual name of the 'Hittite' language and people was Nešili (𒉈𒅆𒇷), which is now rendered in some academic literate as Nesite or Neshite. As early as the mid-1800s some scholars disputed the identification of the Nesites as the Biblical Hittites, including the Orientalist Max Müller, who was one of many claiming the Biblical Hittites were ancient Greeks or some other Mediterranean people. Later in the Septuagint's translation of the Maccabees, the similar term Chettiim (Χεττιιμ) as a reference to all Greek-speaking lands, and therefore the Biblical Hittites were likely the Cypriots or the Achaean Greeks.

In the 1st century AD, the Jewish historian Josephus reported that Cethima was the name of Cyrus in Aramaic, and the Chettim were the descendants of Noah's grandson Chethimus, who had settled on Cyprus. Josephus reported that the name was preserved in the Greek name of the town Cition (Κίτιον). Most historians view it as more likely that the Aramaic name was derived from the city-state of Cition, which was known as Kåtjåy (𓈎𓏏𓇌𓈉) in Egyptian records from the New Kingdom Era in the late Bronze Age, and Kt (𐤊𐤕) or Kty (𐤊𐤕𐤉) in Phoenician records from the early Iron Age. While this may be the origin of the term, by the era of the Neo-Assyrian era, the term must have also referred to other Greek islands, as both the prophets Isaiah and Ezekiel used the term 'Islands of Kittim.' As the term referred to the entire island of Cyprus in Aramaic, the translations of 'Cyprus' and 'Cypriots' are used here.

12 Codex Vaticanus: Iôsaphat o Baethani (ⲓⲱⲥⲁⲫⲁⲧⲟ ⲃⲀⲓⲐⲀⲚⲓ). Translation: Josephat the Bethanite

• Aleppo Codex: ywšpt [r] hmtny [s] (יושפט [ר] המתני [ס]). Translation: ywshpt [R] the mtny [S]

• Leningrad Codex: Yovoshafat hamMitni (יוֹשָׁפָט הַמִּתְנִי). Translation: Yoshapat the Mitni

• Targum of Chronicles: Yoshafat demin Mitan (יוֹשָׁפָט דְּמִן מִתָּן). Translation: Yoshapat who was Mitan

The Septuagint and Masoretic Text disagree on where Josephat was from. The Septuagint uses a Greek transliteration of the Canaanite and Hebrew name for people from Beth-An, a city in Samaria, however, the Masoretic text refers to him as a Mitni. The Greek is clearly a transliteration of an Aramaic version of the name, however, the Hebrew is unrelated, an likely a transliteration of an older, or possibly Edomite term. The term refers to a group of people, meaning the text the Greeks translated would have originated in the Samaritan or Edomite 'people of the House of Ản (𐤉𐤀+𐤕𐤆), a direct Canaanite translation of É An (𒂍𒀭).

In the Amarna Letters, which date to the 1330s BC, the term Éan (𒂍𒀭) was the name of a people, who appear to be the Mitanni, or a group within the Mitanni. The Mitanni Empire seized control of Syria in the middle bronze age, largely composed of Hurrians, although, worshipping Indo-Iranian gods, such as Mitra-Varuna. The cuneiform word Éan (𒂍𒀭) was the Akkadian word meaning 'temple,' suggesting the Éan were the Mitanni priests. According to Israelite sources, the priesthood at Mount Seir was Hurrian, suggesting the Mitanni priesthood in Edom survived long after their empire fell in the north. Like the Israelite God, the Mitanni god Mitra-Varuna was described as being the god of the covenant, and there appears to have been Israelites worshiping at Mount Seir until the era of the prophet Isaiah, who made a pilgrimage to Mount Seir in the late-700s BC. Therefore, it is likely the term Mitanni would have survived longer in Edomite than Samaritan, Judahite, or Aramaic, explaining why it would have been read as 'House of An,' a literal translation of É An (𒂍𒀭).

This also indicates that cuneiform must have still been in use by the priests in Samaria and Judah as late as the time of King David, circa 1000 BC. There are other terms in the books of the Kingdoms of Saul, David, and Solomon that appear to have been transliterated from a cuneiform source, suggesting the now lost Chronicals of the Kings of Samaria, and the Chronicles of the Kings of Judah were written in cuneiform.

1st Paralipomenon: Chapter 12

These are those who came to Ziklag when he still
kept himself close, because of Saul the son of Kish. These
were among the mighty, aiding him in war, and using
the bow with the right hand and with the left, and
slingers of stones, and shooters with bows. Of the brothers of Saul of Benjamin, the chief was Jeezer, and Jeush
son of Asma the Gibeathite, and Joel and Jophalet, sons of
Azmaveth, and Berachah, and Ishuai of Anathoth, and
Shemaiah the Gibeonite a mighty man among the thirty,
and over the thirty; and Jeremiah, and Azarel, and Johanan, and Jehozabad of Gederathiim, Azai and Jerimoth,
and Baalia, and Shemariah, and Shephatiah of Charae-
phiel, Elkanah, and Jesuni, and Azareel, and Joezer, and
Sobocam, and the Korhites, and Joelah and Zebadiah, sons
of Jeroham, and the men of Gedor.

From Gad, these separated themselves to David from
the wilderness, strong mighty men of war, bearing
shields and spears, and their faces were as the face of a
lion, and they were nimble as gazelles on the mountains
in speed. Jazer the chief, Obadiah the second, Elihu the
third, Mishmannah the fourth, Jeremiah the fifth, Attai
the sixth, Eliel the seventh, Johanan the eighth, Elzabad
the ninth, Jeremiah the tenth, Machbanai the eleventh.
These were chiefs of the army of the sons of Gad, the
least one commanded a hundred, and the greatest one a
thousand. These are the men that crossed across the Jor-

dan in the first month, when it had overflowed all its banks, and they drove out all the inhabitants of the valleys, from the east to the west. Some some of the Benjaminites and Judahites came out to the assistance of David. David went out to meet them, and said to them, "If you have come peaceably to me, let my heart be at peace with you, but if you have come to betray me to my enemies unfaithfully, the God of your fathers look on it and reprove it."

The spirit came on Amasai, a captain of the thirty, and he said, "Go, David, son of Jesse, you and your people, peace, peace be to you, and peace to your helpers, for your God has helped you."

David received them and made them captains of the forces. Some came to David from Manasseh, when the Pelesets came against Saul to war, and he helped them not, because the captains of the Pelesets took counsel, saying, "With the heads of those men will he return to his master Saul."

When David was going to Ziklag, there came to him of Manasseh, Adnah and Jehozabad, and Rodiel, and Michael, and Jehozabad, and Elihu, and Semathi. These were the captains of thousands of Manasseh. They fought on the side of David against an army, for they were all men of might, and they were commanders in the army, because of their might.

Every day more men came to David, until they amounted to a great force, like the army of God. These are the names of the commanders of the army, who came to David to Hebron, to turn the kingdom of Saul to him according to the word of the Lord. The sons of Judah, bearing shields and spears, six thousand and eight hundred mighty at war. Of the sons of Simeon mighty for battle, seven thousand and a hundred. Of the sons of Levi, four thousand and six hundred. Jehoiada the chief of the family of Aaron, and with him three thousand and seven hundred. Zadok, a young man mighty in strength, and there were twenty-two leaders of his father's house. Of the Benjaminites, the brothers of Saul, three thousand, and still the greater part of them kept the guard of the house of Saul. Of the sons of Ephraim, twenty thousand and eight hundred mighty men, famous in the houses of their fathers. Of the half-tribe of Manasseh, eighteen thousand, including those who were named by name, to make David king. Of the sons of Issachar having wisdom concerning the times, knowing what Israel should do, two hundred, and all their brothers with them.

Of Zebulun, they that went out to battle, with all weapons of war, were fifty thousand to help David, none weak-handed. Of Naphtali a thousand captains, and with them men with shields and spears, thirty-seven thousand. Of the Danite warriors, twenty-eight thousand and eight hundred. Of Jezer, they that went out to give aid in war, forty thousand. From the country beyond Jordan, from Reuben, and the Gadites, and from the half-tribe of Manasseh, a hundred and twenty thousand, with all weapons of war. All these were men of war, setting the army in battle formation, with a peaceful mind towards him, and they came to Hebron to make David king over all Israel, and the rest of Israel were of one mind to make David king. They were there for three days, eating and drinking, for their brothers had made preparations. Their neighbors, as far as Issachar, Zebulun and Naphtali, brought to them camels, donkeys, mules, and calves, food, meal, cakes of figs, raisins, wine, oil, calves, and sheep in great numbers, for there was joy in Israel.

1st Paralipomenon: Chapter 13

David took counsel with the captains of thousands and captains of hundreds, even with every commander. David said to the whole congregation of Israel, "If it seems good to you, and it should be blessed by Lord the god, let us send to our brothers that are left in all the land of Israel, and let the priests the Levites who are with them in the cities of their possession come, and let them be gathered to us. Let us bring over to us the box of our god, for men have not inquired at it since the days of Saul."

All the congregation said that they would do this, as the saying was right in the eyes of all the people. So David assembled all Israel, from the borders of Egypt even to the entering in of Hama, to bring in the box of God from the city of Jarim. David brought it up, and all Israel went up to the City of David, which belonged to Judah, to bring up to there the box of Lord the god who sits between the sphinxes,[1] and whose name is called on it. They set the box of God on a new wagon brought out of the house of Amminadab, and Uzza and his brothers drove the wagon. David and all Israel were playing before the Lord with all their might, and that together with singers, and with harps, and with lutes, with timbrels, and with cymbals, and with trumpets. They came as far as the threshing floor, and Uzza put out his hand to hold the box because a bull knocked it from its place. The

Lord was very angry with Uzza, and struck him there, because of his reaching out his hand to the box, and he died there before God.

David was depressed, because the Lord had killed Uzza, and he called that place the Breach of Uzza until this day. David was afraid of God that day, saying, "How will I bring the box of God to myself?" So David did not bring the box home to himself to the city of David, but he turned it aside into the house of Obed-Edom the Gethite. The box of God remained in the house of Obed-Edom for three months: and God blessed Obed-Edom and all that he had.

1st Paralipomenon: Chapter 13 Notes

1 Codex Vaticanus: cheroubin (ΧΕΡΟΥΒΙΝ)

- Aleppo Codex: krwbym (כרובים). Translation: cherubs (or griffins, sphinxes)

- Leningrad Codex: keruvim (כְּרוּבִים). Translation: cherubs (or griffins, sphinxes)

- Targum of Chronicles: keruvaya (כְּרוּבַיָא). Translation: cherubs (or griffins, angels)

The word 'cherub' (𐤊𐤓𐤅𐤁 / כרוב / 𐤊𐤓𐤅𐤁 / 𐤊𐤓𐤅𐤁) was the West Semitic term for the mythical creature generally called a 'griffin' in English, which is itself derived from the Hebrew pronunciation. Based in the archaeological record of Canaan, it appears that the concept of the cherub was based on the Egyptian sphinx, as the earliest cherub statues found in Canaan were Egyptian statues of sphinxes. Archaeologists are not sure if the cherubs of Anatolia were based on the Canaanite cherub, or the Egyptian sphinxes directly, however, all three mythical beings are closely related in the archaeological record.

The term cherub was for some reason reinterpreted as 'baby angels' by Christians, although in the books of the Kingdoms, God was described as riding on cherubs, and it is not clear why any god would ride around on 'baby angels,' therefore the alternate translation of 'sphinxes' is used in this translation.

1st Paralipomenon: Chapter 14

King Hiram of Tyre sent messengers[1] to David, and cedar timbers, and masons, and carpenters, to build a temple for him. David knew that the Lord had chosen him to be king over Israel, because his kingdom was highly exalted, on account of his people Israel. David took more wives in Jerusalem, and more sons and daughters were born to David. These are the names of those that were born, who were born to him in Jerusalem: Shammua, Shobab, Nathan, Solomon, Ibhar, Elishua, Eliphalet, Nageth, Naphath, Japhia, Elisamae, Eliade, and Eliphalet.

The Pelesets heard that David was anointed a king over all Israel, and all the Pelesets went to find David, and David heard it and went out to meet them. The Pelesets came and assembled in the valley of the Gigantes. David asked God, "Will I go up against the Pelesets? Will you deliver them into my hand?"

The Lord answered him, "Go, and I will deliver them into your hands."

He went up to Baal Perazim, and David attacked them there, and David said, "God has broken through enemies by my hand like a breach of water, therefore he called the name of that place, the Breach of Perazim."

The Pelesets left their gods there, and David gave orders to burn them with fire. The Pelesets once more assembled themselves in the Valley of the Gigantes. David asked God again, and he said, "You will not go after them, turn away from them, and you will come on them near the pear trees. It will be, when you will hear the sound of their tumult in the tops of the pear trees, then you will go into the battle, as God has gone out before you to slaughter the army of the Pelesets."

He did as God commanded him, and he slaughtered the army of the Pelesets from Gibeon to Gezer. The name of David was famous in all the land, and the Lord put the terror of him on all the nations.

1ˢᵗ Paralipomenon: Chapter 14 Notes

1 Codex Vaticanus: angelous (ⲀⲅⲅⲉⲗⲟⲨⲥ). Translation: messengers

- Aleppo Codex: mlåkym (מלאבים). Translation: messengers

- Leningrad Codex: mal'achim (מַרְאָבִים). Translation: messengers

- Targum of Chronicles: izgadin (אִזְגַדִין). Translation: envoys (or ambassadors)

1st Paralipomenon: Chapter 15

David built for himself houses in the City of David, and he prepared a place for the box of God and made a tent for it. Then David said, "It is not lawful for any to carry the box of God except the Levites, for the Lord has chosen them to carry the box of the Lord, and to minister to him forever."

David assembled all Israel at Jerusalem, to bring up the box of the Lord to the place which he had prepared for it. David gathered together the sons of Aaron the Levites. Of the sons of Kohath, there was Uriel the chief, and his 120 brothers. Of the sons of Merari, Asaiah the chief, and his 230 brothers. Of the sons of Gershon, Joel the chief, and his 130 brothers. Of the sons of Elizaphan, Shimei the chief, and his 200 brothers. Of the sons of Hebron, Eliel the chief, and his 80 brothers. Of the sons of Uzziel, Amminadab the chief, and his 112 brothers.

David called Zadok and Abiathar the priests, and the Levites, Uriel, Asaiah, and Joel, and Shimei, and Eliel, and Amminadab, and said to them, "You are the heads of the families of the Levites, sanctify yourselves, you and your brothers, and you will carry up the box of the god in Israel, to the place which I have prepared for it. Because you were not ready before, our God made a breach with us, because we did not follow his ordinance."

The priests and the Levites sanctified themselves, to bring up the box of the god in Israel. The sons of the Levites took the box of God, (as Moses commanded by the word of God according to the law) on their shoulders with staffs. David said to the chiefs of the Levites, "Set your brothers the singers with musical instruments, lutes, harps, and cymbals, to sound aloud with a voice of joy."

The Levites appointed Heman the son of Joel, Asaph the son of Berechiah was one of his brothers; and Ethan the son of Kushaiah was of the sons of Merari their brothers; and with them their brothers of the second rank, Zachariah, Uzziel, Shemiramoth, Jehiel, Eliel, Elihu, Benaiah, Maaseiah, Mattithiah, Elipheleh, Makellia, Obed-Edom, Jehiel, and Azaziah, the porters. The singers, Heman, Asaph, and Ethan, with bronze cymbals to make a sound to be heard.

Zachariah, and Uzziel, Shemiramoth, Jehiel, Unni, Elihu, Maaseiah, Benaiah with lutes on Alamoth.

Mattithiah, and Elipheleh, Mikneiah, Obed-Edom, Jehiel, and Azaziah with harps of Amasenith, to make a loud noise.

Kenaniah chief of the Levites was master of the bands because he was skillful.

Berechiah and Elkanah were doorkeepers of the box.

Somnia, and Jehoshaphat, Nethanel, Amasai, Zechariah, Benejaakan, and Eliezer, the priests, were sounding with trumpets before the box of God, and Obed-Edom and Jehiah were doorkeepers of the box of God.

So David, and the elders of Israel, and the captains of thousands, went to bring up the box of the covenant from the house of Obed-Edom with joy. It came to pass when God strengthened the Levites bearing the box of the covenant of the Lord, that they sacrificed seven calves and seven rams. David was girded with a fine linen robe, and all the Levites who were bearing the box of the covenant of the Lord, and the singers, and Kenaniah the master of the band of singers, also on David there was a robe of fine linen. All Israel brought up the box of the covenant of the Lord with shouting, and with the sound of a horn, and with trumpets, and with cymbals, playing loudly on lutes and harps. The box of the covenant of the Lord arrived, and came to the City of David, and Michal the daughter of Saul looked down through the window and saw king David dancing and playing, and she despised him in her heart.

1st Paralipomenon: Chapter 16

They brought in the box of God and set it in the tabernacle which David pitched for it, and they offered whole burnt offerings and peace-offerings before God. David finished offering up whole burnt offerings and peace-offerings and blessed the people in the name of the Lord. He divided to every man of Israel (both men and women), for every man one baker's loaf, and a cake. He appointed before the box of the covenant of the Lord, Levites to minister and raise the voice, and to give thanks and praise Lord the god in Israel, Asaph was the chief, and next to him Zachariah, Jehiel, Shemiramoth, and Jehiel, Mattithiah, Elihu, and Benaiah, and Obed-Edom, and Jehiel sounding with musical instruments, lutes and harps, and Asaph with cymbals, and Benaiah and Uzziel the priests sounding continually with trumpets before the box of the covenant of God in that day.

Then David first gave orders to praise the Lord by the hand of Asaph and his brothers. "Sing. Give thanks to the Lord, call on him by his name, make known his designs among the people. Sing songs to him, and sing hymns to him relate to all people his wonderful deeds, which the Lord has worked. Praise his holy name, the heart that seeks his pleasure will rejoice. Seek the Lord and be strong, seek his face continually. Remember his wonderful works which he has worked, his wonders, and the judgments of his mouth, you seed of Israel his servants, you seed of Jacob his chosen ones."

"He is Lord the god! His judgments are in all the earth. Let us remember his covenant forever, his word which he commanded to a thousand generations, which he covenanted with Abraham, and his oath sworn to Isaac. He confirmed it to Jacob for an ordinance, to Israel as an everlasting covenant, saying, 'To you will I give the land of Canaan, the line of your inheritance,' when they were few in number, when they were but little, and lived as strangers in it, and went from nation to nation, and from one kingdom to another people. He didn't allow a man to oppress them, and he punished kings for their sake, saying, 'Don't touch my anointed ones, and don't deal wrongfully with my prophets.' Sing to the Lord, all the earth! Proclaim his salvation from day to day. Declare among the nations his glory, his wondrous deeds among all peoples. For the Lord is great, and greatly to be praised! He is to be feared above all gods. For all the gods of the nations are idols, but our God made the heavens. Glory and praise are in his presence, strength and rejoicing are in his place. Give to the Lord, you families of the nations, give to the Lord glory and strength. Give to the Lord the glory belonging to his name, take gifts and offer them before him, and worship the Lord in his holy courts. Let the whole earth fear before him, let the earth be established, and not be moved. Let the heavens rejoice, and let the earth exult, and let them say among the nations, the Lord reigns. The sea with its fullness will resound and the tree of the field, and all things in it."

"Then the trees of the forest will rejoice before the Lord, for he has come to judge the Earth. Give thanks to the Lord, for it is good, for his mercy is forever. Say, 'Save us, God of our salvation, and gather us, and rescue us from among the heathens, that we may praise your holy name, and glory in your praises.' Blessed is Lord the god in Israel from eternity and to eternity! All the people will say, 'Amen.'"

So they praised the Lord. They left there, Asaph and his brothers before the box of the covenant of the Lord, to minister before the box continually, according to the service of each day, from day to day. Obed-Edom and his brothers were sixty and eight, and Obed-Edom the son of Jeduthun, and Hosah were to be doorkeepers. They appointed Zadok the priest, and his brothers the priests, before the tabernacle of the Lord in the high place in Gibeon, to offer up whole burnt offerings continually morning and evening, and according to all things written in the law of the Lord, which he commanded the Israelites by Moses the servant of God. With him were Heman and Jeduthun, and the rest chose out by name to praise the Lord, for his mercy endures forever. With them, there were trumpets and cymbals to sound aloud, and musical instruments for the songs of God, and the sons of Jeduthun were at the gate. All the people went every one to his home: and David returned to bless his house.

1st Paralipomenon: Chapter 17

When David lived in his palace, David said to Nathan the prophet, "Look, I live in a palace of cedar, but the box of the covenant of the Lord is under curtains of skins."

Nathan replied to David, "Do all that is in your heart, for God is with you."

That night, the word of the Lord came to Nathan, saying, "Go and say to David my servant, the Lord says, 'You will not build me a temple to live in, for I have not lived in a temple from the day that I brought Israel up until today, but I have been in a tabernacle and a tent, in all places through which I have gone with all Israel. Did I ever ask for anyone among the tribe of Israel, whom I commanded to feed my people, 'Why is it that you have not built me a temple of cedar?' Then you will say to my servant David, 'Lord Shaddai[1] says, 'I took you from the sheepfold, from following the flocks, to be a ruler over my people Israel, and I was with you in all places to whatever place you went, and I destroyed all your enemies from before you, and I made for you a name among to the names of the great ones that are on the earth.'"

"I will appoint a place for my people Israel, and I will plant him, and he will live by himself, and will no longer be anxious, and the son of iniquity will no longer afflict him, as at the beginning, and from the days when I appointed judges over my people Israel. Also, I have humiliated all your enemies, and I will increase you, and the Lord will build you a temple. It will come to pass when your days will be fulfilled, and you will sleep with your fathers, that I will raise your seed after you, which will be of your bowels, and I will establish his kingdom. He will build me a house, and I will set up his throne forever. I will be a father to him, and he will be a son to me, and my mercy will I not withdraw from him, as I withdrew it from them that were before you.' I will establish him in my house and his kingdom forever, and his throne will be set up forever.'"

According to all these words, and all this vision, so said Nathan to David. King David came and sat before the Lord, and asked, "Who am I, Lord the god? What is my house, that you have loved me forever? These things were little in your sight, God, you have also spoken concerning the house of your servant for a long time to come, and you have looked on me as a man looks on his fellow, and have exalted me, Lord the god. What will David do to glorify you, so you know your servant? You have worked all this greatness according to your heart.

Lord, there is none like you, and there is no God besides you, according to all things which we have heard with our ears. Neither is there another nation on the earth such as your people Israel, whereas God led him in the way, to redeem a people for himself, to make for himself a great and glorious name, to throw out nations from before your people, whom you redeemed out of Egypt. You have appointed your people Israel as a people to yourself forever, and you, Lord, did become a God to them. Now, Lord, let the word which you spoke to your servant, and concerning his house, be confirmed forever, and do as you have spoken. Let your name be established and magnified forever, men saying, 'Lord Ba'al Shaddai, the God of Israel,'[2] and let the house of your servant David be established before you. For you, Lord my God, have revealed to the ear of your servant that you will build him a house; therefore your servant has found a willingness to pray before you. Now, Lord, you are God, and you have spoken these good things concerning your servant. Now you have begun to bless the house of your servant so that it should continue forever before you, for you, Lord, have blessed it, and you will bless it forever."

1ˢᵗ Paralipomenon: Chapter 17 Notes

1 Codex Vaticanus: cyrios pantocratôr (ΚΥΡΙΟC ΠΑΝΤΟΚΡΑΤωρ). Translation: lord omnipotent (or almighty)

• Aleppo Codex: Yhwh ṣbåwt (יהוה צבאות). Translation: Yhwh forces (or armies)

• Leningrad Codex: Yehvah tzeva'ovt (יְהוָה צְבָאֹות). Translation: Yehwāh forces (or armies)

• Targum of Chronicles: Yya tzeva'ovt (יְיָ צְבָאֹות). Translation: Yahw of desires

The term pantocratôr (παντοκράτωρ), meaning omnipotent, was used as the translation of Šdy (שדי) in the older sections of the Tanakh, including Job, where the terms are mirrored between the Septuagint and Masoretic text 33 times. The Septuagint and Masoretic translations often differ in regards to the name or title Šdy, suggesting that the Aramaic and Canaanite (Judahite or Samaritan) source texts they worked from differed in regards to this word. The term was omitted throughout Cosmic Genesis, suggesting that when the word was first encountered the Greeks did not know how to interpret it, as Cosmic Genesis / Bereshít is the first book of the Torah, the first collection of Israelite texts probably translated at the Library of Alexandria.

It is equally possible that it was the earlier Aramaic translator who had omitted it, however, it was almost certainly in the Canaanite version the translator worked from, as it is used consistently in Bereshít, and is mentioned again when Moses god's name Ān is introduced in the Septuagint's Exodus.

The cause of the confusion over the term šdy, is likely due to the difference between the meaning of the word in Canaanite versus Aramaic. In Akkadian cuneiform, which was adopted as the written script by many cultures, the term was ^{deity}šēdu (✳⊟), however, it referred to a 'protective spirit' or 'lesser god.' In the later Aramaic language, the word became šydå (ᐢᐪᐱᐡ), meaning 'demon' in the classical sense, as a type of muse or nymph. Whereas in Canaanite, šdy (ᙆᐁ) took on different meaning, generally interpreted as 'powerful' by the Early Classical Era, which is likely where the Greeks ultimately derived the term 'omnipotent' (παντοκράτορος), which was used later in the Septuagint where the Masoretic Text generally uses the term šdy.

This alternate interpretation of the šdy (ᙆᐁ) in Canaanite is likely due to the Egyptian New Kingdom era rule over Canaan, when Shed (𓆷𓂝𓏏, transliteration: šd), was worshiped in the region. In the former Amorite lands of northern Canaan, where Aramaic later became dominant, the Hurrians living under the rule of the Mitanni Empire called him Ablu (⊏⧼⊞), generally accepted as a shortened version of aplu ^{ilu}Ellil (⊏⧼⊞ ✳⎸▦), an epithet of Nergal, the son of the Old Babylonian god Ellil. Like Resheph and Nergal, Ablu was a god of both plague and healing. He was also imported to the Neshite (Hittite) and Trojan civilizations, as the god Apaliunas (𒀹𒌋𒈣𒅖𒄿𒊬) was mentioned in a peace treaty between the civilizations in 1280 BC. Homer reported in the

Illiad that Apollôn (Απολλων) was the god that built the wall of Troy, which confirms that the Greeks did view Apaliunas as Apollo. In the Illiad, a priest of Apollo called Chryses, referred to Apollo as the 'Lord of Mice' as he was believed to protect from plagues of mice. This indicates that the Pelesets viewed Shaddai as a version of Apaliunas when they captured the box of the covenant in 1st Kingdoms (Masoretic Samuel), as they returned it with golden statues of mice after their cities were plagued by swarms of mice.

In the Masoretic Book of Job, Eliphaz referred to humanity as the 'sons of Resheph' (בני-רשף) instead of the 'sons of Adam,' and then uses šdy as the name of a god. This god šdy was explicitly listed alongside the god El in Masoretic Job, whereas in the Septuagint's Job they are not explicitly listed as two separate gods. The Greek translation of Šdy (שדי) in Job is consistent with most of the Septuagint, using a term that translates as 'omnipotent' (παντοκράτορος), however, the name El (אל) is generally translated as a word meaning 'strong' (ἰσχυρὸς). It is likely because the Masoretic Text lists them side by side, as 'god El and god Šdy,' (אל-אל ואל-שדי), which the Greek translators did not do, instead routinely dropping the second reference to a god when they were listed together.

The terms 'god Šdy' (אל-שדי) and 'god El' (אל-אל) are repeatedly found in the Masoretic version of Job, and are themselves direct translations of the same terms in Akkadian Cuneiform: deityšēdu (✳⊏⧉) and deityAn (✳✳). Unfortunately, the Akkadian meaning of the word šēdu was 'demonic,' which is likely the cause of its redaction. Based on the linguistics of Masoretic Job, the text book existed in a hieratic Canaanite form during the Hyksos Dynasty, and therefore the name Resheph is not out of place, as Resheph was one of the main gods of the Hyksos rulers.

During the subsequent New Kingdom era, Resheph worship was suppressed due to his association with the earlier Hyksos dynasty. During the early New Kingdom era, holy texts about Resheph would have been updated to Shed (𓈙𓂧𓀭), which would have been transliterated into Canaanite using the Akkadian Cuneiform script in the late New Kingdom era as deityšēdu (𒀭𒆘), before being translated into Canaanite using the Phoenician script in the early iron age as šdy (𐤔𐤃𐤉), resulting in the confusing 'demonic' (𐡔𐡃𐡉𐡀) god in Aramaic.

During the Neo-Babylonian era, after Judah had been occupied by Babylonia, the books of the Kingdoms (Masoretic Samuel and Kings) appear to have been compiled in cuneiform, from the older Canaanite Chronicles of Samaria and Judah. During this translation, Sebittu ([illegible]) appears to have been used as a translation for Shaddai, as deityšēdu (𒀭𒆘) had come to mean 'protective griffin,' during the Neo-Assyrian era. The Assyrian version of the word was Sebitti ([illegible]), the god of war, which was associated with the Phrygian god Sabazdiôs (SA8A↑XOS), which was later reinterpreted as Sabazios (Σαβάζιος) in the Greco-Roman era, who was viewed as the Phrygian version of Sabaoth.

The Babylonian term Sebittu (𒐖𒐈𒐉) did not refer to a war god, but 'cosmic authority' during the Neo-Babylonian era. In the Old Akkadian language, the Sebittu (𒐖𒐉𒐈) had been the seven gods (planets) that ruled the sky, however, this usage had disappeared by the late bronze age, leaving only the vague concept of cosmic authority by the Neo-Babylonian era.

In the Greek translation of the Kingdoms, several terms were used interchangeably, including 'lord god' Sabaoth, Adônae 'Lord' Elôae Sabaôth, 'lord omnipotent', 'lord the forces', and 'Lord' Sabaôth, suggesting the Aramaic text the Greeks translated had previously been redacted more than once. However, in 1ˢᵗ Paralipomenon, only 'omnipotent' (παντοκράτωρ) was used, and in 2ⁿᵈ Paralipomenon, no name or epithet of god was used, indicating that the Aramaic text that were used for the source texts of the Paralipomena and Divrei-hayyamim had not been popular enough to redact. As the Aramaic text appears to have used the term Shaddai, that name is restored in this translation.

2 Codex Vaticanus: Cyrie Cyrie pantocratôr theos Israêl (ΚΥΡΙΕΚΥΡΙΕΠΑΝΤΟΚΡΑΤⲰΡ ΘΕΟC ΙCΡΑΗΛ). Translation: lord lord omnipotent (or almighty) god Israel)

• Aleppo Codex: Yhwh ṣbåwt ålhy Yšrål ålhym lYšrål (יהוה צבאות אלהי ישראל אלהים לישראל). Translation: Yhwh forces (or armies in Hebrew, desires in Aramaic) divine (or

god in Aramaic) Israel divines (or gods in Aramaic or god in
Neo-Babylonian) for Israel

• Leningrad Codex: Yehvah tzeva'ovt elohei Yisra'el
elohim leYisra'el (יְהוָה צְבָאוֹת אֱלֹהֵי יִשְׂרָאֵל אֱלֹהִים לְיִשְׂרָאֵל).
Translation: Yehvah forces (or armies) divine Israel divines
(in Hebrew, or gods in Aramaic, or God in Neo-Assyrian) to
Israel

• Targum of Chronicles: Yya elaha deyIshra'el hu elaha
leyIshra'el (יְיָ אֱלָהָא דְיִשְׂרָאֵל הוּא אֱלָהָא לְיִשְׂרָאֵל). Translation:
Yahw god of Israel forces he is god of Israel

The Greek and Hebrew translations are significantly
different at this point, indicating a difference between the
Aramaic and Hebrew versions of the text. King David also
prays to 'Lord my lord,' (Κύριέ μου κύριε) in 2ⁿᵈ Kingdoms,
which is mirrored in the Dead Sea Scroll 4QSamª with Yhwh
ådny (יהוה אדני), suggesting the name the Hasmoneans
replaced with Yahweh in this verse was Ba'al, which meant
'Lord.'

1st Paralipomenon: Chapter 18

It happened later, that David slaughtered the Pelesets, and routed them, and captured Gath and its villages out of the hand of the Pelesets. He attacked Moab, and the Moabites became servants to David and tributaries. David attacked Hadadezer king of Zobah of Hama, to extend his authority to the Euphrates River. David took against them a thousand chariots, and seven thousand horsemen, and twenty thousand infantry. David hamstrung all the chariot horses, but there were reserved from them a hundred chariots. The Syrians came from Damascus to help Hadadezer king of Zobah, and David slaughtered twenty-two thousand men of the Syrian army. David put a garrison in Syria near Damascus, and they became tributary servants to David, and the Lord delivered David wherever he went.

David took the golden collars that were on the servants of Hadadezer and brought them to Jerusalem. David took out of Tibhath, and out of the chief cities of Hadadezer a great deal of bronze, from this Solomon made the bronze sea, and the pillars, and the bronze vessels. King Taita[1] of Hama heard that David had struck the whole force of Hadadezer king of Zobah. He sent Hadoram his son to king David to ask how he was, and to congratulate him because he had fought against Hadadezer, and struck him, for Taita was the enemy of Hadadezer. All the gold and silver and bronze vessels

King David consecrated to the Lord, along with the silver and the gold which he took from all the nations, from Edom, and Moab, and the Ammonites, and the Pelesets, and Amalekites.

Abishai son of Zeruiah slaughtered eighteen thousand Edomites in the valley of Salt. He put garrisons in the valley, and all the Edomites became David's servants. The Lord delivered David wherever he went. So David reigned over all Israel, and he executed judgment and justice to all his people. Joab the son of Zeruiah was over the army, and Jehoshaphat the son of Ahilud was the recorder. Zadok son of Ahitub, and Ahimelech son of Abiathar were the priests, and Shavsha was the scribe, and Benaiah the son of Jehoiada was over the Cherethite and the Pelethite, and the sons of David were the chief deputies of the king.

1st Paralipomenon: Chapter 18 Notes

1 Codex Vaticanus: Thôa (ⲐⲰⲀ)

- Aleppo Codex: Tôw (תֹעוּ)

- Leningrad Codex: To'u (תֹּעוּ)

- Targum of Chronicles: To'u (תּוֹעוּ)

Ancient records from northern Syria and southeast Turkey record the name of King Taita II of Hama, who is accepted as being the king referenced here.

1st Paralipomenon: Chapter 19

After this Irnahash the king of the Ammonites died, and Hanani his son reigned in his place. David said, "I will act kindly towards Hanani the son of Irnahash, as his father acted kindly towards me."

David sent messengers to console him on the death of his father. So the servants of David came into the land of the Ammonites to Hanani, to comfort him. The chiefs of the Ammonites said to Hanani, "Is it to honor your father before you, that David has sent comforters to you? Have not his servants come to you that they might search the city, and to spy out the land?"

Hanani took the servants of David, and shaved them, and cut off the half of their garments as far as their tunic, and sent them away. There came men to report to David concerning the men, and he sent to meet them, for they were greatly disgraced, and the king said, "Live in Jericho until your beards have grown, and return. The Ammonites saw that the people of David were ashamed, and Hanani and the Ammonites sent a thousand talents of silver to hire for themselves chariots and horsemen out of Mesopotamian Syria, and out of Maachah in Syria, and from Zobah. They hired for themselves two and thirty thousand chariots, and the king of Maachah and his people, and they came and camped before Medeba, and the

Ammonites assembled out of their cities and came to fight.

David heard, and sent Joab and all the army of mighty men. The Ammonites came out, and set themselves in battle formation by the gate of the city, and the kings that were come forth camped by themselves in the plain. Joab saw that they were fronting him to fight against him before and behind, and he chose some out of all the young men of Israel, and they set themselves in array against the Syrian. The rest of the people he gave into the hand of his brother Abishai, and they set themselves in array against the Ammonites.

He said, "If the Syrian should prevail against me, then will you deliver me, and if the Ammonites should prevail against you, then will I deliver you. Be of good courage, and let us be strong, for our people, and the cities of our god, and the Lord will do what is good in his eyes."

Joab and the people that were with him set themselves in battle array against the Syrians, and they fled from them. The Ammonites saw that the Syrians fled, and they also fled from before Abishai, and from before Joab his brother, and they came to the city, and Joab came to Jerusalem. The Syrian saw that Israel had defeated him, and he sent messengers, and they brought out the Syrians from beyond the river, and Shophach the commander-in-chief of the forces of Hadadezer was before them. It was told David, and he gathered all Israel, and crossed across the Jordan, and came on them, and set the battle in array against them. So David set his army in array to fight against the Syrians, and they fought against him. The Syrians fled from before Israel, and David killed of the Syrians seven thousand riders in chariots and forty thousand infantry, and he killed Shophach the commander-in-chief of the forces. The servants of Hadadezer saw that they were defeated before Israel, and they made peace with David and served him, and the Syrians would not anymore help the Ammonites.

1st Paralipomenon: Chapter 20

The following year, at the time that the kings went out to war, Joab gathered the whole force of the army, and they ravaged the land of the Ammonites, and he came and besieged Rabbah. But David remained in Jerusalem. Joab attacked Rabbah and destroyed it. David took the crown of Molchol their king off his head, and the weight of it was found to be a talent of gold, and on it were precious stones, and it was placed on the head of David, and he brought out the spoils of the city which were very great. He brought out the people that were in it, and sawed them to pieces with saws, and choped them with iron axes and with harrows. David did this to all the Ammonites.

David and all his people returned to Jerusalem. It came to pass afterward that there was again war with the Pelesets in Gezer, then Sibbekai the Hushathite struck Sippai of the sons of the Raphites, and laid him low. There was war again with the Pelesets, and Elhanan the son of Jair struck Lahmi the brother of Goliath the Gittite, and the wood of his spear was as a weavers' beam. There was another war in Gath, and there was a man of extraordinary size, and his fingers and toes were six on each hand and foot, 24, and he was descended from the Gigantes. He defied Israel, and Jonathan the son of Shimea the brother of David killed him. These were born to the Rapha[1] in Gath, all four were Raphites, and they fell by the hand of David, and by the hand of his servants.

1st Paralipomenon: Chapter 20 Notes

1 Codex Vaticanus: Rapha (ρ‎ᴧφᴧ)

• Aleppo Codex: rpå (רפא). Translation: healer (in Hebrew and other Canaanite dialects), or loosener (or softener in Aramaic)

• Leningrad Codex: rafa (רָפָא). Translation: healer (in Hebrew and other Canaanite dialects), or loosener (or softener in Aramaic)

• Targum of Chronicles: arepah (עֲרְפָּה)

In this verse, the singular form of Rafa is used in Hebrew, and was also transliterated into Greek. It is not used as the name of an individual, but a title or the name of a god. The most probable explanation is that the original term simply meant healer.

1st Paralipomenon: Chapter 21

The slanderer[1] stood up against Israel and moved David to count Israel. King David said to Joab and the captains of the army, "Go, count Israel from Beersheba to Dan, and bring me the total, and I will know their number."

Joab said, "May the Lord add to his people, a hundredfold as many as they are, and let the eyes of my lord the king see it. All are the servants of my lord. Why does my lord seek this thing? Do not do it, in case it becomes a sin to Israel."

Nevertheless, the king's word prevailed against Joab, and Joab went out and passed through all Israel, and returned to Jerusalem. Joab gave the number of the count of the people to David, and all Israel was one million and one hundred thousand men that drew the sword, and the sons of Judah were four hundred and seventy thousand men that drew the sword. But he did not count Levi and Benjamin among them, for the word of the king was painful to Joab. This thing was evil in the sight of the Lord, and he attacked Israel.

David said to God, "I have sinned greatly, in doing this thing, and now, I beg you, remove the sin of your servant, for I have been exceedingly foolish."

The Lord said to Gad the seer, "Go and tell David, 'The Lord says, I bring three things on you, choose one of them for yourself, and I will do it to you.'"

Gad came to David, and said to him, "The Lord says, 'Choose for yourself, either three years of famine, or that you should flee three months from the face of your enemies, and the sword of your enemies will be employed to destroy you, or that the sword of the Lord and pestilence should be three days in the land, and the messenger of the Lord[2] will destroy all the inheritance of Israel. Now consider what I will answer to him that sent the message.'"

David said to Gad, "They are very hard for me, even all the three, let me fall now into the hands of the Lord, for his mercies are very abundant, and let me not fall by any means into the hands of man."

The Lord brought pestilence on Israel, and seventy thousand Israelite men died. God sent a messenger to Jerusalem to destroy it, and as he was destroying the Lord saw and repented the evil, and said to the messenger of destruction, "Let it be enough for you, withhold your hand."

The messenger of the Lord stood by the threshing floor of Arnan the Jebusite. David lifted his eyes, and saw the messenger of the Lord, standing between the earth and the sky, and his sword drawn in his hand, stretched out over Jerusalem, and David and the elders clothed in sackcloth, fell on their faces.

David said to God, "Was it not I that gave orders to count the people? I am the guilty one! I have greatly sinned! But these sheep, what have they done? Lord the god, let your hand be on me, and my father's house, and not on your people for destruction, my Lord!"

The messenger of the Lord told Gad to tell David, that he should go up to erect an altar to the Lord, in the threshing floor of Arnan the Jebusite. David went up according to the word of Gad, which he spoke in the name of the Lord. Arnan turned and saw the king, and he hid himself and his four sons with him. Now Arnan was threshing wheat. David came to Arnan, and Arnan came forth from the threshing floor and did obeisance to David with his face to the ground.

David said to Arnan, "Give me your section of the threshing floor, and I will build on it an altar to the Lord! Sell it to me for its value in silver, and the plague will cease from among the people."

Arnan said to David, "Take it to yourself and let my lord the king do what is right in his eyes. See, I have given the calves for a whole burnt offering, and the plow for wood, and the grain for a meat-offering! I have given all."

King David replied to Arnan, "No! I will certainly buy it for its worth in silver, for I will not take your property for the Lord, to offer a whole burnt offering to the Lord without cost to myself."

David bought from Arnan his place for six hundred shekels of gold by weight. David built an altar there to the Lord and offered up whole burnt offerings and peace-offerings, and he called to the Lord, and he answered him by fire out of the sky on the altar of whole burnt offerings, and it consumed the whole burnt offering. The Lord spoke to the messenger, and he returned his sword to its sheath. At that time when David saw that the Lord answered him at the threshing floor of Arnan the Jebusite, he also sacrificed there. The tabernacle of the Lord which Moses made in the wilderness, and the altar of whole burnt offerings, were at that time in the high place at Gibeon. David could not go before it to inquire of God. He did not rush because of the sword of the messenger of the Lord.

1ˢᵗ Paralipomenon: Chapter 21 Notes

1 Codex Vaticanus: diabolos (ΔΙΑΒΟΛΟϹ). Translation: slanderer

- Aleppo Codex: štn (שׂטן). Translation: adversary

- Leningrad Codex: satan (שָׂטָן). Translation: adversary (or opponent)

- Targum of Chronicles: Yya sitna (יְיָ סָטָנָא). Translation: Yahw's adversary (or devil)

2 Codex Vaticanus: angelos cyriou (ΑΓΓΕΛΟϹΚΥΡΙΟΥ). Translation: messenger lord

- Aleppo Codex: mlåk yhwh (מלאך יהוה). Translation: messenger Yahweh

- Leningrad Codex: malak Yehvah (מַלְאַךְ יְהוָה). Translation: messenger Yahweh

- Targum of Chronicles: mechabbel (מְחַבֵּל). Translation: destroyer (an evil spirit)

1st Paralipomenon: Chapter 22

David said, "This is the Temple of Lord the god, and this is the altar for all burnt offerings for Israel."

David gave orders to gather all the immigrants that were in the land of Israel, and he appointed stone-masons to cut polished stones to build the Temple for God. David ordered a great deal of iron for the nails of the doors and the gates, and also the hinges, and so much bronze there was no weighing it, and cedar trees without number, for the Sidonians and Tyrians brought cedar trees in great numbers to David.

David said, "My son Solomon is a young child, and the temple I want to build to the Lord is for the greater magnificence of his name and glory through all the earth. I will plan for it." David planned a great deal before his death. He called Solomon his son and commanded him to build the Temple of Lord the god in Israel.

David said to Solomon, "My child, it was in my heart to build a house to the name of Lord the god. But the word of the Lord came to me, saying, 'You have shed a great deal of blood, and have carried on great wars. You will not build a house to my name, because you have shed much blood on the earth for me. Look, a son will be born to you, he will be a man of peace, and I will give him peace from all his enemies all around. His name will be Solomon, and I will give peace and quietness to Israel in his days. He will build a temple in my name, and he will be a son to me, and I will be a father to him, and I will establish the throne of his kingdom in Israel forever."

"Now, my son, the Lord will be with you and prosper you, and you will build a Temple to Lord the god, as he spoke concerning you. Only may the Lord give you wisdom and prudence, and strengthen you over Israel, both to keep and to do the law of Lord the god. Then he will make you prosper, if you pay attention to do the commandments and judgments which the Lord commanded Moses for Israel, be courageous and strong. Don't be afraid, or be terrified."

"See, I have impoverished myself, preparing to build the Temple of the Lord, stockpiling a hundred thousand talents of gold, and a million talents of silver, and so much bronze and iron it cannot be calculated. I have prepared timber and stones, and you will add to these, from that which you will have. Add to the multitude of workmen, let there be artisans and masons, and carpenters, and every skillful workman in every work, in gold and silver, bronze and iron, which is beyond calculating. Rise, and the Lord be with you."

David ordered all the chief men of Israel to help Solomon his son, saying, "Isn't the Lord with you? He has given you peace all around, for he has given into your hands the inhabitants of the land, and the land is subdued before the Lord, and before his people. Now set your hearts and souls to search for Lord the god, and rise, and build a sanctuary to your God to carry in the box of the covenant of the Lord, and the holy vessels of God, into the house that is to be built in the name of the Lord."

1st Paralipomenon: Chapter 23

David was old and full of days, and he made Solomon his son king over Israel in his place. He assembled all the chief men of Israel, and the priests, and the Levites. The Levites counted themselves from thirty years old and upward, and their number by their polls amounted to thirty-eight thousand men. The overseers of the works of the Temple of the Lord were twenty-four thousand. There were six thousand scribes and judges, and four thousand doorkeepers and four thousand to praise the Lord with instruments which he made to praise the Lord. David divided them into daily courses, for the sons of Levi, for Gershon, Kohath, and Merari. From the family of Gershon were Laadan, and Shimei.

The sons of Laadan were Jehiel was the first, and Zethan, and Joel, totaling three. The sons of Shimei were Salomith, Jehiel, and Dan, totaling three These were the chiefs of the families of Laadan.

The sons of Shimei were Jahath, and Zina, and Jeush, and Beriah. These were the four sons of Shimei: Jahath was the first, and Zina the second, and Jeush and Beriah did not have sons, and they each only counted as one in the house of their father.

The sons of Kohath were Amram, and Izhar, and Hebron, and Uzziel, totaling four.

The sons of Amram were Aaron and Moses, and Aaron was appointed for the consecration of the holiest things, he and his sons forever, to burn incense before the Lord, to minister and bless in his name forever.

As for Moses the prophet, his sons were considered of the tribe of Levi.

The sons of Moses were Gershon and Eliezer.

The sons of Gershon were Shubael the first. The sons of Eliezer were Rehabiah the chief, and Eliezer had no other sons, but the sons of Rehabiah were very greatly multiplied.

The son of Izhar was Shelomith the chief.

The sons of Hebron were Jeriah the chief, Omri the second, Azarel the third, Jekameam the fourth.

The sons of Uzziel were Michah the chief, and Isshiah the second.

The sons of Merari were Mahli, and Mushi.

The sons of Mahli were Eleazar, and Kish.

Eleazar died and he had no sons, but daughters: and the sons of Kish, their brothers, took them.

The sons of Mushi were Mahli, Eder, and Jeremoth, totaling three.

These are the sons of Levi according to the houses of their fathers, chiefs of their families according to their count, according to the number of their names, according to their polls, doing the works of service of the Temple of the Lord, from twenty years old and upward, as David said, "Lord the god in Israel has given peace to his people, and has started up living in Jerusalem forever."

The Levites did not carry the tabernacle and all the vessels of it for its service. By the final words of David were the count of the Levites taken from twenty years old and upward. He appointed them to wait on Aaron, to minister in the Temple of the Lord, over the courts, and over the chambers, and over the purification of all the holy things, and over the works of the service of the Temple of God, and for the show-bread, and for the fine flour of the meat-offering, and for the unleavened cakes, and for the fried cake, and for the dough, and for every measure, and to stand in the morning to praise and give thanks to the Lord, and so in the evening, and to be overall the whole burnt offerings that were offered up to the Lord on the sabbaths, and at the new moons, and at the feasts, by number, according to the order given to them, continually before the Lord. They are to keep the charge of the tabernacle of witness, and the charge of the holy place, and the charges of the sons of Aaron their brothers, to minister in the Temple of the Lord.

1st Paralipomenon: Chapter 24

They counted the sons of Aaron in their division, which were Nadab, and Abihud, and Eleazar, and Ithamar.

Nadab and Abihud died before their father, and they had no sons, so Eleazar and Ithamar the sons of Aaron ministered as priests. David divided them, including Zadok of the sons of Eleazar, and Ahimelech of the sons of Ithamar, according to their count, according to their service, according to the houses of their fathers. There were found among the sons of Eleazar more great chiefs, than of the sons of Ithamar, and he divided them, sixteen heads of families among the sons of Eleazar, and eight among the families of the sons of Ithamar.

He divided them according to their lots, one with the other, for there were those who had charge of the holy things, and those who had charge of the Temple of the Lord among the sons of Eleazar, and among the sons of Ithamar. Shemaiah the son of Nethanel, the scribe, of the family of Levi, wrote them down before the king, and the princes, and Zadok the priest, and Ahimelech the son of Abiathar were present, and the heads of the families of the priests and the Levites, each of a household were assigned one to Eleazar, and one to Ithamar.

The first lot came out to Jehoiarib, the second to Jedaiah, the third to Harim, the fourth to Seorim, the fifth to

Malchijah, the sixth to Mijamin, the seventh to Hakkoz, the eighth to Abijah, the ninth to Jesus, the tenth to Shecaniah, the eleventh to Eliashib, the twelfth to Jakim, the thirteenth to Huppah, the fourteenth to Jesbaal, the fifteenth to Bilgah, the sixteenth to Immer, the seventeenth to Hezir, the eighteenth to Aphses, the nineteenth to Pethahiah, the twentieth to Jehezekel, the twenty-first to Ahiam, the twenty-second to Gamul, the twenty-third to Delaiah, the twenty-fourth to Maaziah. This is their numbering according to their service to go into the Temple of the Lord, according to their appointment by the hand of Aaron their father, as Lord the god in Israel commanded.

For the sons of Levi that were left, even for the sons of Amram, Shubael, and for the sons of Shubael, Jedaiah. For Rehabiah: the first was Isshiah, and for Isshiah: Shelomith. For the sons of Shelomith: Jahath. The sons of Ecdiu: Amadia the second, Azarel the third, Jekameam the fourth. For the sons of Uzziel, Micah: the sons of Micah: Shamir. The brother of Michah: Isshiah, the son of Isshiah: Zechariah. The sons of Merari, Mahli, and Mushi: the sons of Uzziah, that is, the sons of Merari by Uzziah, his sons were Shoham, and Zakkur, and Ibri.

To Mahli were born Eleazar and Ithamar, and Eleazar died and had no sons. For Kish, the sons of Kish: Jerahmeel.

The sons of Mushi were Mahli, Eder, and Jerimoth.

These were the sons of the Levites according to the houses of their families. They also received lots as their brothers the sons of Aaron before the king. Zadok also, and Ahimelech, and the chiefs of the families of the priests and the Levites, principal heads of families, even as their younger brothers.

1st Paralipomenon: Chapter 25

King David and the captains of the army appointed to their services the sons of Asaph, Heman, and Jeduthun, prophesiers with harps, and lutes, and cymbals, and their number was according to their polls serving in their ministrations. The sons of Asaph were Zakkur, and Joseph, and Nethaniah, and Asarelah. The sons of Asaph were next to the king. From Jeduthun were thought to be the sons of Jeduthun: Gedaliah, and Hori, and Iseas, and Hashabiah, and Mattithiah, the six followed behind their father Jeduthun, sounding loudly on the harp giving thanks and praise to the Lord.

From Heman were thought to be the sons of Heman: Bukkiah, and Mattaniah, and Uzziel, and Shubael, and Jerimoth, and Hananiah, and Hanani, and Eliathah, and Giddalti, and Romamti-Jazer, and Joshbekashah, and Mallothi, and Hothir, and Mahazioth. All these were the sons of Heman the king's chief player in the praises of God, to lift up the horn. God gave to Heman fourteen sons and three daughters. All these sang hymns with their father in the Temple of God, with cymbals, and lutes, and harps, for the service of the Temple of God, near the king, and Asaph, and Jeduthun, and Heman. The number of them after their brothers, those instructed to sing to God, everyone that understood singing was two hundred and eighty-eight.

They also cast lots for the daily courses, for the great and the small of them, of the perfect ones and the learners. The first lot of his sons and of his brothers came forth to Asaph the son of Joseph, namely, Gedaliah, the second Heneia, his sons and his brothers were twelve.

The third was Zakkur, and his sons and his brothers were twelve.

The fourth was Izri, and his sons and his brothers were twelve.

The fifth was Nathan, and his sons and his brothers were twelve.

The sixth was Bukkiah, and his sons and his brothers were twelve.

The seventh was Iseriel, and his sons and his brothers were twelve.

The eighth was Jeshaiah, and his sons and his brothers were twelve.

The ninth was Mattaniah, and his sons and his brothers were twelve.

The tenth was Shimei, and his sons and his brothers were twelve,

The eleventh was Azarel, and his sons and his brothers were twelve.

The twelfth was Hashabiah, and his sons and his brothers were twelve.

The thirteenth was Shubael, and his sons and his brothers were twelve.

The fourteenth was Mattithiah, and his sons and his brothers were twelve.

The fifteenth was Jerimoth, and his sons and his brothers were twelve.

The sixteenth was Hananiah, and his sons and his brothers were twelve.

The seventeenth was Joshbekashah, and his sons and his brothers were twelve.

The eighteenth was Hananiah, and his sons and his brothers were twelve.

The nineteenth was Mallothi, and his sons and his brothers were twelve.

The twentieth was Eliathah, and his sons and his brothers were twelve.

The twenty-first was Hothir, and his sons and his brothers were twelve.

The twenty-second was Giddalti, and his sons and his brothers were twelve.

The twenty-third was Mahazioth, and his sons and his brothers were twelve.

The twenty-fourth was Romamti-Jazer, and his sons and his brothers were twelve.

1st Paralipomenon: Chapter 26

For the divisions of the gates, the sons of the Korhites were Meshelemiah, of the sons of Asaph. Meshelemiah's firstborn son was Zachariah, the second Jediael, the third Zebadiah, the fourth Jenuel, the fifth Elam, the sixth Jehohanan, the seventh Eliehoenai, the eighth Obed-Edom. To Obed-Edom there were born sons, Shemaiah the firstborn, Jehozabad the second, Joah the third, Sakar the fourth, Nethanel the fifth, Ammiel the sixth, Issachar the seventh, Peullethai the eighth, as God blessed him.

To Shemaiah, his son were chiefs over the house of their father, for they were mighty. The sons of Shemaiah were Othni, and Raphael, and Obed, and Elzabad, and Achiud, mighty men, Elihu, and Shemaiah, and Isbacom. All these were of the sons of Obed-Edom. They and their sons and their brothers, doing mightily in service, in all sixty-two born to Obed-Edom.

Meshelemiah had eighteen sons and brothers, mighty men. To Hosah of the sons of Merari, there were born sons, keeping the dominion, though he was not the firstborn, yet his father made him chief of the second division. Hilkiah the second, Tabaliah the third, Zachariah the fourth, all these were the sons and brothers of Hosah, thirteen. To these were assigned the divisions of the gates, to the chiefs of the mighty men the daily courses for their brothers, to minister in the Temple of the Lord.

They cast lots for the small as well as for the great, for the several gates, according to their families. The lot of the east gates fell to Shelemiah, and Zachariah, the sons of Soaz cast lots for Malchijah, and the lot came out northward. To Obed-Edom they gave by lot the south, opposite the house of Esephim. They gave the lot for the second to Hosah westward, after the gate of the chamber by the ascent, watch against watch. There were six watchmen in the day to the east, and four during the day to the north, and four by the day to the south, and two at the Esephim, as relieve guards. Also for Hosah after the chamber-gate, three to the west.

There was a ward over against the ward of the ascent eastward, six men in a day, and four for the north, and four for the south, and at the Esephim two to relieve guard, and four by the west, and two to relieve guard at the pathway. These are the divisions of the porters for the sons of Korah and to the sons of Merari. The Levites their brothers were over the treasures of the Temple of the Lord, and the treasures of the sacred things. These were the sons of Ladan, the son of the Gershonites, to Ladan belonged the heads of the families.

The son of Ladan the Gershonite was Jehiel. The sons of Jehiel were Zetham and Joel, brothers who were in charge of the treasures of the Temple of the Lord.

To Amram and Izhar belonged Hebron and Uzziel. Shubael the son of Gershon, the son of Moses, was in charge of the treasures, and Rehabiah was the son of his brother Eliezer, and so was Jeshaiah, and Joram, and Zikri, and Shelomith. This Shelomith and his brothers were over all the sacred treasures, which David the king and the heads of families consecrated, and the captains of thousands and captains of hundreds, and princes of the army, things which he took out of cities and from the spoils, and consecrated some of them, so that the building of the Temple of God should not lack supplies, and over-all the holy things of god dedicated by Samuel the prophet, and Saul the son of Kish, and Abner the son of Ner, and Joab the son of Zeruiah, whatever they sanctified was by the hand of Shelomith and his brothers.

For the Izharites, Kenaniah and his sons were over the outward ministration over Israel, to record and to judge. For the Hebronites, Hashabiah and his brothers, a thousand and seven hundred mighty men, were over the charge of Israel beyond Jordan to the west, for all the service of the Lord and work of the king. Of the family of Hebron, Judah[1] was chief of the Hebronites according to their generations, according to their families. In the fortieth year of his reign they were counted, and there were found mighty men among them from Jazer in Gilead. His brothers were two thousand and seven hundred mighty men, chiefs of their families, and King David set them over the Reubenites, and the Gadites, and the half-tribe of Manasseh, for every ordinance of the Lord, and business of the king.

1st Paralipomenon: Chapter 26 Notes

1 Codex Vaticanus: Ioudias (ιογδιας)

- Aleppo Codex: Yryh (ירִיה)

- Leningrad Codex: Yeriyyah (יְרִיָּה)

- Targum of Chronicles: Yeriyah (יְרִיָה)

1st Paralipomenon: Chapter 27

Now the sons of Israel according to their number, heads of families, captains of thousands and captains of hundreds, and scribes ministering to the king, and for every affair of the king according to their divisions, for every ordinance of coming in and going out monthly, for all the months of the year, one division of them was twenty-four thousand.

Over the first division of the first month was Isboaz the son of Zabdiel. In his division were twenty-four thousand. Of the sons of Perez one was chief of all the captains of the army for the first month.

Over the division of the second month was Dodai the son of Ecchoc, and over his division was Mikloth also chief. In his division were twenty-four thousand, chief men of the army.

The third for the third month was Benaiah the son of Jehoiada the chief priest, and in his division were twenty-four thousand. This Benaiah was more mighty than the thirty, and over the thirty. Zabad his son was over his division.

The fourth for the fourth month was Asahel the brother of Joab, and Zebadiah his son, and his brothers, and in his division were twenty-four thousand.

The fifth chief for the fifth month was Shamhuth the Izrahite. In his division were twenty-four thousand.

The sixth for the sixth month was Hoduias the son of Ikkesh the Tekoite. In his division were twenty-four thousand.

The seventh for the seventh month was Helez of Pallu of the children of Ephraim: and in his division were twenty-four thousand.

The eighth for the eighth month was Sibbekai the Hushathite, belonging to Zarai. In his division were twenty-four thousand.

The ninth for the ninth month was Abiezer of Anathoth, of the land of Benjamin: and in his division were twenty-four thousand.

The tenth for the tenth month was Maharai the Netophathite, belonging to Zarai: and in his division were twenty-four thousand.

The eleventh for the eleventh month was Benaiah of Pi-rathon, of the sons of Ephraim, and in his division were twenty-four thousand.

The twelfth for the twelfth month was Heldai the Netophathite, belonging to Othniel, and in his division were twenty-four thousand.

Over the tribes of Israel, the chief for Reuben was Eliezer the son of Zikri.

For Simeon: Shephatiah the son of Maachah.

For Levi: Hashabiah the son of Kemuel.

For Aaron: Zadok.

For Judah: Elihu of the brothers of David.

For Issachar: Omri the son of Michael.

For Zebulun: Ishmaiah the son of Obadiah.

For Naphtali: Jerimoth the son of Uzziel.

For Ephraim: Hoshea the son of Uzziah.

For the half-tribe of Manasseh: Joel the son of Pedaiah.

For the half-tribe of Manasseh in the land of Gilead: Iddo the son of Zechariah.

For the Benjaminites: Jaasiel the son of Abner.

For Dan: Azarel the son of Iroab.

These are the chiefs of the tribes of Israel.

David did not count their count from twenty years old and under, because the Lord said that he would multiply Israel like the stars of the sky. Joab the son of Zeruiah began to count the people, and did not finish the work, for there was subsequently anger on Israel. The number was not recorded in the book of the chronicles of king David.

In charge of the king's treasures was Azmaveth the son of Adiel, and over the treasures in the country, and the towns, and the villages, and the towers, was Jonathan the son of Uzziah. In charge of the farmers who tilled the ground was Esdri the son of Caleb. In charge of the fields was Shimei of Rael, and over the treasures of wine in the fields was Zabdi the son of Sephni. In charge of the olive yards, and over the sycamores in the plain country was Ba'al Hanan the Gedorite, and over the stores of oil was Jeush. In charge of the oxen pasturing in Sharon was Shitrai the Saronite, and over the oxen in the valleys was Shaphat the son of Adlai. In charge of the camels was Obil the Ismaelite, and in charge of the donkeys was Jehdeiah of Merathon. In charge of the sheep was Jaziz the Hagrite.

All these were superintendents of the property of King David. Jonathan, David's uncle by the father's side was a counselor and a wise man. Jehiel the son of Hakmoni was with the king's sons. Ahithophel was the king's counselor, and Hushai the chief friend of the king. After Ahithophel Jehoiada the son of Benaiah came next, and Abiathar. Joab was the king's commander-in-chief.

1ˢᵗ Paralipomenon: Chapter 28

David assembled all the chief men of Israel, the chief of the judges, and all the chief men of the courses of attendance on the person of the king, and the captains of thousands and hundreds, and the treasurers, and the lords of his substance, and of all the king's property, and of his sons, together with the eunuchs, and the mighty men, and the warriors of the army, at Jerusalem.

David stood among the assembly, and said, "Hear me, my brothers, and my people. It was in my heart to build a house of rest for the box of the covenant of the Lord, and a place for the feet of our Lord, and I prepared materials suitable for the building, but God said, 'You will not build me a temple to call my name on it, for you are a man of war, and have shed blood.' Yet Lord the god in Israel chose me out of the whole house of my father to be king over Israel forever, and he chose Judah as the kingly house, and out of the house of Judah, he chose the house of my father, and among the sons of my father he preferred me, that I should be king over all Israel. Of all my sons, (for the Lord has given me many sons,) he has chosen Solomon, my son, to set him on the throne of the kingdom of the Lord over Israel. God said to me, 'Solomon your son will build my temple and my court, for I have chosen him to be my son, and I will be for him a father. I will establish his kingdom forever, if he continues to keep my commandments, and my judgments, as on this day. Now I order you before the whole assembly of the Lord, and in the audience of our God, keep and seek all the commandments of Lord the god, that you may inherit the good land, and leave it for your sons to inherit after you forever. Now, my son Solomon, know the god of your fathers, and serve him with a perfect heart and willing soul, for the Lord searches all hearts, and knows every thought, if you seek him, he will be found of you, but if you should forsake him, he will forsake you forever. See now, for the Lord has chosen you to build him a temple for a sanctuary, be strong and do it."

David gave Solomon his son, the design for the temple, and its buildings, and its treasuries, and its upper chambers, and the inner store-rooms, and the place of the atonement. The design that he had in his mind of the courts of the Temple of the Lord, and of all the chambers around designed for the treasuries of the Temple of God, and of the treasuries of the holy things, and of the chambers for resting. The plan of the courses of the priests and Levites, for all the work of the service of the Temple of the Lord, and of the stores of vessels for the ministration of the service of the Temple of the Lord. He gave him the account of their weight, both of gold and silver vessels. He gave him the weight of the candlesticks, and of the lamps. He gave him likewise the weight of the tables of showbread, of each table of gold, and likewise of the tables of silver: also of the meat-hooks, and vessels for drink-offering, and golden bowls, and the weight of the gold and silver articles, and censers, and bowls, according to the weight of each.

He showed him the weight of the utensils of the altar of incense, which was of pure gold, and the plan of the chariot of the sphinxes that spread out their wings and overshadowed the box of the covenant of the Lord. David gave all to Solomon in the Lord's handwriting, according to the knowledge given to him of the work of the pattern. David said to Solomon his son, "Be strong, and be a man, and don't be afraid or terrified, for Lord the god is with you and he will not forsake you, and will not fail you until you have finished all the work of the service of the Temple of the Lord. See, the design of the temple, including his house, and its treasury, and the upper chambers, and the inner store-rooms, and the place of propitiation, and the plan of the Temple of the Lord. See, here are the courses of the priests and Levites for all the service of the Temple of the Lord, and there will be with you men for every workmanship, and every one from every useful skill, also the chief men and all the people, ready for all your commands."

1st Paralipomenon: Chapter 29

King David said to all the congregation, "Solomon my son, who the Lord has chosen, is young and tender, and the work is great, as it is not for man, but for Lord the god. I have prepared according to all my might for the house of my god gold, silver, bronze, iron, wood, onyx stones, and costly and varied stones for setting, and every precious stone, and a great deal of Parian[1] marble. Still farther, because I took pleasure in the temple of my god, I have gold and silver which I have procured for myself, and, look, I have given them to the house of my god over and above, beyond what I have prepared for the holy house. Three thousand talents of gold of Sauvira,[2] and seven thousand talents of fine silver, for the over-laying of the walls of the sanctuary, for you to use the gold for things of gold, and the silver for things of silver, and every work by the hand of the artificers. Who is willing to dedicate himself to work this day for the Lord?"

Then the heads of families, and the princes of the Is-raelites, and the captains of thousands and captains of hundreds, and the overseers of the works, and the king's builders offered willingly.

They gave for the works of the Temple of the Lord five thousand talents of gold, and ten thousand gold pieces, and ten thousand talents of silver, and eighteen thousand talents of bronze, and a hundred thousand talents of iron. They who had precious stone gave it into the treasuries of the Temple of the Lord by the hand of Jehiel the Gedsonite.

The people rejoiced because of the willingness, for they offered willingly to the Lord with a full heart, and King David rejoiced greatly.

King David blessed the Lord before the congregation, saying, "Blessed are you, Lord the god in Israel, our father, from century and to century. You, Lord, are the greatness and the power and the glory and the victory and the might, for you are the lord of all things that are in the sky and on the earth. Before your face every king and nation is troubled. From you come wealth and glory, you govern everything, Lord governing all governors, and in your hand are strength and power, and your hand, Shaddai,[3] enlarges and overpowers everything. Now, Lord, we give thanks to you and praise your glorious name. But who am I, and what are my people, that we have been able to be so forward in offering to you? For all things are yours, and from your own have we given you, for we are strangers before you, and travelers, as all our fathers were, our days on the earth are like a shadow, and there is nothing remaining. Lord the god, as for all this abundance which I have prepared that a house should be built to your holy name, it is of your hand, and all is yours. I know, Lord, that you are he that searches the hearts, and you love righteousness. I have willingly offered all these things with honesty of heart, and now I have seen with joy your people here present, willingly offering to you. Lord the god, god of Abraham, Isaac, and Israel, our fathers, preserve these things in the thought of the heart of your people forever and direct their hearts to you. To Solomon my son give a good heart, to perform your commandments, and to observe your testimonies, and your ordinances, and to accomplish the building of your house."

David said to the whole congregation, "Bless you, Lord the god."

All the congregation blessed Lord the god of their fathers, and they bowed the knee and worshiped the Lord, and bowed towards the king. David sacrificed to the Lord, and offered up whole burnt offerings to the Lord on the morning after the first day, a thousand calves, a thousand rams, a thousand lambs, and their drink-offerings, and sacrifices in abundance for all Israel. They ate and drank joyfully that day before the Lord, and they made Solomon the son of David king a second time and anointed him king before the Lord, and Zadok to the priesthood.

Solomon sat on the throne of his father David, and was highly honored, and all Israel obeyed him. The princes, and the mighty men, and all the sons of king David his father, were subject to him. The Lord magnified Solomon over all Israel, and gave him royal glory, such as was not on any king before him. David the son of Jesse reigned over Israel forty years, seven years in Hebron, and thirty-three years in Jerusalem. He died in a good old age, full of days, in wealth, and glory and Solomon his son reigned in his place. The rest of the acts of David, the former and the latter, are written in the Book of Samuel the seer, and in the Book of Nathan the prophet, and in the Book of Gad the seer, concerning all his reign, and his power, and the times which went over him, and over Israel, and over all the kingdoms of the earth.

1st Paralipomenon: Chapter 29 Notes

1 Codex Vaticanus: parion (ΠΑΡΙΟΝ)

The Masoretic Text does not mention where the marble came from. Parian Marble was from the Island of Paros in the Aegean Sea. It was highly prized by the Greeks, and many ancient statues were carved in it, including the Winged Victory of Samothrace. The mines of Paros were in use since at least the 6th century BC. It is unclear if they were in the 10th century BC.

2 Codex Vaticanus: Souphir (ϹΟΥΦΙΡ)

- Aleppo Codex: Åwpyr (אופיר)

- Leningrad Codex: Ovfir (אֹופִיר)

- Targum of Chronicles: Ofir (אֹופִיר)

The spelling of the name in the this book of the Septuagint supports this book having been translated from Phoenician (probably Samaritan) instead of Aramaic, like most of the Septuagint. In most of the Septuagint's books that mention the land it is transliterated as Sôphêra (Σωφηρα) from the Aramaic spelling.

The location of this civilization has been a matter of debate for centuries. Given the list of items imported from Sôphêra/Åwpyr, it was likely the ancient Pakistani Kingdom of Sauvira on the Indus River. Imported items include gold, silver, sandalwood, pearls, ivory, apes, and peacocks. Sandalwood trees are indigenous to South and Southeast Asia and have traditionally been considered sacred by the Hindus,

Jainists, Buddhists, and Zoroastrians, as well as other Asian cultures. Peacocks are indigenous to South and Southeast Asia, as well as the Congo Rain-forest, however, Sandalwood trees are not found in the Congo Rain-forest. Apes were still living in South and Southeast Asia circa 1000 BC, along with most of Africa.

An alternate theory regarding the location of Sôphêra was that is was a trading port in Southern Arabia or Somalia, however, the ships of Solomon were said to take three years to travel between Edom and Sôphêra/Ofir, which makes the location of Sauvira more likely. The Kingdom of Sauvira is listed in ancient Late Vedic period and early Buddhist literature, as well as the Mahabharata, based around its capital of Rohri in the modern Pakistani state of Sindh. This civilization is recorded as having existed from the Early Vedic period, before 1100 BC, meaning it would have existed in the time of Solomon.

3 Codex Vaticanus: pantocratôr (ΠΑΝΤΟΚΡΑΤΩΡ). Translation: omnipotent (or almighty)

The Masoretic test does not include a name or epithet in this verse. For information on the relationship of Shaddai and pantocratôr, please see the note on Lord Shaddai in Chapter 17.

2nd Paralipomenon: Chapter 1

Solomon the son of David was established over his kingdom, and Lord the god[1] was with him and increased him greatly. Solomon spoke to Israel, to the captains of thousands, the captains of hundreds, the judges, all the rulers over Israel, including the heads of the families, and Solomon and all the congregation went to the bamah[2] that was in Gibeon, where the tabernacle of testimony of the God,[3] that Moses the servant of the Lord[4] made in the wilderness. However, David had taken up the box of God[5] out of the city of the village of groves,[6] for David had prepared a place for it and had pitched a tabernacle for it in Jerusalem.

The bronze altar which Bezalel the son of Orion,[7] the son of Hur, had made was there before the tabernacle of the Lord, and Solomon and the congregation inquired at it. Solomon brought victims to the bronze altar that was before the Lord in the tabernacle and offered on it a thousand whole burnt offerings. That night God appeared to Solomon, and said to him, "Ask what I will give you."

Solomon answered God, "You have dealt very mercifully with my father David, and have made me king in his place. Now, Lord the god, let, I beg you, your name be established on David my father, for you have made me king over people numerous as the dust of the earth.

Now give me wisdom and understanding, that I may go out and come in before these people. For who will judge this your great people?"

God said to Solomon, "Because this was in your heart, and you have not asked great wealth, or glory, or the life of your enemies, and you have not asked long life, but have asked for yourself wisdom and understanding, that you might judge my people, over whom I have made you king, I give you this wisdom and understanding, and I will give you wealth, and riches, and glory, so that there will not have been any like you among the kings before you, neither will there be such after you."

Solomon came from the bamah that was in Gibeon to Jerusalem, from before the tabernacle of witness, and reigned over Israel. Solomon counted chariots and cavalry, and he had fourteen hundred chariots and twelve thousand cavalry and he set them in the cities of chariots, and the people were with the king in Jerusalem. The king made silver and gold in Jerusalem as common as stones, and cedars in Judea like the sycamores of the plain in numbers. Solomon imported horses from Egypt, and the orders of the king's merchants were as follows: they traded, and went and brought out of Egypt a chariot for six hundred pieces of silver, and a horse for a hundred and fifty pieces of silver. They also brought for all the kings of the Cypriots,[8] and for the kings of Syria by their means.

2nd Paralipomenon: Chapter 1 Notes

1 Codex Vaticanus: cyrios ho theos (ΚΥΡΙΟCΟΘΕΟC). Translation: Lord the god

- Aleppo Codex: Yhwh ålhyw (**יהוה אלהיו**). Translation: Yhwh his god

- Leningrad Codex: Yhvah elohav (יְהֹוָה אֱלֹהָיו). Translation: Yhwah his god

- Targum of Chronicles: Yya (״). Translation: Yahw

The name Aramaic name Yhw (𐤉𐤄𐤅) was transliterated as Iaw (Ιαω) in the Septuagint, and as Yhwah (יְהוָה) in the Masoretic text. This name was later transliterated as Iaw by the Pre-Christian Romans from the Greek translation. The name Iaw is found in fragments of the 3rd century AD Papyrus Oxyrhynchus 1007, however, is represented by a double Yod (״), meaning it was copied from a later Hebrew or Aramaic text from that era. After the sixth century AD the occasional copy of the Septuagint is found which uses the name, either written as ΙΑΩ or a Greek approximation of יהוה (ΠΙΠΙ), however, all of these can be traced back to the Hexapla, Quinta, Sextus, and/or Septima, which attempted to retranslate and harmonize the Old Testament in the 3rd through 6th centuries AD. There are no early surviving copies of the Septuagint's version of Paralipomena which have the name Iaw (Ιαω / יְהֹוָה) in it, like some of the other books of the Septuagint, and therefore it cannot be proven if the name was in the Septuagint's Genesis or not, however, several other books in the Septuagint appear to retain older versions of the Hebrew scriptures that pre-date the redaction during the Hasmonean dynasty, which replaced many older names of gods with Yahweh or Yahweh Sabaoth, the national god of Hasmonean Judea.

The Septuagint's version of 2nd Paralipomenon was translated circa 200 BC, before the Hasmonean redaction, and contains the term Lord the god (Κυριος ο θεος), which, if correctly translated from the Canaanite source texts, would have read Adon Elim (𐤟𐤋𐤀 𐤉𐤀𐤃). If the source text had Yahweh Elohim (𐤉𐤆𐤀𐤋𐤀 𐤀𐤉𐤀𐤆), the Greeks would have translated it as 'Iaw your God' (Ιαω ο θεος σου). Adon Elim (𐤟𐤋𐤀 𐤉𐤀𐤃) was a Canaanite epithet for El, found in the Ugaritic Texts. In the polytheistic Canaanite religion, the term translates as 'Father of the gods' as El was the father of the 70 Elohim (gods) and creator of the world in the Canaanite religion. Within Judaism, the concept of multiple gods became anachronistic, and the word Elohim was reinterpreted to mean 'powers' and considered a euphemism for the one God Yahweh. The term 'father of the gods' subsequently became Lord the god in the early Second Temple era, before being replaced by Yahweh Elohim in the Hasmonean dynasty. El is also mentioned in later books of the Septuagint and appears to have been one of the main gods worshiped by the ancient Hebrews. As Κυριος ο θεος translates directly as Lord the god, that term is used in this translation.

2 Codex Vaticanus: ypsêlên (ΥϯΗΧΗΝ). Translation: highness

- Aleppo Codex: bmh (במה). Translation: high place

- Leningrad Codex: bamah (בָּמָה). Translation: high place

- Targum of Chronicles: ramta (רָמְתָא). Translation: hill

Bamahs were stone platforms built at the tops of hills, where sacrifices were made to gods in ancient Canaan and Assyria. These Bamahs generally included an altar for barbecuing the sacrifices, a stele, a seat for the god (which the priest would sit on), a tree representing Asherah (Ashteroth), and a cistern for water. These Bamahs were also generally accompanied by a banquet hall, and a 'low stone' used for slaughtering and butchering the animal.

3 Codex Vaticanus: scênê tou martyriou tou theou (CKHNH TOY MAPTYPIOY TOY ⊝EOY). Translation: tabernacle of martyrdom (or testimony, evidence, proof, shrine) of the god

- Aleppo Codex: åhl mwôd hålhym (אהל מועד האלהים). Translation: tent of the assembly (or festival, or meeting) of the gods

- Leningrad Codex: ohel mov'ed ha'elohim (אֹהֶל מוֹעֵד הָאֱלֹהִים). Translation: tent of the assembly (or festival, or meeting) of the gods

- Targum of Chronicles: mashkan zimna daYya (מַשְׁכַּן זִמְנָא דַיְיָ). Translation: dwelling of time of the Yahw

4 Codex Vaticanus: cyriou (ⲕⲨⲢⲒⲞⲨ). Translation: lord (or main, chief, dominant, master)

- Aleppo Codex: Yhwh (יהוה)

- Leningrad Codex: Yehvah (יְהוָה)

- Targum of Chronicles: Yya (יי). Translation: Yahw

There are no early surviving copies of the Septuagint's version of 1st Paralipomenon which have the name Iaw (Ιαω) in it, like some of the other books of the Septuagint, and therefore it cannot be known conclusively if the name was ever in the Septuagint's 1st Paralipomenon or not. Based on textual comparisons between the Septuagint, and the Masoretic Texts, it is likely the Aramaic text used to translate 1st Paralipomenon circa 180 BC, used the term Adon, which the Greeks translated as Lord, and the Hasmoneans replaced with Yahweh.

5 Codex Vaticanus: cibôton tou theou (ⲕⲒⲃⲰⲦⲞⲚⲦⲞⲨ ⲐⲈⲞⲨ). Translation: box of the god

- Aleppo Codex: ârwn hâlhym (ארון האלהים). Translation: box (or cabinet) of the gods

- Leningrad Codex: arovn ha'elohim (אֲרוֹן הָאֱלֹהִים). Translation: box (or cabinet) of the gods

- Targum of Chronicles: arona Yya (אֲרוֹנָא דַיי). Translation: box (or cabinet) of Yahw

6 Codex Vaticanus: Cariathiarim (ΚΑΡΙΑΘΙΑΡΙΜ)

- Aleppo Codex: qryt yôrym (קרית יערים). Translation: village (in Aramaic) of groves (or forest, thicket)

- Leningrad Codex: qiryat ye'arim (קִרְיַת יְעָרִים).
Translation: village (in Aramaic) of groves (or forest, thicket)

- Targum of Chronicles: qiryat ye'arim (קִרְיַת יְעָרִים).
Translation: village of groves (or forest, thicket)

Various ancient texts, including the book of Joshua (chapter 15, and 1st Paralipomenon (chapter 13, refer to this town as 'Baalah,' implying this verse should have been referring to Baalah when it was originally written, however, by the time of the Greek translation, this name had already been updated to the post-Baalist name of the city. This suggests the text of 2nd Paralipomenon was redacted during the reign of King Josiah or later.

7 Codex Vaticanus: Oyriou (ΟΥΡΙΟΥ)

- Aleppo Codex: Åwry (אורי)

- Leningrad Codex: Uri (אוּרִי)

- Targum of Chronicles: Uri (אוּרִי)

This name is spelled as Oyrian (Ουριαν) in 2nd Kingdoms, and Åwryh (אוריה) in the Masoretic version of 1st Paralipomenon, indicating that the Aramaic name was Åwrôån (אוןעשׂל) before the Hebrew translation. This suggests that the Hebrew translators substituted 'Yah' (יה) for

'An' (אֵל), in this name, which is consistent with other changes made when the Hebrew translation was made. In this verse An was simply dropped in the the Masoretic version.

The Septuagint's Exodus includes Moses' god identifying himself as Ôn (Ὤν), a name later found in the Septuagint's Book of Hosea, which is mirrored in the Masoretic Text by the name Aven (אָוֶן) / Åwn (אוֹן). Therefore, the original name of this person was likely the Akkadian name úru An (𒌷𒀭), meaning 'Light of An,' which was imported to Greece in the early Iron Age as Orion (Ὠρίων). As Orion is more common than Uru-An, the name used in this translation is Orion.

8 Codex Vaticanus: Chettaeôn (ⲭⲉⲧⲧⲁⲓⲱⲛ)

- Aleppo Codex: Ḥtym (חתים). Translation: Cypriots

- Leningrad Codex: Chittim (חִתָּים). Translation: Cypriots

- Targum of Chronicles: Chitta'ei (חִתָּאֵי)

This term has created a great deal of confusion since the misidentification of the ruins of the Neshites as being 'Hittite' in the 1800s. The modern archaeological name 'Hittite,' is not derived from an ancient name for the culture applied by themselves, or anyone else, but rather adopted from the biblical reference to a then-unknown civilization somewhere in the region. There an ancient culture in the region called the Hattians, however, they were conquered by the

Nesites before 1700 BC, and subsequently disappeared from the historic records. The name was applied to culture today referred to as 'Hittites,' before the 'Hittite' language had been translated, and is incorrect. Since 1906, excavations at Boğazköy, the ancient 'Hittite' capital Hattusa have uncovered more than 10,000 'Hittite' texts, including the royal achieve.

The actual name of the 'Hittite' language and people was Nešili (𒉈𒅆𒇷), which is now rendered in some academic literate as Nesite or Neshite. As early as the mid-1800s some scholars disputed the identification of the Nesites as the Biblical Hittites, including the Orientalist Max Müller, who was one of many claiming the Biblical Hittites were ancient Greeks or some other Mediterranean people. Later in the Septuagint's translation of the Maccabees, the similar term Chettiim (Χεττιιμ) as a reference to all Greek-speaking lands, and therefore the Biblical Hittites were likely the Cypriots or the Achaean Greeks.

In the 1st century AD, the Jewish historian Josephus reported that Cethima was the name of Cyrus in Aramaic, and the Chettim were the descendants of Noah's grandson Chethimus, who had settled on Cyprus. Josephus reported that the name was preserved in the Greek name of the town Cition (Κίτιον). Most historians view it as more likely that the Aramaic name was derived from the city-state of Cition, which was known as Kåtjåy (𓈖𓏤𓊪𓈖) in Egyptian records from the New Kingdom Era in the late Bronze Age, and Kt (𐤊𐤕) or Kty (𐤊𐤕𐤉) in Phoenician records from the early Iron Age. While this may be the origin of the term, by the era of the Neo-Assyrian era, the term must have also referred to other Greek islands, as both the prophets Isaiah and Ezekiel used the term 'Islands of Kittim.' As the term referred to the entire island of Cyprus in Aramaic, the translations of 'Cyprus' and 'Cypriots' are used here.

2ⁿᵈ Paralipomenon: Chapter 2

Solomon said that he would build a temple to the name of the Lord, and a palace for his kingdom. Solomon gathered seventy thousand laborers and eighty thousand stone-masons in the mountains, and there were three thousand and six hundred superintendents over them.

Solomon sent to King Hiram of Tyre, a message saying, "Whereas you dealt favorably with David my father, and did send him cedars to build for himself a palace to live in, look, I also his son am building a temple in the name of the Lord my god, to consecrate it to him, to burn incense before him, and to offer showbread continually, and to offer up whole burnt offerings continually morning and evening, and on the sabbaths, and at the new moons, and at the feasts of Lord the god. This is a perpetual statute for Israel. The temple which I am building is to be great, for Lord the god is great beyond all gods. Who will be able to build him a house? The sky, and the sky of Shamayim[1] do not contain his glory, and who am I, that I should build him a temple, just to burn incense before him? Now send me a man wise and skilled to work in gold, and in silver, and in bronze, and in iron, and in purple, and in scarlet, and in blue, and one that knows how to grave together with the craftsmen who are with me in Judah and in Jerusalem, which materials my father David prepared. Send me from Lebanon cedarwood, and wood of juniper, and pine, for I know that your servants are skilled in cutting timber in Lebanon, and, look, your servants will go with my servants, to prepare timber for me in abundance. The temple which I am building must be great and glorious. And, look, I have given freely to your servants that work and cut the wood, grain for food, including twenty thousand measures of wheat, and twenty thousand measures of barley, and twenty thousand measures of wine, and twenty thousand measures of oil."

King Hiram of Tyre answered in writing and sent a message to Solomon saying, "Because the Lord loved his people, he made you king over them. Blessed be Lord the god in Israel, who made the sky and earth, who has given to king David a wise son, and one endowed with knowledge and understanding, who will build a house for the Lord, and a house for his kingdom. Now I have sent you a wise and understanding man who belonged to Hiram, my father (his mother was of the daughters of Dan, and his father was a Tyrian), skilled to work in gold, and in silver, and in bronze, and in iron, and in stones and wood, and to weave with purple, and blue, and fine linen, and scarlet, and to engrave, and to understand every device, whatever you will give him to do with your craftsmen, and the craftsmen of my lord David your father. Now, the wheat, and the barley, and the oil, and the wine which my lord mentioned let him send to his servants. We will cut timber out of Lebanon according to all your needs, and we will bring it on rafts to the sea of Jaffa, and you will bring it to Jerusalem."

Solomon gathered all the foreigners that were in the land of Israel, after the accounting when David his father counted them, and there were found a hundred and fifty-three thousand and six hundred. He made from them seventy thousand laborers, and eighty thousand stone-masons, and three thousand and six hundred taskmasters over the people.

2ⁿᵈ Paralipomenon: Chapter 2 Notes

1 Codex Vaticanus: ouranos cae ho ouranos tou ouranou (ΟΥΡΑΝΟCΚΑΙΟΟΥΡΑΝΟCΤΟΥΟΥΡΑΝΟΥ). Translation: sky and the skies of the sky (or Uranus)

- Aleppo Codex: šmym wšmy hšmym (שמים ושמי השמים). Translation: skies and sky of skies (or Shamayim)

- Leningrad Codex: Shamayim ushemei haShamayim (שָׁמַיִם וּשְׁמֵי הַשָּׁמָיִם). Translation: skies and sky of skies (or Shamayim)

- Targum of Chronicles: shemaya ar'ita ushemaya metzi'ita ushemaya ila (שְׁמַיָּא אַרְעִיתָא וּשְׁמַיָּא מְצִיעִיתָא וּשְׁמַיָּא עִלָּא). Translation: lower sky and middle sky and upper sky

This section mirrors the archaic belief that there were several skies above several and worlds, above our sky. In the Secrets of Enoch, there were seven worlds and skies above our sky.

2nd Paralipomenon: Chapter 3

Solomon began to build the Temple of the Lord in Jerusalem on Mount Moriah, where the Lord appeared to his father David, in the place which David had prepared in the threshing floor of Araunah the Jebusite. He began to build in the second month, in the fourth year of his reign. Solomon began to build the Temple of God,[1] the length in cubits, the first measurement from end to end, was sixty cubits, and the width was twenty cubits. The portico in front of the house, its length in front of the width of the temple was twenty cubits, and its height a hundred and twenty cubits, and he gilded it within with pure gold.

He lined the great temple with cedar-wood, and gilded it with pure gold, and carved on it phoenixes[2] and chains. He garnished the temple with precious stones for beauty, and he gilded it with gold, and in the gold were glowing gemstones.[3] He gilded the house, and its inner walls, and the door-posts, and the roofs, and the doors with gold, and he carved sphinxes[4] on the walls. He built the sacred of sacreds, its length was like the front of the other temple, the width of the temple was twenty cubits and the length twenty cubits, and he gilded it with pure gold for sphinxes, weighing six hundred talents.

The weight of the nails, even the weight of each was fifty shekels of gold, and he gilded the upper chamber with gold. He made two sphinxes in the holiest temple, wood-work, and he gilded them with gold. The wings of the sphinxes were twenty cubits in length, and one wing of five cubits touched the wall of the house, and the other wing of five cubits touched the wing of the other sphinx. The wings of these sphinxes stretched out a length of twenty cubits, and they stood on their feet, and their faces were towards the temple. He made the veil of blue, and purple, and scarlet, and fine linen, and wove sphinxes in it.

Also, he made in front of the temple two steles, thirty-five cubits in height, and their chapters of five cubits. He made chains, like in the oracle, and put them on the tops of the steles, and he made a hundred pomegranates and put them on the chains. He set up the steles in front of the temple, one on the right hand and the other on the left, and he called the name of the one on the right hand Correction,[5] and the name of the one on the left Power.[6]

2nd Paralipomenon: Chapter 3 Notes

1 Codex Vaticanus: oecon tou theou (ΟΙΚΟΝΤΟΥΘΕΟΥ). Translation: house (or temple, home) the god

- Aleppo Codex: byt hålhym (בית האלהים). Translation: house (or temple, abode) of gods

- Leningrad Codex: beit ha'elohim (בֵּית הָאֱלֹהִים). Translations: house (or temple, abode) of gods

- Targum of Chronicles: beit makdesha (בֵּית מַקְדְּשָׁא). Translation: house (or temple, abode) of sanctuary

As this is a reference to Solomon's Temple in Jerusalem, it appears to be the older name, pre-dating King Josiah's removal of the statues of the gods from the temple, circa 625 BC, meaning this section of the book likely dates back to before Josiah's reforms.

2 Codex Vaticanus: phoenicas (ΦΟΙΝΙΚΑC). Translation: phoenixes (or Phoenicians, dates)

- Aleppo Codex: tmrym (תמרים). Translation: dates (or date palms)

- Leningrad Codex: timorim (תְּמֹרִים). Translation: dates (or date palms)

- Targum of Chronicles: diklin (דִּקְלִין). Translation: palm trees

Unlike in the parallel verse in 3rd Kingdoms (Masoretic Kings), the Masoretic term is the proper Hebrew term for 'dates' or 'date palms,' and therefore, a common English translation is 'palm tree.' The Greek translation of 'Phoenixes' is the same as in 3rd Kingdoms, but no more illuminating, as 'Phoenixes' has multiple meanings, one of which was 'dates,' as the Greeks imported dates from Phoenicia. As a result, most translators settle for the translation of 'palm trees,' however, rabbinical and academic interpretations have disagreed for more than a thousand years, as the interpretation of 'date palm' is anachronistic to the era of Solomon. The proto-Semitic root term 'tamar' relates to 'being awake' or 'standing watch,' suggesting that the term referred to engravings of 'guardians,' and not 'palm trees.' If these 'guardians' were anything like the Greek concept of the Phoenix fire-bird, they were probably the Winged Suns that are found engraved on the important buildings in Canaan from the era.

The Winged Sun iconography seems to have originated in the Egyptian Old Kingdom, were Egyptologts label it as 'Behdety.' At the time, the Behdety represented the sun god Horus in the southern Egyptian city of Edfu. Later it was imported into the Old Assyrian and Old Babylonian Empires, where it represented royal power. It appears to have been used the same way in Samaria and Judah until the Neo-Babylonian Empire conquered Judah and destroyed Jerusalem.

The Greek term phoenix is also paradoxical as the Hebrew 'tamar,' as the Greeks believed the mythical Phoenix fire-bird came from Egypt, yet they named it 'Phoenician,' suggesting that they learned the myth of the Phoenix from Phoenicians.

Egyptologists believe the root of the Phoenix fire-bird myth originates in the myth of the Bennu solar-bird (𓃀𓏤𓅬𓏏), one of the creator gods worshiped in Heliopolis. The Old Kingdom era Pyramid Texts refer to the Bennu solar-bird as an aspect of the creator Atum, similar to the eye of Horus-Ra, of the later New-Kingdom era. During the New Kingdom era, the Bennu was depicted as a heron in Egyptian artwork, meaning that if the Winged Sun was based on the Bennu, it had to have been adopted into Canaan before the fall of the Hyksos Dynasty, circa 1550 BC.

Both the north Egyptian Bennu and south Egyptian Behdety probably have a common origin in pre-Dynastic Egypt, although Egyptologists are not sure what the root of the story would have been. As the term 'Phoenix' is probably not related to palm trees, the Greek translation of phoenixes is imported into this translation.

3 Codex Vaticanus: cae chrysiô chrysiou tou ec Pharouaem (ΚΑΙΧΡΥϹΙѠΧΡΥϹΙΟΥΤΟΥΕΚΦΑΡΟΥΑΙΜ). Translation: and gold is gold the from Pharauaem

• Aleppo Codex: whzhb zhb prwym (וחזהב זהב פרוים). Translation: and the gold gold pharaohs

• Leningrad Codex: vehazzahav zehav parvayim (וְהַזָּהָב זְהַב פַּרְוָיִם). Translation: and the gold gold Parvayim

• Targum of Chronicles: bedahava dehav parvayim (בְּדַהֲבָא דְהַב פַּרְוָיִם). Translation: with gold gold Parwayim

This meaning of this term has been considered lost since the early Christian era, however, the Greek translators don't appear to have known what the term meant either, so it may have already have been unknown by their time. Both the Syriac Peshitta and Latin Vulgate substituted the term for 'fine gold' for 'gold from the Pharouaem.' The Greeks treated the term Pharouaem as the name of a land, however, the Hebrew translation does not indicate that. The Greek term is clearly a transliteration of the same term that is found in the Masoretic text, however, that term is neither Hebrew nor Aramaic. It is sometimes interpreted as a spelling error of the Hebrew word purim (פּוּרִים), meaning pure, however, if that is where the word originated the spelling error must have existed in the Greek translation was made from the Aramaic text, which the Hebrew translators wound have corrected. The section may have been copied from one of the various books of Solomon that were later destroyed by Judan leaders for being heretical, as reported in the Talmud, Shabbat 30b.

Based on the Greek interpretation, it is generally interpreted as the name of an unknown land, however, a simpler explanation is that prwym (𐤐𐤓𐤅𐤉𐤌) was the Canaanite term for 'pharaohs.' Solomon was described as deeply involved with trade in northern Egypt at the time, and his first wife was recorded as being an Egyptian princess. The era was one of chaos, referred to as the Third Intermediate Period by Egyptologists. The Egyptian empire had collapsed a couple of centuries earlier, and the Libyans had occupied northern Egypt. Nevertheless, this 'gold of the Pharoahs,' described as being a gemstone, and not gold itself.

The Sanhedrin tractate (103b:12 in the Talmud may shed light on this, as tells the story of King Jehoiakim's heresy when claiming that man no longer needed God, as men had glowing gemstones that created light. The god he was talking about was clearly the sun, however, it's not clear what the glowing gemstones were. The tractate uses the term zhb prwyym (זהב פרויים), which is virtually identical term used in this verse.

In the book of Isaiah, the prophet described the future gate of the city being built to incorporate a gemstones named ekdach (אֶקְדָּח), which the Greeks translated as anthrax (ἄνθραξ). The term is not otherwise used in the Masoretic text, however, the commentary on Isaiah in the Talmud (Bava Batra 75a:10, Sanhedrin 100a:7 confirm that it has traditionally been viewed as a gemstone. The Torah commentary of Rabbi Bahya (Shemot 28:15:3 claims that the light that Noah used in his ark was an ekdach stone, and disputes the correlation of the ekdach and 'turquoise of Nubia,' which the Greeks also translated as anthrax in the Septuagint. The Greek word anthrax (ἄνθραξ) translates directly as coal, however, also referred to a mythical glowing stone from centuries before coal became common.

The gemstone in question was likely calcite, a stable carbonate mineral that may occasionally show phosphorescence or fluorescence. Calcite-alabaster, also called Egyptian alabaster, is a gemstone that the Egyptians were using in the New Kingdom era. Several Egyptian alabaster perfume jars were discovered in the tomb of Tutankhamun from circa 1323 BC, however, the gemstone was mainly used to carve figures of the guardian goddess Bast, from which the name 'alabaster' is ultimately derived.

Calcite stones that glow in the dark are somewhat rare, however, can glow in a variety of colors. The Greek legends about the anthrax gemstone referred to it had a reddish-orange hue, while the term 'gold of the pharaohs' suggests it was a yellowish-orange. It suggests that all the glowing gemstones the ancient Egyptians had access to came from the same mine, however, it is not clear where that would have been. As Egypt was already thousands of years old, it could have imported the stones at any point during its history. There is evidence of an orange calcite mine in bronze age Iberia, and so it is possible that they imported the stones from there.

It is possible that the original author was simply stating that the gold in question was the gold of the pharaohs, purchased in Egypt by Solomon's merchants, however, that is not the traditional interpretation. Neither the Greek nor Hebrew translations treat this term as simply the 'gold of the pharaohs,' nor Isaiah ekdach gemstone as simply coal. Based on this, and the commentary in the Talmud, the translation of 'glowing gemstones' is used.

4 Codex Vaticanus: cheroubin (ⲭⲉⲣⲟⲩⲃⲓⲛ)

• Aleppo Codex: krwbym (כרובים). Translation: sphinxes (or griffins, sphinxes)

- Leningrad Codex: keruvim (כְּרוּבִים). Translation: sphinxes (or griffins, sphinxes)

- Targum of Chronicles: keruvin (כְּרוּבִין). Translation: sphinxes (or griffins, sphinxes)

The word 'cherub' (ܟܪܘܒܐ / כרוב / 𐤊𐤓𐤁 / 𐤊𐤓𐤁) was the West Semitic term for the mythical creature generally called a 'griffin' today. Based in the archaeological record of Canaan, it appears that the concept of the cherub was based on the Egyptian sphinx, as the earliest cherub statues found in Canaan were Egyptian statues of sphinxes. Archaeologists are not sure if the cherubs of Anatolia were based on the Canaanite cherub, or the Egyptian sphinxes directly, however, all three mythical beings are closely related in the archaeological record. The term cherub was for some reason reinterpreted as 'baby angels' by Christians, although in the books of the Kingdoms, God was described as riding on cherubs, and it is not clear why any god would ride around on 'baby angels,' therefore the alternate translation of 'sphinxes' is used.

5 Codex Vaticanus: catorthôsis (ΚΑΤΟΡΘΩϹΙϹ). Translation: correction

- Aleppo Codex: ykyn (יכין). Translation: prepare

- Leningrad Codex: ykyn (יכין). Translation: prepare

- Targum of Chronicles: yachin (יְכִין). Translation: preparation

6 Codex Vaticanus: ischys (ιϲχγϲ). Translation: power (or strength, might)

- Aleppo Codex: bôz (בֹעז). Translation: here

- Leningrad Codex: bōaz (בְּעַז). Translation: here

- Targum of Chronicles: malchuta (מַלְכוּתָא). Translation: governance

2ⁿᵈ Paralipomenon: Chapter 4

He made a bronze altar, twenty cubits long, and twenty cubits wide, and ten cubits high. He made the molten sea, ten cubits in diameter, entirely round. It was five cubits high, and its circumference was thirty cubits. Beneath it were statues of calves, and they surrounded it. The laver around it was ten cubits ,and they cast the calves in two rows. They made twelve calves; three looking north, and three looking west, and three looking south, and three looking east, and the sea was on top of them, and their hind parts were inward. Is was a handwidth thick, and its brim was like the brim of a cup, engraved with lily blossoms. It held three thousand baths[1] when he finished it.

He made ten lavers and set five on the right hand, and five on the left, to wash in them the instruments of the whole burnt offerings, and to rinse the vessels in them, and the sea was for the priests to wash in. He made the ten golden candlesticks according to their pattern, and he put them in the temple, five on the right hand, and five on the left. He made ten tables and put them in the temple, five on the right hand, and five on the left, and he made a hundred golden bowls. Also, he made the priests' court, and the great court, and doors to the court, and their panels were overlaid with bronze. He set the sea at the corner of the house on the right, as it was facing the east.

Hiram made the meat-hooks, and the fire-pans, and the grate of the altar, and all its instruments, and Hiram finished doing all the work which he worked for King Solomon in the Temple of God, two steles, and on them an embossed work for the chapiters on the heads of the two steles, and two nets to cover the heads of the chapiters which are on the heads of the steles, and four hundred golden bells for the two nets, and two rows of pomegranates in each net, to cover the two embossed rims of the chapiters which are on the steles. He made the ten bases, and he made the lavers on the bases, and the one sea, and the twelve calves under it, and the foot-baths, and the buckets, and the cauldrons, and the meat-hooks, and all their furniture (which Hiram made, and brought to King Solomon in the Temple of the Lord) of pure bronze.

In the country around the Jordan, the king cast them in the clay ground in the house of Booths, and between that and Saredatha. Solomon made all these vessels in great abundance, as the quantity of bronze did not run out. Solomon made all the vessels of the Temple of the Lord, and the golden altar, and the tables, and on them were to be the loaves of showbread, also the candlesticks, and the lamps to give light according to the pattern, and in front of the oracle, of pure gold. Their snuffers and their lamps were made, and he made the bowls, and the censers, and the fire-pans, of pure gold. There was the inner door of the house opening into the holy of holies, and he made the inner doors of the temple from gold. Then all the work in which Solomon worked for the Temple of the Lord was finished.

2nd Paralipomenon: Chapter 4 Notes

1 Codex Vaticanus: metrêtas (ΜΕΤΡΗΤΔC). Translation: measures (or meters, measurements)

- Aleppo Codex: btym (בתים). Translation: baths

- Leningrad Codex: battim (בַּתִּים). Translation: baths

- Targum of Chronicles: battin (בַּתִּין). Translation: baths

The bat (בַּת) was a unit of liquid measurement used in the Middle East, also called the batu (𒂍𒈝𒄷) in Neo-Babylonian, and baṭium (𒁁𒌑𒌐) in Old Akkadian. It appears to have originally been the size of a large mixing cauldron used in Akkad, however, by the Persian era had become standardized to approximately 22 liters (5¾ gallons). If this measurement was consistent during the era of Solomon, the cauldron would have been large enough to hold 66,000 liters (17,250 gallons). The name of the measurement was imported into many languages, however, not always with the exact same meaning. It was known variously as the bṭytå (𐡁𐡈𐡉𐡕𐡀) in Aramaic, bātiyaka (𐎲𐎠𐎫𐎡𐎹𐎣) in Persian, bat (בַּת) in Hebrew, and bāṭīṭā (ܒܛܝܛܐ) in Syriac. It was imported to Greek as batiacê (βατιάκη), however, meant 'cup,' explaining why the Greeks substituted metrêtas. The standard English term for the ancient measurement is 'bath,' which is used in this translation.

2nd Paralipomenon: Chapter 5

Solomon brought in the holy things of his father David, the silver, and the gold, and the other vessels, and put them in the treasury of the Temple of the Lord. Then Solomon assembled all the elders of Israel, and all the heads of the tribes, the leaders of the families of the Israelites, to Jerusalem, to bring up the box of the covenant of the Lord out of the City of David (this is Zion). All Israel assembled to the king in the feast in the seventh month. All the elders of Israel came, and the Levites lifted the box, and the tabernacle of witness, and all the holy vessels that were in the tabernacle, and the priests and the Levites carried it up.

King Solomon and all the elders of Israel and the religious men among them gathered before the box, were sacrificing calves and sheep in great numbers which could not be counted for multitude. The priests brought in the box of the covenant of the Lord into its place, into the oracle of the house, even into the holy of holies, under the wings of the sphinxes. The sphinxes stretched out their wings over the place of the box, and the sphinxes covered the box and its staffs above. The staffs projected, and the heads of the staffs were seen from the holy place in front of the oracle, they were not seen outside, and there they remain to this day.

There was nothing in the box, except the two tables which Moses placed there in Horeb, which God gave in covenant with the Israelites when they left the land of Egypt. When the priests left the holy place, (for all the priests that were found were sanctified, they were not then arranged according to their daily schedule), that all the singing Levites assigned to the sons of Asaph, Heman, Jeduthun, and his sons, and to his brothers, of them that were clothed in linen garments, with cymbals and lutes and harps, were standing before the altar, and with them a hundred and twenty priests, blowing trumpets. There was one voice in the trumpeting and the singing, and in the loud utterance with one voice to give thanks and praise the Lord.

When they raised their voice together with trumpets and cymbals, and instruments of music, and said, "Give thanks to the Lord, for it is good, for his mercy endures forever," then the house was filled with the cloud of the glory of the Lord. The priests could not stand to minister because of the cloud, for the glory of the Lord filled the Temple of God.Solomon brought in the holy things of his father David, the silver, and the gold, and the other vessels, and put them in the treasury of the Temple of the Lord. Then Solomon assembled all the elders of Israel, and all the heads of the tribes, the leaders of the families of the Israelites, to Jerusalem, to bring up the box of the covenant of the Lord out of the City of David, (this is Zion). All Israel assembled to the king in the feast in the seventh month. All the elders of Israel came, and the Levites lifted the box, and the tabernacle of witness, and all the holy vessels that were in the tabernacle, and the priests and the Levites carried it up.

King Solomon and all the elders of Israel and the religious men among them gathered before the box, were sacrificing calves and sheep in great numbers which could not be counted for multitude. The priests brought in the box of the covenant of the Lord into its place, into the oracle of the house, even into the holy of holies, under the wings of the sphinxes. The sphinxes stretched out their wings over the place of the box, and the sphinxes covered the box and its staffs above. The staffs projected, and the heads of the staffs were seen from the holy place in front of the oracle, they were not seen outside, and there they remain to this day.

There was nothing in the box, except the two tables which Moses placed there in Horeb, which God gave in covenant with the Israelites when they left the land of Egypt. When the priests left the holy place, (for all the priests that were found were sanctified, they were not then arranged according to their daily schedule), that all the singing Levites assigned to the sons of Asaph, Heman, Jeduthun, and his sons, and to his brothers, of them that were clothed in linen garments, with cymbals and lutes and harps, were standing before the altar, and with them a hundred and twenty priests, blowing trumpets.

There was one voice in the trumpeting and the singing, and in the loud utterance with one voice to give thanks and praise the Lord. When they raised their voice together with trumpets and cymbals, and instruments of music, and said, "Give thanks to the Lord, for it is good, for his mercy endures forever," then the house was filled with the cloud of the glory of the Lord. The priests could not stand to minister because of the cloud, for the glory of the Lord filled the Temple of God.

2nd Paralipomenon: Chapter 6

Then Solomon said, "The Lord said that he would live in thick darkness. But I have built a temple to your name, holy to you, and prepared for you to live in forever."

The king turned his face and blessed all the congregation of Israel, and all the congregation of Israel stood by. He said, "Blessed is Lord the god in Israel. He has even fulfilled with his hands as he said with his mouth to my father David, 'From the day when I brought up my people out of the land of Egypt, I chose no city of all the tribes of Israel, to build a house that my name should be there, neither did I choose a man to be a leader over my people Israel. But I chose Jerusalem that my name should be there, and I chose David to be over my people Israel.' It came into the heart of David my father, to build a temple for the name of Lord the god in Israel. But the Lord said to my father David, 'Whereas it came into your heart to build a temple for my name, you did well that it came into your heart. Nevertheless, you will not build the temple, for your son who will come from your body, he will build the temple for my name.' The Lord has confirmed this word, which he spoke, and I am raised up in the place of my father David, and I sit on the throne of Israel as the Lord said, and I have built the temple for the name of Lord the god in Israel, and I have set there the box in which is the covenant of the Lord, which he made with Israel."

He stood before the altar of the Lord in the presence of all the congregation of Israel and spread out his hands. Solomon had made a bronze stage, and placed it in the middle of the court of the sanctuary. It was five cubits long, and five cubits wide, and three cubits high. He stood on it, and fell on his knees before the whole congregation of Israel, and spread out his hands to the sky, and said, "Lord the god in Israel, there is no god like you in the sky, or on the earth, keeping covenant and mercy with your servants that walk before you with their whole heart. Even as you have kept them with your servant David my father, as you have spoken to him in words. You have both spoken with your mouth, and have fulfilled it with your hands, as it is this day. Now, Lord the god in Israel, keep with your servant David my father the things when you said to him, 'There will not fail you a man before me sitting on the throne of Israel, if only your sons will pay attention to their way to walk in my law, as you did walk before me.'"

"Now, Lord the god of Israel, let, I beg you, your word be confirmed, when you asked your servant David, 'Will God live with men on the earth?'"

"If the sky, and the sky of Shamayim, will not be enough for you, what then is this temple which I have built? Nevertheless, you will pay attention to the prayers of your servant, and to my petition. Lord the god, listen to the petition and the prayer which your servant prays before you today. Open your eyes over this house by day and by night. Hear the prayers towards this place, on which you said your name should be called, which your servant prays towards this temple. Hear the supplication of your servant, and of your people Israel, whatever prayers they will make towards this place. Listen from your abode in the sky. Yes, hear and be merciful. If a man sins against his neighbor and he brings an oath on him to make him swear, and he comes and swears before the altar in this temple, then listen out of the sky and judge your servants, to repay the transgressor, to turn his ways on his head, and to justify the righteous and repay him according to his righteousness. If your people Israel should be defeated by an enemy, if they should sin against you, and then turn and confess to your name, and pray and make supplication before you in this temple, then listen out of the sky and be merciful to the sins of your people Israel, and return them to the land which you gave them and to their fathers."

"When the sky is restrained, and there is no rain, because they will have sinned against you, and when they will pray towards this place, and praise your name, and will turn from their sins, because you will afflict them, then you will listen from the sky, and you will be merciful to the sins of your servants, and of your people Israel. You will show them the good way in which they will walk, and you will send rain on your land, which you gave to your people for an inheritance. If there should be famine on the land, if there should be death, a pestilent wind and blight, if there should be locust and caterpillar, and if enemies should attack them before their cities, in whatever plague and whatever distress they may be, then whatever prayer and whatever supplication will be made by any man and all your people Israel, if a man should know his own plague and his own sickness, and should spread forth his hands towards this house, then you will hear from the sky, out of your prepared abode, and will be merciful, and will repay to the man according to his ways, as you will know his heart. You alone know the heart of the children of men, that they may reverence all your ways all the days which they live on the face of the land, which you gave to our fathers."

"Every foreigner who is not himself from your people Israel, and who will have come from a distant land because of your great name, and your mighty hand, and your strong arm; when they come and worship at this place, then will you listen out of the sky, out of your abode, and will do according to all that the foreigner will call on you for, that all the nations of the earth may know your name, and that they may fear you, as your people Israel do, and that they may know that your name is called on at this temple which I have built."

"If your people will go out to war against their enemies by the roads by which you will send them, and will pray to you towards this city which you have chosen, and towards the temple which I have built to your name, then you will hear out of the sky their prayer and their supplication, and maintain their cause. Whereas if they will sin against you, (for there is no man who will not sin), and you will strike them, and deliver them up before their enemies, and they that take them captive will carry them away into a land of enemies, to a land far off or near, and if they will repent in their land to whatever place they were carried captive, and will also turn and make supplication to you in their captivity, saying, 'We have sinned, we have transgressed, we have worked unrighteously,' and if they will turn to you with all their heart and all their soul in the land of them that carried them captives, to whatever place they carried them captives, and will pray towards their land which you gave to their fathers, and the city which you did choose, and the house which I built to your name, then you will hear out of the sky, out of your abode, their prayer and their supplication, and you will execute justice, and will be merciful to your people that sin against you."

"Now Lord, I beg you, let your eyes be opened, and your ears be attentive to the petition made in this place. Now, Lord the god, rise into your resting-place, you, and the box of your strength, let your priests, Lord the god, clothe themselves with salvation, and your sons rejoice in prosperity. Lord the god, don't turn away from the face of your anointed. Remember the mercies of your servant David."

2ⁿᵈ Paralipomenon: Chapter 7

When Solomon had finished praying, then fire came down from the sky and devoured the whole burnt offerings and the sacrifices, and the glory of the Lord filled the house. The priests could not enter into the Temple of the Lord at that time, for the glory of the Lord filled the house. All the Israelites saw the fire descending, and the glory of the Lord was on the house, and they fell on their face to the ground on the pavement, and worshiped, and praised the Lord, for it is good to do so because his mercy endures forever.

The king and all the people were offering sacrifices before the Lord. King Solomon offered a sacrifice of twenty-two thousand calves, and a hundred and twenty thousand sheep, so the king and all the people dedicated the Temple of God. The priests were standing at their watches, and the Levites with instruments of music of the Lord, belonging to King David, to give thanks before the Lord, for his mercy endures forever, with the hymns of David, by their ministry, and the priests were blowing the trumpets before them, and all Israel standing.

Solomon consecrated the middle of the court that was in the Temple of the Lord, for he offered there the whole burnt offerings and the fat of the peace-offerings, for the bronze altar which Solomon had made was not sufficient to receive the whole burnt offerings, and the meat-offerings, and the fat. Solomon kept the feast at that time seven days, and all Israel with him, a very great assembly, from the entering in of Hama, and as far as the river of Egypt. On the eighth day, he kept a solemn assembly, for he kept a feast of seven days as the dedication of the altar. On the twenty-third day of the seventh month, he dismissed the people to their tents, rejoicing, and with a glad heart because of the good deeds which the Lord had done to David, and to Solomon, and to Israel his people.

So Solomon finished the Temple of the Lord and the king's palace, and in whatever Solomon wished in his heart to do in the Temple of the Lord and in his own house, he prospered. The Lord appeared to Solomon by night, and said to him, "I have heard your prayer, and I have chosen this place to myself for a house of sacrifice. If I should restrain the sky and there should be no rain, and if I should command the locust to devour the trees, and if I should send pestilence on my people, then if my people, on whom my name is called, should repent, and pray, and seek my face, and turn from their evil ways, I also will hear in the sky, and I will be merciful to their sins, and I will heal their land. Now my eyes will be open, and my ears attentive to the prayer of this place.'"

"'Now I have chosen and sanctified this temple, that my name should be there forever, and my eyes and my heart will be there always. If you will walk before me as David your father did, and will do according to all that I have commanded you, and will keep my ordinances and my judgments, then I will establish the throne of your kingdom, as I covenanted with David your father, saying, 'There will not fail from you, a man ruling in Israel.' But if you should turn away, and ignore my ordinances and my commandments, which I have set before you, and go and serve other gods, and worship them, then I will remove you from the land which I gave them, and this temple which I have consecrated to my name I will remove out of my sight, and I will make it a proverb and an insult among all nations. As for this great temple, every one that passes by it will be amazed, and will ask, 'Why has the Lord done this to this land, and to this temple?' Men will say, 'Because they forgot Lord the god of their fathers, who brought them out of the land of Egypt, and they attached themselves to other gods, and worshiped them, and served them. Therefore he has brought on them all this evil.'"

2ⁿᵈ Paralipomenon: Chapter 8

In the twenty years after Solomon built the Temple of the Lord, and his own palace, Solomon rebuilt the cities which Hiram had given to Solomon and settled the Israelites in them. Solomon went to Baesoba and fortified it. He rebuilt Tadmor in the wilderness and all the fortified cities which he rebuilt in Hama. He built the Upper House of Horon, and the Lower House of Horon, two fortified cities with walls, gates, and bars, and Baalath, and all the fortified cities which Solomon had, and all his chariot cities, and cities of cavalry, and all things that Solomon desired according to his desire of building, in Jerusalem, and in Lebanon, and in all his kingdom.

As for all the people that were left from the Cypriots, and Amorites, and Perizzites, and Mitanni,[1] and Jebusites, who are not of Israel, but were of the descendants of those who the children of Israel did not destroy, and were left from those in the land, Solomon made them tributaries until today. But Solomon did not make any of the Israelites slaves in his kingdom, for they were warriors and rulers, and mighty men, and captains of chariots and cavalry. These were the chiefs of the officers of King Solomon, two hundred and fifty overseeing the work among the people. Solomon brought up the daughter of Pharaoh from the City of David to the palace which he had built for her, and he said, "My wife will not live in the City of David, the king of Israel, for the place is sacred into which the box of the Lord has entered."

Then Solomon offered up to the Lord whole burnt offerings on the altar which he had built to the Lord before the temple, according to the daily rate, to offer up sacrifices according to the commandments of Moses, on the sabbaths, and at the new moons, and at the feasts, three times in the year, at the feast of unleavened bread, and at the feast of weeks, and at the feast of tabernacles. He established, according to the order of his father David, the courses of the priests, and that according to their public ministrations, and the Levites were appointed over their charges, to praise and minister before the priests according to the daily order, and the porters were appointed according to their courses to the different gates, for these were the commandments of David the prophet.[2]

They did not transgress the commandments of the king concerning the priests and the Levites with regard to everything else, and with regard to the treasures. Now all the work had been prepared from the day when the foundation was laid until Solomon finished the Temple of the Lord. Then Solomon went to Ezion Geber, and to Elath near the sea in the land of Edom. Hiram sent by the hand of his servants' ships, and servants skilled in naval affairs, and they went with the servants of

Solomon to Sauvira,[3] and brought there four hundred and fifty talents of gold, and they returned to King Solomon.

2ⁿᵈ Paralipomenon: Chapter 8 Notes

1 Codex Vaticanus: Euaiou (ΕΥΑΙΟΥ)

- Aleppo Codex: Hwy (חוי)

- Leningrad Codex: Chivvi (חִוִּי)

- Targum of Chronicles: chiva'ei (חִוָאֵי). Translation: farmer

The term is believed to have been derived from the name of the Hurrians, however, is derived separately from the other term Chori (חֹרִי). As the Euaiou / Hwy are routinely reported to be rulers, the term appears to represent the Mitanni nobility. The Mitanni Empire was conquered by the Middle Assyrian Empire circa 1350 BC, and the Mitanni people disappeared from the historic record circa 1260 BC.

In the Amarna Letters, which date to the 1330s BC, the term Éan (𒂊𒀭) was the name of a people, who appear to be the Mitanni, or a group within the Mitanni. The Mitanni Empire seized control of Syria in the middle bronze age, largely composed of Hurrians, although, worshipping Indo-Iranian gods, such as Mitra-Varuna. The cuneiform word Éan (𒂊𒀭) was the Akkadian word meaning 'temple,' suggesting the Éan were the Mitanni priests. According to Israelite sources, the priesthood at Mount Seir was Hurrian, suggesting the Mitanni priesthood in Edom survived long after their empire fell in the north. Like the Israelite God, the Mitanni god Mitra-Varuna was described as being the god of the covenant, and there appears to have been Israelites worshiping at Mount Seir until the era of the prophet Isaiah, who made a pilgrimage to Mount Seir in the late 700s BC.

2 Codex Vaticanus: Dauid anthrôpou tou theou (ᴅᴀʏɪᴅ ᴀɴꭼᴩⲱⲡⲟʏ ⲧⲟʏ ⲑⲉⲟʏ). Translation: David man of the god

• Aleppo Codex: Dwyd åyš hålhym (דויד איש האלהים).
Translation: David prophet (or man of the gods)

• Leningrad Codex: David ish-ha'elohim (דְּוִיד אִישׁ־
הָאֱלֹהִים). Translation: David prophet (or man of the gods)

• Targum of Chronicles: David neviya daYay (דְוִד נְבִיָא דַיְיָ).
Translation: David prophet of Yahw

3 Codex Vaticanus: Sôphira (ⲥⲱϕɪⲣᴀ)

• Aleppo Codex: Åwpyrh (אופירה)

• Leningrad Codex: Ovfirah (אֹופִירָה)

• Targum of Chronicles: Ofir (אֹופִיר)

The difference between the way this name is transliterated in 1ˢᵗ and 2ⁿᵈ Paralipomenon indicates that 2ⁿᵈ Paralipomenon was translated from an Aramaic source, while 1ˢᵗ Paralipomenon was most likely translated from a Samaritan source. The differences in the spelling are also found in the equivalent sections of Divrei-hayyamim indicating the Hebrew translation used the same sources.

The location of this civilization has been a matter of debate for centuries. Given the list of items imported from Sôphira/Åwpyrh, it was likely the ancient Pakistani Kingdom of Sauvira on the Indus River. Imported items include gold, silver, sandalwood, pearls, ivory, apes, and peacocks. Sandalwood trees are indigenous to South and Southeast Asia and have traditionally been considered sacred by the Hindus, Jainists, Buddhists, and Zoroastrians, as well as other Asian cultures. Peacocks are indigenous to South and Southeast Asia, as well as the Congo Rain-forest, however, Sandalwood trees are not found in the Congo Rain-forest. Apes were still living in South and Southeast Asia circa 1000 BC, along with most of Africa.

An alternate theory regarding the location of Sôphêra was that is was a trading port in Southern Arabia or Somalia, however, the ships of Solomon were said to take three years to travel between Edom and Sôphêra/Åwpyrh, which makes the location of Sauvira more likely. The Kingdom of Sauvira is listed in ancient Late Vedic period and early Buddhist literature, as well as the Mahabharata, based around its capital of Rohri in the modern Pakistani state of Sindh. This civilization is recorded as having existed from the Early Vedic period, before 1100 BC, meaning it would have existed in the time of Solomon.

2nd Paralipomenon: Chapter 9

The Queen of Saba[1] heard of the name of Solomon, and she came to Jerusalem with a very large force, to test Solomon with difficult questions. She had camels bearing spices in great quantities, and gold, and precious stones. She came to Solomon and asked him all that was in her mind. Solomon told her all her words, and there passed not a word from Solomon which he did not tell her. The Queen of Saba saw the wisdom of Solomon, and the temple which he had built, and the meat of the tables, and the sitting of his servants, and the standing of his ministers, and their clothing, and his cupbearers, and their apparel, and the whole burnt offerings which he offered up in the Temple of the Lord, and she was in ecstasy.

She said to the king, "It was a true report which I heard in my land concerning your words, and concerning your wisdom. Yet I did not believe the reports until I came and saw that half of the abundance of your wisdom was not told me, you have exceeded the report which I heard. Blessed are your men, blessed are these your servants, who stand before you continually, and hear your wisdom. Blessed be the Lord your god, who took pleasure in you, to set you on his throne for a king, to the Lord your god, inasmuch as the Lord your god loved Israel to establish them forever, therefore he has set you over them for a king to execute judgment and justice."

She gave the king a hundred and twenty talents of gold, and spices in very great abundance, and precious stones, and there were not anywhere else such spices as those which the Queen of Saba gave to King Solomon. The servants of Solomon and the servants of Hiram brought gold to Solomon out of Sauvira, and pine timber, and precious stones. The king made of the pine timber steps to the Temple of the Lord, and to the king's house, and harps and lutes for the singers, and such were not seen before in the land of Judah. King Solomon gave to the Queen of Saba all that she requested, besides all that she brought to king Solomon, and she returned to her own land. The weight of the gold that was brought to Solomon in one year was six hundred and sixty-six talents of gold, besides what the men who were regularly appointed and the merchants brought, and all the kings of Arabia and princes of the land brought gold and silver to king Solomon.

King Solomon made two hundred shields of beaten gold, there were six hundred shekels of pure gold in each shield. Three hundred buckles of beaten gold, the weight of three hundred gold shekels went to one buckler, and the king placed them in the palace in the forest of Lebanon. The king made a great throne of ivory, and he gilded it with pure gold. There were six steps to the throne, riveted with gold, and elbows on either side of the seat of the throne, and two lions standing by the elbows, and twelve lions standing there on the six steps on each side. There was nothing like it in any other kingdom. All king Solomon's vessels were of gold, and all the vessels of the palace in the forest of Lebanon were covered with gold, and silver was not worth anything of in the days of Solomon.

A ship went for the king to Tartessos[2] with the servants of Hiram. Once every three years came vessels from Tartessos to the king, laden with gold, and silver, and ivory, and apes. Solomon exceeded all other kings both in riches and wisdom. All the kings of the earth wanted the presence of Solomon, to hear his wisdom, which God had put in his heart. They brought everyone his gifts, silver vessels and golden vessels, and clothing, myrrh and spices, horses and mules, a percentage every year. Solomon had four thousand mares for chariots and twelve thousand cavalry, and he stationed the chariots in the cities, and with the king in Jerusalem. He ruled over all the kings from the river all the way to the land of the Pelesets,[3] and to the borders of Egypt.

The king made gold and silver in Jerusalem as common as stones and cedars as common as the sycamore trees in the plain. Solomon imported horses from Egypt, and from every other country. The rest of the acts of Solomon, the first and the last, look, these are written in the words of Nathan the prophet, and in the words of Ahijah the Shilonite, and in the visions of Joel the seer concerning Jeroboam the son of Nebat. Solomon reigned over all Israel forty years. Solomon fell asleep, and they buried him in the City of David his father, and Rehoboam his son reigned in his place.

2nd Paralipomenon: Chapter 9 Notes

1 Codex Vaticanus: Saba (cᴀʙᴀ)

- Aleppo Codex: Šbå (שבא)

- Leningrad Codex: Sheva (שְׁבָא)

- Targum of Chronicles: Zemargad (זְמַרְגַד)

Saba was a country in the territory of modern Yemen between 1200 BC and 275 AD. This nation is later mentioned in the Septuagint's books of Job, Joel, Ezekiel, and Isaiah, as well as the Quran's An-Naml and Saba surahs. This country was ultimately conquered by the neighboring Himyarite Kingdom around 275 AD, which was itself then conquered by the Ethiopian Axumite Empire around 525 AD. The Himyarite Kingdom was an officially Jewish State after 390 AD and is likely the origin of the early Arabic language version of the Kebra Nagast, which was later translated into Ge'ez, and Ethiopianized, making the 'Queen of Saba' a monarch from the Ethiopian Highlands. The Kebra Nagast has never been used by the Beta Israel community in Ethiopia, who consider it a later Christian work.

The Targum of Chronicles's use of Zemargad (זְמַרְגַד) is less clear. The general interpretation of the Aramaic word, it that it was a transliteration of the Greek word smáragdos (σμάραγδος), meaning 'emerald.' The Syriac word for emerald continues to be zmrgdå (ܐܝܕܓܪܡܙ), supporting the claim, however, the Greek word itself is generally accepted as an adopted term, although the origin of the term is not clear. The geographical location of Zemargad, may refer to Mount Smaragdus the Greek name for the 'mountain of emeralds,' in the Sinai, where the Egyptians had been mining emeralds since at least the Middle Kingdom, however, there is no evidence of a significant kingdom existing in the region at any point, and it is unlikely the Aramaic translator was thinking of that location.

In the first chapter of the Targum of Chronicles (1st Paralipomenon, chapter 1, the translator used Demeregad (דְּמֶרְגַד) as a translation of Saba (Σαβα) / Šbå (שבא), indicating that either Demeregad or Zemargad was a spelling error. Immediately preceding Demeregad in that list, was Mavreyatinos as a translation of Regma (Ρεγμα) from the Septuagint and Ra'ma (רַעְמָא) from the Masoretic text. An alternate reading, found in Targum of Chronicles Scroll A, uses the translation of Zemarged (זְמַרְגַד) instead of Mavreyatinos. Mavreyatinos was the Aramaic name of the ancient Amazigh (Berber) kingdom in the Atlas mountains of Northwest Africa, known in Latin as Mauretania, and Greek as Mauroúsii (Μαυρούσιοι). As the Canaanites dominated the trade between the Mauretanians and the Mediterranean, and the Mauretanians were a gender neutral society, with both kings and queens ruling at different times, it is plausible that a Mauretanian queen visited Solomon, however, no other ancient sources list Mauretania as the land the queen came from.

Medieval Aramaic sources occasionally reference a land of Zemarged somewhere in the Indian Ocean, and are often assumed to be referring to region along the Zambezi-Kafubu river system of Mozambique and Zambia, as the Kafubu region is the largest sources for emeralds in the eastern hemisphere. Trade in the Kafubu region flowed along the Zambezi river into the Indian Ocean, as it later did for the Zimbabwe civilization to the south. However, if the Medival Arameans were referring to Kafubu as Zemarged, it indicates the Greeks had already established trade with the region by the Greco-Roman era, as the Arameans used the Greek name for the civilization. Alternative suggestions for the location of Zemarged include Madagascar, which fell under the control of the Indonesians during the Greco-Roman era, or other smaller emerald mining locations in Somalia, Tanzania, or Mozambique.

The name does not appear in the 1st century AD Periplus of the Erythraean Sea, a Greek description of the trade routes and ports in the Red Sea and Indian Ocean. The African ports listed only go as far south as Rhapta, believed to have been the Rufiji River region of modern Tanzania, where a Greoco-Roman era trade port has been excavated. The book does claim it is possible to sail south around the continent and return to the Mediterranean that way, indicating that there had been attempts to find more trading partners to the south. In the book, the name of East Africa is Azania, and therefore, if Smáragdos was applied to a region the Greeks later open trade with, it must have been south of Azania, in the region of Madagascar, or the Zambezi-Kafubu region. If the translator of Scroll A was using the name Zemarged in this context, it suggests that he viewed Sheba as a sub-Saharan African state along the east coast of Africa, however, the queen was described as traveling over land to Jerusalem, making this interpretation unlikely.

The medieval Arabs called the region south of Azania the Sea of Zinj, meaning 'sea of Blacks,' while the medieval Persians knew the regions collectively as Zangbâr, meaning 'Black land.' This suggests that the Aramaic term Zemarged was already antiquated by the medieval era, and implies that Scroll A was translated during the early Christian era.

2 Codex Vaticanus: Tharsis (ΘΑΡϹΙϹ)

- Aleppo Codex: Tršyš (תרשיש)

- Leningrad Codex: Tarshish (תַרְשִׁישׁ)

- Targum of Chronicles: le'afarkaya {s"a le'afrika} (לְאַפְרְקְיָא {ס"א לְאַפְרִיקָא}). Translation: the Aparqaya {scroll A: the Africa}

This civilization was mentioned in a number of ancient documents, including the inscriptions of Esarhaddon from Assyria where it was called Tarsisi (𒋼𒅈𒋛𒋛), and the Nora Stone from Phoenicia where is was called Tršš (𐤅𐤅𐤔𐤕). Based on the various descriptions of the land in Phoenician, Hebrew, and Assyrian sources, Tharsis was in the Mediterranean or the Atlantic Ocean, somewhere west of Malta.

The Greek historian Herodotus recorded that at his time, circa 450 BC, the city of Tartessos was a major trading center, past the 'Pillars of Herakles' or in modern terms, outside the

Mediterranean, on the Atlantic Coast somewhere. This is generally considered to be the same civilization, implying it existed from at least 1000 BC to at least 450 BC. The dominant theory of the past century is that it was the 'Tartessos' culture of southwest Spain. The name Tartessos was adopted from the Greek geography by modern archaeologists, and it is unclear if they called their civilization something that sounded like Tartessos.

A number of ancient ruins and inscriptions have been found in the area, using the Phoenician script, but written in a language dubbed 'Tartessian.' The records of the Hebrews, Phoenicians, and Assyrians all record that Tarshish/Tarsisi was a metal-rich land, which exported large amounts of silver, iron, tin, and other metals. The records of the ancient Greeks reported the same about Tartessos. Modern archaeology in the region around Cadiz does support that this was a metal exporting nation, and therefore the evidence is strongly supportive of this being the civilization referred to in the Septuagint. Several other locations have historically been proposed as the potential location of Tharsis, including Sardinia, Italy, Britain, West Africa, and Southern India. Most of these proposals predated the discovery of the Assyrian and Phoenician records of Tarsisi/Tršš, however, the proposal that Tharsis was in Britain is still supported by some, as the British were also exporting tin to the Phoenicians at the time, however, it is unlikely that the Canaanites would have imported ivory and apes from Britain. The Canaanites did explore the Atlantic coast of Africa, and could have been importing apes to Spain at the time.

This translation uses the name Tartessos, it is generally agreed by archaeologists that this was the civilization being referred to.

3 Codex Vaticanus: allophylôn (ΑΛΛΟΦΥΛѠΝ).
Translation: tribals (or nationals)

- Aleppo Codex: plštym (פלשתים). Translation: Palestinians (or Pelesets)

- Leningrad Codex: Felishtim (פְּלִשְׁתִּים). Translation: Palestinians (or Pelesets)

- Targum of Chronicles: Felishta'ei (פְּלִשְׁתָּאֵי). Translation: Palestinians (or Pelesets)

The Pelesets were an ancient people based in the region of the modern Gaza Strip of the Palestinian Territories. The earliest surviving mention of them is from the reliefs of the Temple of Ramses III at Medinet Habu in Egypt that dates back to some time between 1186 and 1155 BC, in which they were called Pwråsåtj (𓂋𓏤𓊪𓈖𓈙𓏏), commonly angiclized as Pelesets.

In Akkadian cuneiform texts they were called the ^{kur}Palastu (𒆳𒉺𒆷𒊍𒌓). It is unclear where they came from, however, one theory is that they were the Pala, a Luwian people from the Black Sea coast of Anatolia. The region was an independent country called Palaa (𒉺𒆷𒀀) in the Hittite (Neshite) records from the 1600s BC, however, had become part of the Nesite Empire by the 1500s BC. Around the time the Pelesets invaded Canaan, the Pala were driven from their homeland by the neighboring Kaskians from northeast Anatolia, which supports the connection between the groups, however, it has yet to be proven conclusively.

They were later taken as captives by the Babylonians and resettled in Mesopotamia in 604 BC. After the Jewish-Romans war, the Romans renamed the province Palestine and recolonized the area with Greeks, Romans, Egyptians, and Syrians. Modern Palestinians descend from these colonists.

2nd Paralipomenon: Chapter 10

Rehoboam traveled to Shechem, and all Israel traveled to Shechem to make him king. It came to pass when Jeroboam the son of Nebat heard it, (at the time, he was in Egypt, as he had fled there from King Solomon, and had lived in Egypt), that Jeroboam returned out of Egypt. They sent and called him, and Jeroboam and all the congregation came to Rehoboam, saying, "Your father made our workload terrible, now then remove some of your father's terrible rule, and of his heavy workload which he put on us, and we will serve you."

He said to them, "Go away for three days, and then return to me."

So the people departed. King Rehoboam assembled the elders that stood before his father Solomon in his lifetime and asked, "How do you counsel me to answer these people?"

They answered him, "If you would this day befriend these people, and be kind to them, and speak to them good words, then will they be your servants forever."

But he ignored the advice of the old men, who took counsel with him, and he took counsel with the young men who had been brought up with him, who stood around him. He asked them, "What do you advise that I should answer these people, who said to me, "Ease the workload which your father laid on us?"

The young men that had been brought up with him answered him, "Say this to the people that asked you, 'Your father made our workload heavy, will you lighten some of it from us?' answer, "My little finger will be thicker than my father's loins! Where my father punished you with a heavy workload, I will also add to your workload! My father punished you with whips, and I will punish you with scorpions!"

Jeroboam and all the people came to Rehoboam on the third day, as the king had said, 'Return to me on the third day.'

The king answered harshly. King Rehoboam ignored the counsel of the old men, and spoke to them according to the counsel of the young men, saying, "My father made your workload heavy, but I will add to it! My father chastised you with whips, but I will chastise you with scorpions!"

The king did not listen to the people, for there was a change of their minds from God, saying, "The Lord has confirmed his word, which he spoke by the hand of Ahijah the Shilonite concerning Jeroboam the son of Nebat, and concerning all Israel, for the king did not listen to them. The people answered the king, "What portion have we in David, nor inheritance in the son of Jesse?

To your tents, Israel! now see to your own house, David!"

So all Israel went to their tents. But the men of Israel, including those who lived in the cities of Judah, remained and made Rehoboam king over them. King Rehoboam sent to them Adoniram that was in charge of the tribute, and the Israelites stoned him with stones until he died. King Rehoboam rushed and mounted his chariot and fled to Jerusalem. So Israel rebelled against the house of David until today.

2nd Paralipomenon: Chapter 11

Rehoboam traveled to Jerusalem, and he assembled Judah and Benjamin, a hundred and eighty thousand young men fit for war, and he invaded Israel to recover the kingdom to Rehoboam. The word of the Lord came to Shemaiah the prophet, saying, "Speak to Rehoboam the son of Solomon, and all Judah and Benjamin, saying, 'The Lord says, You will not go up, and you will not war against your brothers. Return everyone to his home, for this thing is of me.'"

They listened to the word of the Lord and returned from going against Jeroboam. Rehoboam lived in Jerusalem, and he built walled cities in Judea. He built Bethlehem, and Etam and Tekoah, and Beth Zur, and Succoth, and Adullam, and Gath, and Mareshah, and Ziph, and Adoraim, and Lachish, and Azekah, and Zorah, and Elon, and Hebron, which belong to Judah and Benjamin. He fortified them with walls and placed in them captains, and stores of provisions, oil and wine, shields and spears in every several cities, and he fortified them very strongly, and he had on his side, Judah and Benjamin.

The priests and the Levites who were in all Israel were gathered to him from all of the frontiers. For the Levites left the tents of their possession and went to Judah to Jerusalem because Jeroboam and his sons had ejected them so that they should not minister to the Lord. He made for himself priests of the bamahs, and for the idols, and the vanities, and for the calves which Jeroboam made. He threw out from the tribes of Israel those who set their hearts to seek Lord the god in Israel, and they came to Jerusalem, to sacrifice to Lord the god of their fathers. They strengthened the kingdom of Judah, and Judah strengthened Rehoboam the son of Solomon for three years, as he followed in the ways of David and Solomon for three years.

Rehoboam took from himself as a wife Mahalath the daughter of Jarmuth the son of David, and Abigail the daughter of Eliab the son of Jesse. She carried him three sons: Jeush, Shelomith, and Zaham. Afterward, he took to himself Maakah the daughter of Absalom, and she carried him Abiah, and Attai, and Ziza, and Shelomith. Rehoboam loved Maakah the daughter of Absalom more than all his wives and all his concubines, as he had eighteen wives and sixty concubines, and he fathered twenty-eight sons, and sixty daughters. He made Abiah the son of Maakah chief, even a leader among his brothers, for he intended to make him king. He was exalted beyond all his other sons within all the frontiers of Judah and Benjamin, and in the fortified cities, and he gave them provisions in great abundance, and he desired many wives.

2nd Paralipomenon: Chapter 12

When the kingdom of Rehoboam was established, and after he had grown strong, he forgot the commandments of the Lord and all Israel with him. In the fifth year of the reign of Rehoboam, King Shoshenq[1] of Egypt came up against Jerusalem, because they had sinned against the Lord, with twelve hundred chariots and sixty thousand cavalry, and there was no counting of the multitude that came with him from Egypt, including Libyans,[2] Sags,[3] and Kushites.[4] They captured the fortified cities that were in Judah and approached Jerusalem. Shemaiah the prophet came to Rehoboam, and to the princes of Judah that were gathered to Jerusalem for fear of Shoshenq, and said to them, "The Lord says, 'You have left me, and I will leave you in the hand of Shoshenq!'"

The elders of Israel and the king were ashamed, and said, "The Lord is righteous!"

When the Lord saw that they repented, then the word of the Lord came to Shemaiah, saying, "They have repented. I will not destroy them, but I will set them in safety for a little while, and my anger will not be poured out on Jerusalem. Nevertheless, they will be servants, and know my service, and the service of the kings of the earth."

King Shoshenq of Egypt attacked Jerusalem and took the treasures that were in the Temple of the Lord and the treasures that were in the king's house. He took everything. He took the golden shields which Solomon had made, and King Rehoboam replaced them with bronze shields. Shoshenq set over him captains of infantry, as keepers of the gate of the king. It came to pass, when the king went into the Temple of the Lord, the guards and the infantry went in, and they that returned to meet the infantry. When he repented, the anger of the Lord turned from him and did not destroy him completely, for there were good things in Judah.

So King Rehoboam strengthened himself in Jerusalem and reigned, and Rehoboam was forty-one years old when he began to reign, and he reigned seventeen years in Jerusalem, in the city which the Lord chose out of all the tribes of the Israelites to call his name there, and his mother's name was Naamah the Ammonitess. He did evil, as he did not seek the Lord. The acts of Rehoboam, the first and the last, look, are they not written in the book of Shemaiah the prophet, and Iddo the seer, with his achievements. Rehoboam made war with Jeroboam all his days. Rehoboam died with his fathers and was buried in the City of David, and Abiah his son reigned in his place.

2ⁿᵈ Paralipomenon: Chapter 12 Notes

1 Codex Vaticanus: Sousacim (**ϹΟΥϹΑΚΙΜ**)

* Aleppo Codex: šyšq (שׁישׁק)

* Leningrad Codex: Shishak (שִׁישַׁק)

* Targum of Chronicles: Sheishak (שֵׁישַׁק)

These references are generally accepted as denoting King Hedjkheperre Setepenre Shoshenq I, of the 22ⁿᵈ dynasty, who ruled Egypt circa 943 to 922 BC, and invaded Canaan in 925 BC.

2 Codex Vaticanus: Libyes (**ΛΙΒΥΕϹ**)

* Aleppo Codex: Lwbym (לובים)

* Leningrad Codex: Luvim (לוּבִים)

* Targum of Chronicles: Luva'ei (לוּבָאֵי)

The term 'Libyans' was at that time a reference to the Amazigh (Berber) people. The 'Libyan' 22ⁿᵈ Dynasty of Egypt, founded by Shoshneq I ruled Egypt between 943 and 720 AD. Modern descendants include the Shila, Kabyle, Tamazight, Riffians, Shawiya, and Tuareg, who range across Algeria, Morocco, Tunisia, Libya, Chad, Niger, Mali, and Mauritania.

The specific spelling of the word in the Masoretic Text confirms that the Masoretic version of this verse was translated from Aramaic Lwbåm (𐤋𐤅𐤁𐤀𐤌), not Judahite or Samaritan, as the Canaanite spelling was Lbym (𐤋𐤁𐤉𐤌).

3 Codex Vaticanus: Trôglodytae (Ⲧⲣⲱⲅⲗⲟⲇ**Ⲩ**Ⲧ**Ⲁ**ⲓ).
Translation: cave-dweller (or caveman)

- Aleppo Codex: skyym (סכיים)

- Leningrad Codex: Sukkiyyim (סֻכִּיִּים)

- Targum of Chronicles: Sucha'ei (סוּכָאֵי)

Troglodyte was a Greek term that referred to any group of cave-dwelling people. Greek geographers recorded the existence of several groups of troglodytes, along in Red Sea coast of Africa, in the Balkans, and Sahara. The Troglodytes in question were likely the Troglodytes that Aristotle mentioned living in the upper Nile, and believed to be the then mythical Pygmies. The Egyptians called these people the Såg (🏺⚒), which is likely the origin of the Masoretic name, and is used in this translation. It is not clear where they lived, however, the Egyptian name for their homeland was the 'Såg marshes' (🏺⚒𓈗), suggesting they came from the Sudd swampland of South Sudan, which was the farthest south the Greeks and Romans were able to explore the White Nile. This location is supported by the fact that they must have been located somewhere in the Kushite empire, as they disappeared from Egyptian records after the Assyrians defeated the Kushites.

During the Persian era, the name Såg (🏺⚒) was often conflated with the Sek (𓊹⚒), however, that name was adopted from the Persian name Saka (𐎿𐎣), their name for all Iranian nations to the north of the Persian empire, today known as Scythians in historical texts from their Greek name

Scythicê (Σκυθικη). The Scythians did maraud through Samaria and Judea between 623 and 616 BC, when the Assyrian Empire was collapsing, however, that Scythian force was the enemy of Egypt, not their ally. In the 10th century BC, the Scythians were north of the Caucasus Mountains, and there is no evidence the Egyptians knew of them. Clearly the Greek translators in the 3rd century BC did not believe the reference was to the Scythians, or they would have used that name.

4 Codex Vaticanus: Aithiopes (ⲀⲒⲐⲒⲞⲠⲈⲤ). Translation: dark-skinned people

• Aleppo Codex: Kwšym (כּושׁים). Translation: Kushites (or black people, Nubians)

• Leningrad Codex: Chushim (כּוּשִׁים). Translation: Kushites (or black people, Nubians)

• Targum of Chronicles: Chusha'ei (כּוּשָׁאֵי). Translation: Kushites (or black people, Nubians)

The term 'Aethiopians' was applied to all dark-skinned nations that the Greeks encountered, both in Sub-Saharan Africa and Southern Asia. The Hebrew term Chushim refers to the people of the Kingdom of Kush, south of Egypt, which were undoubtedly the Kushites referred to in this chapter.

2nd Paralipomenon: Chapter 13

In the eighteenth year of the reign of Jeroboam, Abiah began to reign over Judah, and he reigned three years in Jerusalem. His mother's name was Maakah, daughter of Uriel of Gibeon. There was a war between Abiah and Jeroboam. Abiah set the battle formation of the army, with mighty men of war, all four hundred thousand mighty men, and Jeroboam set the battle formation against him with eight hundred thousand, they were mighty warriors of the army.

Abiah rose up from Mount Zemaraim, which is in the mountains of Ephraim, and said, "Listen, Jeroboam, and all Israel. Do you not know that Lord the god in Israel has set David as king over Israel forever, and to his sons, by a covenant of salt? But Jeroboam the son of Nebat, the servant of Solomon the son of David, has risen and has revolted from his master, and there are gathered to him pestilent men, transgressors, and he has risen against Rehoboam the son of Solomon, while Rehoboam was young and fearful in heart, and he could not withstand him."

"Now you profess to resist the kingdom of the Lord in the hand of the sons of David, and you are a great multitude, and with you are golden calves, which Jeroboam made as gods for you. Did you not throw out the priests of the Lord, the sons of Aaron, and the Levites, and make to yourselves priests of the people of any other land?"

"Whoever came to consecrate himself with a calf of the heard and seven rams, he immediately became a priest to that which is no god. But we have not forgotten Lord the god, and his priests, the sons of Aaron, and the Levites, minister to the Lord, and in their daily courses they sacrifice to the Lord whole burnt offering, morning and evening, and compound incense, and set the show-bread on the pure table, and there is the golden candle-stick, and the lamps for burning, to light in the evening, for we keep the orders of Lord the god of our fathers, but you have forgotten him. And look, the Lord and his priests are with us at our head, and the signal trumpets to sound an alarm over us. Israelites, don't fight against Lord the god of our fathers, for you will not win."

Now Jeroboam had planed an ambush to circle around against him from behind, while he was in front of Judah, and the ambush behind. Judah looked back, and saw the battle was against them before and behind, and they cried to the Lord, and the priests sounded with the trumpets.

The men of Judah shouted, and when the men of Judah shouted, the Lord struck Jeroboam and Israel before Abiah and Judah. The Israelites fled from before Judah, and the Lord delivered them into their hands. Abiah and his people struck them with a great slaughter, and five hundred thousand warriors of Israel fell dead that day. So the Israelites were brought down on that day, and the children of Judah prevailed because they trusted on Lord the god of their fathers. Abiah chased after Jeroboam, and he took from him the cities, Bethel and her towns, and Jeshanah and her towns, and Ephron and her towns. Jeroboam did not recover strength again all the days of Abiah, and the Lord struck him, and he died. But Abiah strengthened himself and took to himself fourteen wives, and he fathered twenty-two sons, and sixteen daughters. The rest of the acts of Abiah, and his deeds, and his sayings are written in the book of the prophet Iddo.

2nd Paralipomenon: Chapter 14

Abiah died with his fathers, and they buried him in the City of David, and Asa his son reigned in his place. In the days of Asa, the land of Judah had rest ten years. He did that which was good and right in the sight of Lord the god. He removed the altars of the foreign gods and the bamahs, and broke the steles in pieces, and cut down Asherahs,[1] and he told Judah to seek earnestly Lord the god of their fathers and to perform the law and commandments. He removed from all the cities of Judah the altars and the idols, and established in quietness fortified cities in the land of Judah, for the land was quiet, and he had no war in these years, as the Lord gave him peace.

He said to Judah, "Let us fortify these cities, and make walls, and towers, and gates, and bars. We will prevail over the land, for as we have served Lord the god, he has served us and has given us peace all around and we prospered."

Asa had a force of armed men bearing shields and spears in the land of Judah, numbering three hundred thousand, and in the land of Benjamin two hundred and eighty thousand slingers and archers, all these were mighty warriors. Osorkon I the Egyptian[2] attacked them with a force of a million, and three hundred chariots, and came to Mareshah. Asa went out to meet him and set a battle formation in the valley north of Mareshah.

Asa cried to Lord the god, "Lord, it is not impossible with you to save by many or by few. Strengthen us, Lord the god, for we trust in you, and in your name have we come against this great multitude. Lord the god, don't let men prevail against you!"

The Lord struck the Egyptians before Judah, and the Egyptians fled. Asa and his people pursued them to Gerar,[3] and the Egyptians fell. They could not recover themselves, for they were crushed before the Lord, and before his army, and they took a lot of plunder. They destroyed their towns around Gerar, for a terror of the Lord was on them, and they ruined all their cities, for they carried off great spoils. Also, they destroyed the tents and livestock of the Libyans[4] and took many sheep and camels, and returned to Jerusalem.

2nd Paralipomenon: Chapter 14 Notes

1 Codex Vaticanus: alsê (ᴧᴧᴄн). Translation: grove (or copse)

- Aleppo Codex: Ăšrym (אשרים). Translation: Asherahs

- Leningrad Codex: Asherim (אֲשֵׁרִים). Translation: Asherahs

- Targum of Chronicles: Asheirata (אֲשֵׁירָתָא)

Asherah was the name of an Israelite goddess before the time of Elijah in the 9th century, described as the mother of Yahweh, as well as the wife of El. It is unclear exactly how Asherah was worshiped, however, is is believed she was worshiped by planting oak trees, similar to her Egyptian counterpart Iusaaset, who was worshiped by planting acacia trees. If so, then these asherahs would have been oak trees. Oak trees were used as grave markers in ancient Canaan.

2 Codex Vaticanus: Zare o aethiops (ᴢᴧᵽᴇoᴧɪϴɪo†). Translation: Zare the Aethiopian

- Aleppo Codex: Zrh hKwšy (זרח הכושי). Translation: Zare the Kwshy

- Leningrad Codex: Zerach hakKushi (זֶרַח הַכּוּשִׁי). Translation: Zerach the Kwshy

- Targum of Chronicles: Zerach Kusha'ah (זֶרַח כּוּשָׁאָה). Translation: Zerach Kushaah

The Egyptian king at the time was Osorkon I, which the Hebrew name Zrh (זרח) appears to be a corruption of.

However, Osorkon was not a Kushite, but a Libyan. He was the second king in the Libyan 22nd Dynasty of Egypt, which ruled most of northern Egypt between 943 and 716 BC. Late in the 22nd dynasty's rule, the country broke up into smaller kingdoms, and ultimately the Kushites occupied all of Egypt. The Kushite Empire took control of Egypt between 743 and 712 BC, and then Egypt was part of the Kushite Empire until the Neo-Assyrian Empire occupied Egypt in 673 BC. During the era that Egypt was part of Kush, it was common for all Egyptians to be called Kushites. This indicates that this section was originally written sometime between 712 and 673 BC. As Osorkon was not a Kushite, the term Zrḥ hKwšy (זרח הכושי) is interpreted as 'Osorkon I the Egyptian' in this translation. Likewise, the later mentions of the Kushites in the chapter are interpreted as Egyptians.

3 Codex Vaticanus: Gedôr (ܓܕܘܪ)

- Aleppo Codex: Grr (גרר)

- Leningrad Codex: Gerar (גְרָר)

- Targum of Chronicles: Gerar (גְרָר)

The location of this town is debated, however it is generally agreed to have been a town in the territory southern modern Israel, likely south of the Palestinian Gaza Strip. The current view is that was in the valley of Nahal Gerar, at the site of Tel Haror.

4 Codex Vaticanus: Amazonis (ΛΜΛΖΟΝЄΙϹ). Translation: Amazons

The Masoretic version of the verse, as well as the version in the Targum of Chronicles, do not specify whose livestock was plundered. The Greek term is a variation of the name Amazones (Ἀμαζόνες), which referred to several tribes the Greeks recorded around the edge their known world, with tribes listed from Eastern Europe to North Africa. Several Greek historians claimed that there were briefly Amazons in Egypt, which was probably a corruption of the name Amazigh (oᴄoⵯⵉⴴ), the name the Libyan (Berber) tribes call themselves. In the ancient Libyco-Berber script, it was recorded as Mzyɣ (ⴵⵣⵣⵉ), which gave rise to the Classical Latin name Mazices. The older script, had no vowels in it, although the å (o) and ô (ⴴ) were added to the modern Tifinagh script to clarify pronunciation. Based on the ancient spelling of Mzyɣ (ⴵⵣⵣⵉ), and the modern spoken forms, it is certain that their name would have been pronounced as something like Amazygh at the time. The Greek legends of female warriors are at least partially correct, as the ancient Amazigh we a gender neutral society, with both male and female warriors and monarchs.

In this verse, it appears that the source texts the Greeks translated were reporting that the Judahites seized the livestock of the Libyan invaders, not the inhabitants of Gerer. This reading does confirm that it was Osorkon I, the Libyan king of Egypt that was identified as 'Zrḥ the Kushite' earlier in the chapter. It is unclear why the term is missing from the

Hebrew translation, however, it is likely it would not have been understood by the time the Hasmonean dynasty standardized the Hebrew translation circa 140 BC. As the Amazigh are generally referred to as Libyans in Egyptology, 'Libyans' is used as an interpretation of 'Amazons.'

2ⁿᵈ Paralipomenon: Chapter 15

The spirit of the Lord came into Azariah the son of Oded, and he went out to meet Asa, and all Judah and Benjamin, and said, "Hear me, Asa, and all Judah and Benjamin! The Lord is with you, while you are with him! If you seek him out, he will be found of you! If you forsake him, he will forsake you! Israel has been a long time without the true God, and without a priest to expound the truth, and without the law. But he will turn them to Lord the god in Israel, and he will be found of them. In that time there will be no peace to one going out, or to one coming in, for the terror of the Lord will be in all that inhabit the lands. Nation will fight against nation, and city against city, because God has confounded them with every kind of affliction! But be strong, and don't let your hands be weakened, for there is a reward for your work."

When Asa heard these words, and the prophecy of Hadad the prophet, then he strengthened himself, and threw out the abominations from all the land of Judah and Benjamin, and from the cities which Jeroboam possessed in the mountains of Ephraim, and he restored the altar of the Lord, which was in front of the temple of the Lord. He assembled Judah and Benjamin, and the foreigners that lived with him, of Ephraim, and Manasseh, and of Simeon, for many of Israel were joined to him when they saw that Lord the god was with him. They assembled at Jerusalem in the third month, in the fifteenth year of the reign of Asa. He sacrificed to the Lord on that day of the spoils which they brought, seven hundred calves and seven thousand sheep. He entered into a covenant that they should seek Lord the god of their fathers with all their hearts and with all their souls. That whoever should not seek Lord the god in Israel, should be murdered, whether young or old, whether man or woman.

They swore to the Lord with a loud voice, and with trumpets, and with cornets. All Judah rejoiced concerning the oath, for they swore with all their hearts, and they wanted him with all their desires, and he was found of them, and the Lord gave them peace all around. He removed Maakah his mother from being a priestess of Asherah,[1] and he cut down the idol and burnt it in the brook of Kidron. Nevertheless, they did not remove the bamahs, they still existed in Israel. The heart of Asa was perfect all his days. He brought in the holy things of David his father, and the holy things of the Temple of God, silver, and gold, and vessels. There was no war waged with him until the thirty-fifth year of the reign of Asa.

2nd Paralipomenon: Chapter 15 Notes

1 Codex Vaticanus: Astartê (ΑϹΤΑΡΤΗ)

- Aleppo Codex: åšrh (אשרה)

- Leningrad Codex: Asherah (אֲשֵׁרָה)

- Targum of Chronicles: Asherata (אֲשֵׁרְתָא)

Astarte was the Greek name of the Canaanite goddess Ôštrt (𐤏𐤕𐤔𐤕 / 𐎓𐎘𐎚𐎚). Local versions of her were worshiped throughout the Middle East and the Mediterranean Sea. In Akkadian she was a god known as ᵃⁿAsdartú (𒀭𒀸𒁯𒌈), while in Babylonian she was known as ᵃⁿIštar (𒀭𒈹), and in Etruscan she was known as Uni-al-Astres (𐌔𐌄𐌐𐌕𐌔𐌀𐌋𐌀𐌉𐌍𐌖). The Greek goddess Aphrodite appears to be derived from an early Cypriot version of her, while the Roman goddess Venus appears to be derived indirectly through the Etruscan Uni-al-Astres. During the New Kingdom era of Egyptian history, circa 1549 to 1077 AD, Astarte was incorporated into the Egyptian pantheon as one of the daughters of Ra, as she appeared in the book entitled the 'Contest between Horus and Set.' According to the Phoenician scholar Sanchuniathon, who supposedly lived circa 1200 BC, Astarte's sister was Asherah. The word Asherah also appears in the Septuagint many times and appears to be widely worshiped by the early Israelites.

2nd Paralipomenon: Chapter 16

In the thirty-eighth year of the reign of Asa, the king of Israel attacked Judah and built Ramah, so as not to allow King Asa of Judah to invade. Asa stole the silver and gold out of the treasures of the Temple of the Lord, and the king's palace, and sent them to the son of Arad king of Syria, who lived in Damascus, saying, "Make a treaty between you and I, and between my father and your father. Look, I have sent you gold and silver. Come, and break your treaty with Baasha king of Israel, and make him leave from me."

The son of Arad listened to king Asa, and sent the captains of his army against the cities of Israel, and struck Ijon, Dan, Abelmain, and all the country around Naphtali. When Baasha heard it he abandoned building Ramah and stopped his work. Then king Asa took all Judah and took the stones of Ramah, and its timber, with which Baasha had built, and he built with them Gibeah and Mizpeh. At that time Hanani the prophet went to King Asa of Judah, and said to him, "Because you trusted in the king of Syria, and did not trust in the Lord your god, therefore the army of Syria has escaped out of your hand. Were not the Kushites and Libyans a great force, in courage, in cavalry, in great numbers? Didn't he deliver them into your hands, because you trusted in the Lord? For the eyes of the Lord look on all the earth, to strengthen every heart that is perfect towards him. In this, you have done foolishly, and from now on there will be war with you."

Asa was angry with the prophet and put him in prison. He was angry at this, and Asa tortured some of the people at that time. And look, the acts of Asa, the first and the last, are written in the Book of the Kings of Judah and Israel. Asa became diseased in his feet in the thirty-ninth year of his reign, until he was very ill, but in his disease did not call out to the Lord, but the physicians. Asa slept with his fathers and died in the fortieth year of his reign. They buried him in the sepulcher which he had dug for himself in the City of David, and they laid him on a bed and filled it with spices and all kinds of perfumes of the apothecaries, and they made for him a very great funeral.

2ⁿᵈ Paralipomenon: Chapter 17

Jehoshaphat his son reigned in his place, and Jehoshaphat strengthened himself against Israel. He put garrisons in all the fortified cities of Judah and appointed captains in all the cities of Judah, and in the cities of Ephraim, which Asa his father had taken. The Lord was with Jehoshaphat, for he followed the first ways of his father, and did not follow idols, but he served Lord the god of his father, and followed the commandments of his father, and not according to the works of Israel.

The Lord prospered the kingdom in his hand, and all Judah gave gifts to Jehoshaphat, and he had great wealth and glory. His heart was exalted in the way of the Lord, and he removed the bamahs and Asherah from the land of Judah. In the third year of his reign, he sent his chief men, and his mighty men, Obadiah Zachariah, Nethanel, and Micah, to teach in the cities of Judah. With them were the Levites: Shemaiah, Manthaniah, Zebadiah, Asahel, Shemiramot, Johnathan, Adonian, (Tobiah,) and Tob Adoniah,[1] Levites, and with them Elishama and Jeroham, the priests.

They taught in Judah, and there was with them the book of the law of the Lord, and they passed through the cities of Judah and taught the people. A terror of the Lord was on all the kingdoms of the land around Judah, and they made no war against Jehoshaphat. Some of the

Pelesets brought to Jehoshaphat gifts, and silver, and presents and the Arabians brought him seven thousand and seven hundred rams. Jehoshaphat increased in greatness greatly and built in Judea palaces and fortified cities. He had many works in Judea, and the mighty men of war, the men of strength, were in Jerusalem.

This is their number according to the houses of their fathers. The captains of thousands in Judah were: Adnah the chief, and with him mighty men of strength three hundred thousand. After him, Jehohanan the captain, and with him two hundred and eighty thousand. After him Amasiah the son of Zari, who was zealous for the Lord, and with him two hundred thousand mighty men of strength. Out of Benjamin, there was a mighty man of strength named Eliada, and with him two hundred thousand archers and slingers. After him Jehozabad, and with him a hundred and eighty thousand mighty men of war. These were the king's servants besides those which the king stationed in the fortified cities in all Judea.

2ⁿᵈ Paralipomenon: Chapter 17 Notes

1 Codex Vaticanus: Samouas cae Manthanias cae Zabdias cae Iasiêl cae Samiramôth cae Iônathan cae Adônian cae Tôbadôbia (ϹΑΜΟΥΑϹΚΑΙΜΑΝΘΑΝΙΑϹΚΑΙΖΑΒΔΕΙΑϹΚΑΙΙΑϹΕΙΗΛ ΚΑΙ ϹΑΜΕΙΡΑΜΩΘ ΚΑΙ ΙΩΝΑΘΑΝ ΚΑΙ ΑΔΩΝΙΑΝ ΚΑΙ ΤΩΒΑΔΩΒΕΙΑ). Translation: Samouas and Manthanias and Zabdias and Iasiêl and Samiramôth and Iônathan and Adônian and Tôbadôbia

- Codex Alexandrinus: Samaeas cae Nathanias cae Zabdias cae Asiêl cae Semiramôth cae Iônathan cae Adônias cae Tôbias (ϹΑΜΑΙΑϹ ΚΑΙ ΝΑΘΑΝΙΑϹ ΚΑΙ ΖΑΒΔΙΑϹ ΚΑΙ ΑϹΙΗΛ ΚΑΙ ϹΕΜΙΡΑΜΩΘ ΚΑΙ ΙΩΝΑΘΑΝ ΚΑΙ ΑΔΩΝΙΑϹ ΚΑΙ ΤΩΒΙΑϹ). Translation: Samaeas and Nathanias and Zabdias and Asiêl and Semiramôth and Iônathan and Adônias and Tôbias

- Aleppo Codex: šmôhw wntnhw wzbdhw wôšhål wšmrmwt {wšmrmwt} wyhwntn wådnhw wtwbhw wtwb ådwnyh (שמעיהו ונתניהו וזבדיהו ועשהאל ושמרימות {ושמירמות} ויהונתן ואדניהו וטוביהו וטוב אדוניה). Translation: Šmôyhw and Ntnyhw and Zbdyhw and Ôšhål and Šmrymwt {and Šmyrmwt} and Yhwntn and Ådnyhw and Twbyhw and Twb Ådwnyh

- Leningrad Codex: shema'yahu unetanyahu uzevadyahu va'asahel [ushemirimovt K] {ushemiramovt Q} vihovnatan va'adoniyyahu vetovviyyahu vetovv adovniyyah (שְׁמַֽעְיָ֡הוּ וּנְתַנְיָ֩הוּ֩ וּזְבַדְיָ֨הוּ וַעֲשָׂהאֵ֜ל ׀וְשֽׁמִרִימוֹת {וּשְׁמִירָמ֣וֹת ק} ׀וִיהוֹנָתָ֗ן וַאֲדֹנִיָּ֧הוּ וְטֽוֹבִיָּ֛הוּ וְט֥וֹב אֲדוֹנִיָּ֖ה). Translation: Shema'yahu and Netanyahu and Zevadyahu and Asahel [and Shemirimovt K]

285

{and Shemiramovt Q} and Ihovnatan and Adoniyyahu and Tovviyyahu and Tovv Adovniyyah

• Targum of Chronicles: shema'yah unetanyah uzecharyah (s"ā uzevadyahu) va'ashahel ushemiramot vihonatan va'adoniyahu vetoviyah vetov adoniyah (שְׁמַעְיָה וּנְתַנְיָה וּזְכַרְיָה {ס"א וּזְבַדְיָהוּ} וַעֲשָׂהאֵל וּשְׁמִירָמוֹת וִיהוֹנָתָן וַאֲדוֹנִיָהוּ וְטוֹבִיָה וְטוֹב אֲדוֹנִיָה). Translation: Shema'yah and Netanyah and Zecharyah (alternate: and Zevadyahu) and Ashahel and Shemiramot and Ihonatan and Adoniyahu and Toviyah and Tov Adoniyah

All sources have a different list, or refer to variant lists in their source texts. Both Greek lists include eight names, while the Hebrew and Aramaic lists include nine, along with an alternate spelling for one of the names. The Codex Alexandrinus dates to the 5th century, and includes corrections based on the Hebrew translations of the time, however, is still missing the extra name. In most cases, the Greek names appear to be transliterations of the names found in the Masoretic text, however, there are a few differences.

The oldest Greek source uses 'Manthanias' instead of 'Nathanias,' which may have resulted from a scribal error, but the error is not obvious. The older Greek Adonian is a transliteration of a different name than the Hebrew Adoniyahu. Both names a based on the name of a god, the older Greek version is 'Lord An,' while the later Hebrew translation is 'Lord Yahw.' Ôn / Åwn (Ων / אוֹן) was a god that the prophet Hosea told the Judahites to stop worshiping, and whose worship was later banned under King Hosea. However, all of this happened long after the events in this verse, suggesting the name was altered in the text during or after Josiah's reforms. The final older Greek name, Tôbadôbia (Τωβαδωβεια), is a mistransliteration of the final Hebrew name Twb Ådwnyh (טוב אדוניה), resulting from reading an N (נ / ן) as a B (ב / ך). While both Tobiah and Tob Adoniyah are included in the Hebrew and Aramaic translations, only one is included in the Greek translations, and they do not include the same name. As the Codex Alexandrinus is a modified version of the Septuagint, the name Tobiah is listed in parentheses.

2nd Paralipomenon: Chapter 18

Jehoshaphat had great wealth and glory, and he connected himself by marriage with the house of Ahab. He went down after a term of years to Ahab in Samaria, and Ahab killed for him sheep and calves, in great numbers, and also for the people with him, and he greatly desired him to go up with him to Ramoth of the country of Gilead.

Ahab king of Israel asked Jehoshaphat king of Judah, "Will you go with me to Ramoth of the country of Gilead?"

He answered him, "As I am, so are you. As your people, so are my people with you for the war."

Jehoshaphat said to the king of Israel, "Seek today, I beg you, the Lord."

The king of Israel gathered the prophets, all four hundred men, and asked them, "Will I go to Ramoth in Gilead to battle, or won't I?"

They answered, "Go up, and God will deliver it into the hands of the king."

Jehoshaphat asked, "Is there not here a prophet of the Lord also, that we may inquire of him?"

The king of Israel answered Jehoshaphat, "There is still one man by whom to inquire of the Lord, but I hate him, for he does not prophesy good for me, and all his days are for evil. This is Micah the son of Imlah."

Jehoshaphat said, "Don't let the king say that!"

The king called a eunuch, and said, "Fetch quickly Micah the son of Imlah."

The king of Israel and Jehoshaphat king of Judah were sitting each on his throne, and clothed in their robes, sitting in the open space at the entrance of the gate of Samaria, and all the prophets were prophesying before them. Zedekiah son of Canaan made for himself iron horns, and said, "The Lord says, 'With these, you will thrust Syria until it is consumed.'"

All the prophets prophesied so, saying, "Go up to Ramoth in Gilead, and you will prosper, and the Lord will deliver it into the hands of the king."

The messenger that went to call Micah spoke to him, saying, "Look, the prophets have spoken favorably concerning the king with one mouth, let now, I beg you, your words be as the words of one of them, and you should speak good things."

Micah replied, "As the Lord lives, whatever God will say to me, that I will state."

He went to the king, and the king asked him, "Micah, will I go up to Ramoth in Gilead to battle, or won't I?"

He answered, "Go up, and you will prosper, and they will be given into your hands!"

The king asked him, "How often will I solemnly charge you, that you speak to me nothing but the truth in the name of the Lord?"

He answered, "I saw Israel scattered on the mountains, like sheep without a shepherd, and the Lord said, 'These have no commander, let each return to his home in peace.'"

The king of Israel said to Jehoshaphat, "Did I not tell you, that he would not prophesy concerning me good, but evil?"

Yet he replied, "Not so. Hear the word of the Lord. I saw the Lord sitting on his throne, and all the army of the sky stood by on his right hand and his left. The Lord said, 'Who will deceive Ahab king of Israel, that he may go up, and fall in Ramoth in Gilead?' One spoke this way, and another spoke that way. There came out a spirit, and stood before the Lord, and said, 'I will deceive him.' The Lord asked, 'How?' He answered, 'I will go out, and will be a lying spirit in the mouth of all his prophets.' The Lord said, 'You will deceive him, and will prevail. Go out, and do so.' Now, look, the Lord has put a false spirit in the mouth of these your prophets, and the Lord has spoken evil against you."

Then Zedekiah the son of Canaan approached, and slapped Micah on the cheek, and asked him, "How did the spirit of the Lord pass from me to speak through you?"

Micah answered, "Look, you will see in that day when you will go from chamber to chamber to hide."

The king of Israel ordered, "Take Micah, and carry him back to Emer the governor of the city, and to Joash the captain, the king's son, and you will say, 'This says the king, 'Put this fellow into the prison house, and let him eat the bread of affliction, and drink the water of affliction, until I return in peace.'"

Micah said, "If you do at all return in peace, the Lord has not spoken by me."

He said, "Hear, all you people."

So the king of Israel and Jehoshaphat king of Judah went up to Ramoth in Gilead. The king of Israel said to Jehoshaphat, "Disguise me, and I will enter into the battle, and you put on my clothing," so the king of Israel disguised himself, and entered into the battle.

The king of Syria had commanded the captains of the chariots that were with him, saying, "Don't attack the small or great, but only against the king of Israel. When the captains of the chariots saw Jehoshaphat, they said, "It is the king of Israel!" They surrounded him to attack him, and Jehoshaphat cried out, and the Lord delivered him, and god turned them away from him. When the captains of the chariots saw that it was not the king of Israel, that they turned away from him. A man drew a bow with a good aim and struck the king of Israel between the lungs and the breast-plate, and he said to the charioteer, "Turn your hand, drive me out of the battle, for I am wounded."

The battle turned in that day, and the king of Israel remained on the chariot against Syria until evening and died at sunset.

2nd Paralipomenon: Chapter 19

King Jehoshaphat of Judah returned to his palace in Jerusalem. Jehu the prophet, the son of Hanani, went out to meet him, and said to him, "King Jehoshaphat. You helped a sinner, and acted friendly towards one hated by the Lord! Therefore anger has come on you from the Lord. Nevertheless, some good things have been found in you, in that you did remove Asherah from the land of Judah, and did direct your heart to seek after the Lord."

Jehoshaphat lived in Jerusalem, and he again went out among the people from Beersheba to the mountains in Ephraim and turned them back to Lord the god of their fathers. He appointed judges in all the fortified cities of Judah, city by city. He said to the judges, "Pay close attention to what you do, for you judge not for man, but the Lord, and with you are matters of judgment. Now let the fear of the Lord be on you, and be wary, and do your duty, for there is no unrighteousness with Lord the god, neither is it for him to respect persons nor take bribes."

Moreover, Jehoshaphat appointed in Jerusalem some of the priests, and Levites, and heads of houses of Israel, for the judgment of the Lord, and to judge the residents in Jerusalem. He ordered them, "This you will do in the fear of the Lord, in truth and with a perfect heart. Whatever man of your brothers that live in their cities will bring the cause that comes before you, between blood and blood, and between precept and commandment, and ordinances and judgments, you will even decide for them, so they will not sin against the Lord, and there will not be anger on you, and your brothers. This you will do, and you will not sin. And, look, Omri the priest is head over you in every matter of the Lord, and Zebadiah the son of Ishmael is head over the house of Judah in every matter of the king, and the scribes and Levites are before you, be strong and active, and the Lord will be with the good."

2ⁿᵈ Paralipomenon: Chapter 20

After this came the Moabites, and the Ammonites and with them some Minaeans[1] to attack Jehoshaphat. They came and told Jehoshaphat, "There has come against you a great multitude from Syria, and from beyond the sea, and they are in Hazazon Tamar," (this is Ein Gedi.)[2]

Jehoshaphat was alarmed and set his face to seek the Lord earnestly, and he proclaimed a fast in all Judah. Judah gathered themselves together to seek after the Lord, even from all the cities of Judah they came to seek the Lord. Jehoshaphat stood up in the assembly of Judah in Jerusalem, in the Temple of the Lord, in front of the new court.

He said, "Lord the god of my fathers, are you not God in the sky above, and are you not lord of all the kingdoms of the nations? Is there not in your hand the might of dominion, and there is no one who can resist you? Are you not the Lord that destroyed the inhabitants of this land before the face of your people Israel, and gave it to your beloved seed of Abraham forever? They lived in it, and built in it a sanctuary to your name, saying, 'If there should come on us evils, sword, judgment, pestilence, famine, we will stand before this house, and before you, (for your name is on this house,) and we will cry to you because of the affliction, and you will hear, and deliver. Now, look, the Ammonites, and Moab, and mount Seir, with regard to whom you did not permit Israel to pass through their border, when they had come out of the land of Egypt, (for they turned away from them, and did not destroy them) yet now, look, they make attempts against us, to come forth to cast us out from our inheritance which you gave us. Lord the god, will you not judge them? We have no strength to resist this great multitude that is come against us, and we don't know what we will do to them, but our eyes are towards you."

All Judah was standing before the Lord, and their children, and their wives. Uzziel the son of Zachariah, of the children of Benaiah, of the sons of Eliel, the sons of Mattaniah the Levite, of the sons of Asaph, into him came to the spirit of the Lord in the assembly, and he said, "Hear you, all Judah, and the residents in Jerusalem, and King Jehoshaphat. The Lord says to you, even you, 'Don't be afraid or be alarmed, before all this great multitude, for the battle is not years, but God's. Tomorrow is against them. See, they will come up by the ascent of Ziz, and you will find them at the edge of the river in the wilderness of Jeruel.' It is not for you to fight, understand these things, and see the deliverance of the Lord. Judah and Jerusalem, don't be afraid. Don't be afraid to go out tomorrow to meet them, and the Lord will be with you."

Jehoshaphat bowed with his face to the ground with all Judah and the residents in Jerusalem, and they fell before the Lord to worship the Lord. The Levites of the children of Kohath, and they of the sons of Korah rose up to praise Lord the god in Israel with a loud voice on high. They rose early in the morning and went out to the wilderness of Tekoah, and as they went out, Jehoshaphat stood and cried, "Hear me, Judah, and the residents in Jerusalem, put your trust in Lord the god, and your trust will be honored, trust in his prophet, and you will prosper."

He took counsel with the people and set appointed men to sing psalms and praises, to give thanks, and sing the holy songs of praise in going out before the army, and they said, "Give thanks to the Lord, for his mercy endures forever. When they began the praise, and gave thanks, the Lord caused the Ammonites to fight against the Moabites, and the inhabitants of mount Seir that came out against Judah, and they were routed. Then the Ammonites and Moabites rose up against the residents in mount Seir, to destroy and consume them, and when they had made an end of destroying the inhabitants of Seir, they rose up against one another so that they were destroyed.

Judah came to the watch-tower of the wilderness, and looked, and saw the multitude, and, look, they were all fallen dead on the earth, not one escaped. Jehoshaphat and his people went out to plunder them, and they found a great deal of livestock, and furniture, and spoils, and precious things, and they plundered them. They were three days gathering the spoils, for it was abundant. On the fourth day, they were gathered to the Valley of Blessing and blessed the Lord, and therefore they called the name of the place the Valley of Blessing, until this day.

All the men of Judah returned to Jerusalem, and Jehoshaphat led them with great joy, for the Lord gave them joy over their enemies. They entered into Jerusalem with lutes and harps and trumpets, going into the Temple of the Lord. There was a terror of the Lord on all the kingdoms of the land when they heard that the Lord fought against the enemies of Israel. The kingdom of Jehoshaphat was at peace, and his god gave him peace all around. Jehoshaphat reigned over Judah, being thirty-five years old when he began to reign, and he reigned twenty-five years in Jerusalem. His mother's name was Azubah, daughter of Shilhi. He followed the ways of his father Asa and did not turn away from doing that which was right in the sight of the Lord. Nevertheless, the bamahs yet remained, and as yet the people did not direct their heart to Lord the god of their fathers.

The rest of the acts of Jehoshaphat, the first and the last, look, they are written in the Book of Jehu the son of Hanani, who wrote the Book of the Kings of Israel.

Afterward, Jehoshaphat king of Judah allied with Ahaziah king of Israel, (now this was an unrighteous man), by acting with and going to him, to build ships to go to Tartessos, and he built ships in Ezion Geber. Eliezer you son of Dodavah of Mareshah prophesied against Jehoshaphat, saying, "In that, you have allied yourself with Ahaziah, the Lord has broken your work, and your vessels have been wrecked," and they could not go to Tartessos.

2nd Paralipomenon: Chapter 20 Notes

1 Codex Vaticanus: Minaeôn (ΜΙΝΑΙΩΝ). Translation: Minaeans

- Aleppo Codex: ômhm mhômwnym (עמהם מהעמונים). Translation: nations in other columns
- Leningrad Codex: immahem meha'ammonim (עִמָּהֶם מֵהָֽעַמּוֹנִים). Translation: nations in other columns
- Targum of Chronicles: imhon min Edoma'ei (עִמְהוֹן מִן אֱדוֹמָאֵי). Translation: nations from the Edom

The Minaeans were the people of the Kingdom of Ma'in in modern Yemen. They appeared in several ancient Greek works, including the work of Eratosthenes. The region of Ma'in appears to have been part of the Kingdom of Saba until after 400 BC, and therefore if Minaeans were in the alliance against Jehoshaphat, this would be reference to a Saban group.

2 Codex Vaticanus: Engaddi (ΕΝΓΑΔΔΙ)

- Aleppo Codex: ôyn gdy (עין גדי)
- Leningrad Codex: Ein Gedi (עֵין גֶּדִי)
- Targum of Chronicles: Ein Gedi (עֵין גֶּדִי)

Ein Gedi is an oasis in modern Israel west of the Dead Sea. This note was added to the Septuagint when it was translated.

2ⁿᵈ Paralipomenon: Chapter 21

Jehoshaphat slept with his fathers and was buried in the City of David, and Jeroham his son reigned in his place. He had brothers, the six sons of Jehoshaphat: Azariah, and Jehiel, and Zachariah, and Azariah, and Michael, and Shephatiah, all these were the sons of Jehoshaphat king of Judah. Their father gave them many gifts, silver, and gold, and arms, together with fortified cities in Judah, but he gave the kingdom to Jeroham, for he was the firstborn. Jeroham entered on his kingdom, and strengthened himself, and murdered all his brothers with the sword, and some of the princes of Israel.

When he was thirty-two years old, Jeroham succeeded to his kingdom, and he reigned eight years in Jerusalem. He followed the way of the kings of Israel, like the house of Ahab did, as his wife was a daughter of Ahab, and he did that which was evil in the sight of the Lord. Nevertheless, the Lord would not destroy the house of David, because of the covenant which he made with David, and as he said to him that he would give a light to him and his sons forever.

In those days Edom revolted from Judah, and they made a king over themselves. Jeroham went with the princes and all the cavalry with him, and he arose by night, and attacked Edom which was surrounding him, and the captains of the chariots and the people fled to their tents. Edom revolted from Judah until today. Then Libnah revolted from under his hand because he forgot Lord the god of his fathers. He had built bamahs in the cities of Judah, and caused the residents in Jerusalem to fornicate, and led Judah astray.

There came to him a message in writing from Elijah the prophet, saying, "Lord the god of your father David says, 'Because you have not followed the way of your father Jehoshaphat, nor in the ways of Asa king of Judah, but have followed the ways of the kings of Israel, and have caused Judah and the residents in Jerusalem to fornicate, like the house of Ahab had caused Israel to fornicate, and you have slain your brothers, the sons of your father, who were better than yourself, look, the Lord will strike you with a great plague among your people, and your sons, and your wives, and all your store, and you will be afflicted with a terrible disease, with a disease of the bowels, until your bowels will fall out day by day with the sickness.'"

So the Lord stirred up the Pelesets against Jeroham, and the Arabians, and those who bordered on the Kushites, and they went up against Judah, and prevailed against them, and took away all the store which they found in the house of the king, and his sons, and his daughters, and there was no son left to him but Ahaziah the youngest of his sons. After all these things the Lord struck him in the bowels with an incurable disease. It continued from day to day, and after two year his bowels fell out from the disease, and he died in terrible fever. His people performed no funeral, like the funeral of his fathers. He was thirty-two years old when he began to reign, and he reigned eight years in Jerusalem. He departed without honor, and was buried in the City of David, but not in the tombs of the kings.

2nd Paralipomenon: Chapter 22

The inhabitants of Jerusalem made Ahaziah, his youngest son, king in his place, for the band of robbers that came against them, including Arabs and Libyans,[1] had slain all the elder ones. So Ahaziah son of Jeroham king of Judah reigned. Ahaziah began to reign when he was twenty years old, and he reigned one year in Jerusalem, and his mother's name was Athaliah, the daughter of Omri. He followed the way of the house of Ahab, as his mother counseled him to do evil. He did that which was evil in the sight of the Lord as the house of Ahab had done, for they were his counselors after the death of his father, until his destruction.

He followed their counsel, and he went with Jeroham son of Ahab king of Israel to war against Hazael king of Syria to Ramoth in Gilead, and the archers struck Jeroham. Jeroham returned to Jezreel to be healed of the wounds where the Syrians struck him in Ramoth when he fought against Hazael king of Syria. Ahaziah son of Jeroham, king of Judah, went down to see Jeroham the son of Ahab at Jezreel because he was sick. Destruction from God came on Ahaziah in his coming to Jeroham, for when he had come, Jeroham went out with him against Jehu the son of Nimshi, the anointed of the Lord against the house of Ahab. When Jehu was taking vengeance on the house of Ahab, he found the princes of Judah and the brothers of Ahaziah ministering to Ahaziah, and he killed them. He gave orders to seek Ahaziah, and they took him while he was healing his wounds in Samaria, and they brought him to Jehu, and he killed him, and they buried him, for they said, "He is the son of Jehoshaphat, who wanted the Lord with all his heart."

So there was none in the house of Ahaziah to secure their power in the kingdom. Athaliah the mother of Ahaziah saw that her son was dead, and she rose and destroyed all the royal seed in the house of Judah. But Jehoshabeath, the daughter of the king, took Joash the son of Ahaziah and rescued him secretly out from among the sons of the king that were put to death, and she placed him and his nurse in a bedchamber. So Jehoshabeath daughter of king Jeroham, sister of Ahaziah, wife of Jehoiada the priest, hid him, and she even hid him from Athaliah, and she could not kill him. He was hidden in the Temple of God for six years, and Athaliah reigned over the land.

2nd Paralipomenon: Chapter 22 Notes

1 Codex Vaticanus: Alimazonis (ⲀⲗⲓⲘⲀⳤⲞⲚⲉⲓⲥ)

- Aleppo Codex: lmhnh (לְמַחֲנֵה). Translation: to encampment (or campsite)

- Leningrad Codex: lammachaneh (לְמַחֲנֵה). Translation: to encampment (or campsite)

- Targum of Chronicles: lemashiryat Pelishta'ei ve'Afrika'ei (לְמַשְׁרְיַת פְּלִשְׁתָּאֵי וְאַפְרִיקָאֵי). Translation: to the camp of the Pelesets (or Palestinians) and Africans (or Carthaginians)

The Greek and Hebrew terms do not appear to be related. There is no Alimazoneis tribe known to had lived in the Middle East, and is likely a transliteration of the word l (ⳤ), meaning 'to.' followed by the same term as the Amazonis (Ἀμαζονεῖσ) listed in 2nd Paralipomenon Chapter 14. As the term is likely derived from the name of the Amazigh (Berber) people who were ruling Egypt, the translation of 'Libyans' is used.

2nd Paralipomenon: Chapter 23

In the eighth year, Jehoiada strengthened himself and took the captains of hundreds, Azariah the son of Jeroham, and Ishmael the son of Jehohanan, and Azariah the son of Obed, and Maaseiah the son of Adaiah, and Elizaphan the son of Zachariah, with him in his home. They traveled around Judah and gathered the Levites out of all the cities of Judah, and heads of the families of Israel, and they came to Jerusalem, and all the congregation of Judah made a covenant with the king in the Temple of God.

He showed them the king's son, and said to them, "Look, let the king's son reign, as the Lord said concerning the house of David. Now, this is the thing which you will do. Let a third part of you, even of the priests and of the Levites, enter in on the sabbath, even into the gates of the entrances, and let a third part be in the house of the king, and another third at the middle gate, and all the people in the courts of the Lord's house. Don't let anyone enter into the Temple of the Lord, except the priests and the Levites, and the servants of the Levites, they will enter in, because they are holy, and let all the people keep the watch of the Lord. The Levites will surround the king, each man with his weapon in hand, and whoever else goes into the house will die, but they will be with the king when he goes out, and when he comes in."

The Levites and all Judah did according to all that the priest Jehoiada commanded them, and they took each his men from the beginning of the sabbath to the end of the sabbath, for Jehoiada the priest did not dismiss the courses. Jehoiada gave to the men the swords, and the shields, and the arms, which had belonged to King David, in the Temple of God. He set all people, every man with his arms, from the right side of the temple to the left side of the altar and the temple, near the king and around him. He brought out the king's son and put on him the crown and the testimony, and Jehoiada the priest and his sons proclaimed him king, and anointed him, and said, "Long live the king!"

Athaliah heard the sound of the people running, and acknowledging and praising the king, and she went to the king into the Temple of the Lord. She looked and saw the king stood in his place, and the princes and trumpets were at the entrance, and the princes were round the king, and all the people of the land rejoiced, and sounded the trumpets, and there were the singers singing with instruments, and singing hymns of praise, and Athaliah tore her robe, and cried, "You certainly are plotting against me!"

Jehoiada the priest went out, and Jehoiada the priest ordered the captains of hundreds, even the captains of the army, and said to them, "Throw her out of the temple, and follow her, and murder her with the sword," and the priest said, "Don't let her be murdered in the Temple of the Lord."

So they let her leave, and she went through the horses' gate to the palace of the king, and they killed her there. Jehoiada made a covenant between himself, and the people, and the king, that the people should be the Lord's. All the people of the land went into the Temple of Ba'al and tore it down and its altars, and they ground his images to powder, and they killed Mattan the priest of Ba'al before his altars. Jehoiada the priest committed the works of the Temple of the Lord into the and of the priests and Levites, and he re-established the courses of the priests and Levites which David appointed over the Temple of the Lord, and he appointed them to offer whole burnt offerings to the Lord, as it is written in the law of Moses, with gladness, and with songs by the hand of David. The porters stood at the gates of the Temple of the Lord, that no one unclean in any respect should enter in. He took the heads of families, and the mighty men, and the chiefs of the people, and all the people of the land, and they conducted the king into the Temple of the Lord, and he went through the inner gate into the king's house, and they seated the king on the throne of the kingdom. All the people of the land rejoiced, and the city was quiet. And so they had murdered Athaliah.

2nd Paralipomenon: Chapter 24

Joash was seven years old when he began to reign, and he reigned forty years in Jerusalem. His mother's name was Zibiah of Beersheba. Joash did that which was right in the sight of the Lord all the days of Jehoiada the priest. Jehoiada took to himself two wives, and they carried sons and daughters. It came to pass afterward that it came into the heart of Joash to repair the Temple of the Lord. He gathered the priests and the Levites, and said to them, "Go out into the cities of Judah, and collect money of all Israel to repair the Temple of the Lord from year to year, and rush to tell everyone of it."

But the Levites did not rush, so King Joash called Jehoiada the chief, and asked him, "Why have you not looked after the Levites so that they should bring from Judah and Jerusalem that which was prescribed by Moses the prophet when he assembled Israel at the tabernacle of witness? For Athaliah was a transgressor, and her sons tore down the Temple of God, for they offered the holy things of the Temple of the Lord to Ba'als."

The king added, "Let a box be made, and let it be put outside the gate of the Temple of the Lord. Let men proclaim in Judah and Jerusalem, that the people should bring to the Lord, as Moses the servant of God spoke concerning Israel in the wilderness."

All the princes and all the people gave, and brought in, and dropped into the box until it was filled. It came to pass, when they brought in the box to the officers of the king by the hand of the Levites, and when they saw that the money was more than sufficient, then came the king's scribe, and the officer of the high priest, and emptied the box, and restored it to its place. This they did day by day and collected a great deal of money. The king and Jehoiada the priest gave it to the workmen employed in the service of the Temple of the Lord, and they hired masons and carpenters to repair the Temple of the Lord, also smiths and jewelers to repair the Temple of the Lord. The workmen worked, and the works proceeded in their hands, and they established the Temple of the Lord on its foundation and strengthened it. When they had finished it, they brought to the king and Jehoiada the remainder of the money, and they made vessels for the Temple of the Lord, vessels of service for whole burnt offerings, and gold and silver censers, and they offered up whole burnt offerings in the Temple of the Lord continually all the days of Jehoiada.

Jehoiada grew old, being full of days, and he died, being a hundred and thirty years old at his death. They buried him with the kings in the City of David because he had dealt well with Israel, and with God and his house. It came to pass after the death of Jehoiada, that the princes of Judah went in, and did obeisance to the king. Then the king listened to them. They forgot the Temple of Lord the god of their fathers and served the Asherahs[1] and idols, and there was anger on Judah and Jerusalem on that day. Yet he sent prophets to them, to turn them to the Lord, but they did not listen, and he testified to them, but they did not obey. The spirit of God came on Azariah the son of Jehoiada the priest, and he stood up above the people, and said, "The Lord says, 'Why do you transgress the commandments of the Lord?' You will not prosper, for you have forgotten the Lord, and he will forsake you."

They conspired against him, and stoned him by command of king Joash in the court of the Lord's house. Joash did not remember the kindness which his father Jehoiada had exercised towards him but killed his son. As he died, he said, the Lord look on it, and judge. It came to pass after the end of the year, that the army of Syria went up against him, and came against Judah and Jerusalem, and they killed all the chiefs of the people from among the people, and all their spoils they sent to the king of Damascus. For the army of Syria came with few men, yet God gave into their hands a very large army, because they had forgotten the God of their fathers, and he brought judgments on Joash. After they had departed from him, when they had left him in sore diseases, then his servants conspired against him because of the blood of the son of Jehoiada the priest, and killed him on his bed, and he died, and they buried him in the City of David, but they did not bury him in the sepulcher of the kings.

They who conspired against him were Zabad the son of Shimeath the Ammonitess, and Jehozabad the son of Shimrith the Moabitess. All his sons and the five came to him, and the other matters, look, they are written in the Book of the Kings. Amasiah his son reigned in his place.

2nd Paralipomenon: Chapter 24 Notes

1 Codex Vaticanus: Astartaes (ⲀⲤⲦⲀⲢⲦⲀⲓⲤ). Translation: Astarte

- Aleppo Codex: Åšrym (אשרים). Translation: Asherahs

- Leningrad Codex: Asherim (אֲשֵׁרִים). Translation: Asherahs

- Targum of Chronicles: Asherata (אֲשֵׁרָתָא)

Astarte was the Greek name of the Canaanite goddess Ôštrt (𐤕𐤓𐤕𐤔𐤏), known earlier in the Bronze age as Ôṯtrt-Ym (𐎓𐎘𐎚𐎗𐎚𐎊𐎎) in Ugaritic. Ôṯtrt-Ym was one of the two wives of El, the Canaanite father-god, his other wife being Ôṯtrt (𐎓𐎘𐎚𐎗𐎚), who was later known as Asherah (אשרה) in Hebrew. In the Bronze, these were two fertility goddesses, Ôṯtrt representing the fertility of the land, and Ôṯtrt-Ym representing the fertility of the sea. Local versions of them were worshiped throughout the Middle East and the Mediterranean Sea.

In Akkadian, Asherah was a god known as [an]Asdartú (𒀭𒊭𒁯𒌈), while in Babylonian she was known as [an]Ištar (𒀭𒌋), and in Etruscan Astarte was known as Uni-al-Astres (𐌔𐌄𐌐𐌕𐌔𐌀𐌋𐌃𐌀𐌉𐌍𐌖). The Greek goddess Aphrodite appears to be derived from an early Cypriot version of Astarte, while the Roman goddess Venus appears to be derived from her indirectly through Uni-al-Astres. During the New Kingdom era of Egyptian history, circa 1549 to 1077 BC, Astarte was incorporated into the Egyptian pantheon as one of the daughters of Ra, as she appeared in the book entitled the 'Contest between Horus and Set.' According to the Phoenician scholar Sanchuniathon, who supposedly lived circa 1200 BC, Astarte's sister was Asherah. The word Asherah also appears in the Septuagint many times and appears to be widely worshiped by the early Israelites.

2nd Paralipomenon: Chapter 25

Amasiah began to reign when he was twenty-five years old, and he reigned twenty-nine years in Jerusalem. His mother's name was Jehoaddan of Jerusalem. He did that which was right in the sight of the Lord, but not with a perfect heart. When the kingdom was established in his hand, he murdered his servants who had slain the king, his father. But he did not murder their sons, according to the covenant of the law of the Lord, as it is written, and as the Lord commanded, saying, "The fathers will not die for the children, and the sons will not die for the fathers, but they will die each for his sin."

Amasiah assembled the house of Judah and appointed them according to the houses of their families for captains of thousands and captains of hundreds in all Judah and Jerusalem, and he counted them from twenty years old and upward, and found them three hundred thousand able to go out to war, holding spear and shield. Also, he hired of Israel a hundred thousand mercenaries for a hundred talents of silver.

A prophet came to him, saying, "King, don't let the army of Israel go with you, for the Lord is not with Israel, including all the sons of Ephraim. For if you will undertake to strengthen yourself with these, then the

Lord will put you to flight before the enemies, for it is of the Lord both to strengthen and to put to flight."

Amasiah said to the prophet, "But what will I do for the hundred talents which I have given to the army of Israel?"

The prophet said, "The Lord can give you much more than these."

Amasiah separated out the army that came to him from Ephraim, that they might go away to their home, and they were very angry with Judah, and they returned to their homes with great anger. Amasiah strengthened himself, and took his people, and went to the valley of salt, and while there slaughtered ten thousand children of Seir. The Judahites took ten thousand prisoners, and they carried them to the top of the mountain, and threw them headlong from the top of the montain, and they were all dashed to pieces.

The men of the army who Amasiah sent back so that they should not go with him to battle, went and attacked the cities of Judah, from Samaria to the House of Horon, and they struck three thousand among them and took a great deal of spoil. After Amasiah had returned from striking Edom, he brought home the gods of the children of Seir, and set them up for himself as gods, and bowed down before them, and he sacrificed to them.

The anger of the Lord came on Amasiah, and he sent him a prophet, and he said to him, "Why have you wanted the gods of the people, which have not rescued their people out of your hand? It came to pass when the prophet was speaking to him, that he said to him, have I made you a king's counselor? Pay attention in case you be scourged, I know that God is disposed against you to destroy you, because you have done this thing, and have not listened to my counsel."

King Amasiah of Judah accepted the counsel, and sent to Joash, son of Joahaz, son of Jehu, king of Israel, saying, "Come, and let us meet face to face."

Joash king of Israel sent to Amasiah king of Judah, saying, "The thistle that was in Lebanon sent to the cedar that was in Lebanon, saying, 'Give your daughter to my son as wife, but, look, your wild beasts of the field that are in Lebanon will come, and the wild beasts did come, and trod down the thistle.' You have said, 'Look, I have struck Edom, and your stout heart exalts you,' now stay at home, for why do you implicate yourself in mischief, that you should fall, and Judah with you."

Nevertheless, Amasiah did not listen, for it was of the Lord to deliver him into the enemy's hands, because he worshiped the gods of the Edomites. So Joash king of Israel went up, and they met one another, he and King

Amasiah of Judah, in the Temple of Shemesh in of Judah. Judah was put to flight before Israel, and they fled every man to his tent. King Joash of Israel took prisoner King Amasiah of Judah, son of Joash, son of Joahaz, in the Temple of Shemesh, and brought him to Jerusalem. He pulled down part of the wall of Jerusalem from the gate of Ephraim to the corner gate, four hundred cubits. He took all the gold and the silver, and all the vessels that were found in the Temple of the Lord and with Obed-edom, and the treasures of the king's house, and the hostages, and he returned to Samaria.

Amasiah the son of Joash king of Judah lived after the death of Joash the son of King Joahaz of Israel for fifteen years. The rest of the acts of Amasiah, the first and the last, look, are they not written in the book of the kings of Judah and Israel? At the time when Amasiah departed from the Lord, then they formed a conspiracy against him, and he fled from Jerusalem to Lachish, and they sent after him to Lachish and killed him there. They took him up on horses and buried him with his fathers in the City of David.

2nd Paralipomenon: Chapter 26

Then all the people of the land took Uzziah, when he was sixteen years old, and they made him king in place of his father Amasiah. He built Elath, he recovered it to Judah, after the king slept with his fathers. Uzziah began to reign at the age of sixteen years, and he reigned fifty-two years in Jerusalem: and his mother's name was Jecholiah of Jerusalem. He did that which was correct in the sight of the Lord, like all that Amasiah his father did. He served the Lord in the days of Zachariah, who understood the fear of the Lord, and in his days he served the Lord, and the Lord prospered him.

He went out and fought against the Pelesets, and pulled down the walls of Gath, Jabneh, and Ashdod, and he built cities near Ashdod, and among the Pelesets. The Lord strengthened him against the Pelesets, and against the Arabians that lived on the rock, and against the Minaeans. The Minaeans gave gifts to Uzziah, and his fame spread as far as the entering in of Egypt, for he strengthened himself greatly.

Uzziah built towers in Jerusalem at the gate of the corners and the valley gate and the corners and he fortified them. He built towers in the wilderness and dug many wells for he had a great deal of livestock in the low country and the plain, and vineyards in the mountain country and in Carmel, for he was a husbandman.

Uzziah had an army of warriors, and that went out orderly to war and returned orderly in number, and their number was made by the hand of Jehiel the scribe, and Masseiah the judge, by the hand of Hananiah the king's deputy. The whole number of the chiefs of families of the mighty men of war were two thousand and six hundred, and with them was a warrior force, three hundred thousand and seven thousand and five hundred, these great waged wars to help the king against his enemies.

Uzziah prepared for them, even for all the army, shields, and spears, and helmets, and breastplates, and bows, and slings for stones. He made in Jerusalem machines invented by a wise inventor, to be on the towers and on the corners, to hurl bolts and huge stones, and the fame of their preparation was heard at a distance, for he was wonderfully helped, until he was strong. When he was strong, his heart was lifted to his destruction, and he transgressed against Lord the god and went into the temple of the Lord to burn incense on the altar of incense. There went in after him Azariah the priest and with him eighty priests of the Lord, mighty men.

They resisted Uzziah the king, and said to him, "It is not for you, Uzziah, to burn incense to the Lord, but only for the priests the sons of Aaron, who are consecrated to sacrifice. Get out of the sanctuary, for you have departed from the Lord, and this will not be for glory to you from Lord the god."

Uzziah was angry, and in his hand was the censer to burn incense in the temple, and when he was angry with the priests, then leprosy rose up in his forehead before the priests in the Temple of the Lord, over the altar of incense. Azariah the chief priest, and the other priests turned to look at him, and saw he was leprous in his forehead. They got him out of there quickly, as he rushed to leave because the Lord had rebuked him. Uzziah the king was a leper until the day of his death, and he lived as a leper in a separate house, for he was cut off from the Temple of the Lord, and Jotham his son was set over his kingdom, judging the people of the land. The rest of the acts of Uzziah, the first and the last, are written by Isaiah the prophet. Uzziah slept with his fathers, and they buried him with his fathers in the field of the burial place of the kings, for they said, "He is a leper," and Jotham his son reigned in his place.

2nd Paralipomenon: Chapter 27

Jotham was twenty-five years old when he began to reign, and he reigned sixteen years in Jerusalem. His mother's name was Jerusha, daughter of Zadok. He did that which was right in the sight of the Lord, like all that his father Uzziah did, but he went not into the temple of the Lord. Still, the people corrupted themselves. He built the high gate of the Temple of the Lord, and he built a great amount of the wall of Ophel.

In the mountain of Judah and the woods, he built both living-places and towers. He fought against the king of the Ammonites and prevailed against him, and the Ammonites gave him even annually a hundred talents of silver, and ten thousand measures of wheat, and ten thousand of barley. These the king of the Ammonites brought to him annually in the first and second and third years. Jotham grew strong because he prepared his ways before Lord the god. The rest of the acts of Jotham, and his war, and his deeds look, they are written in the Book of the Kings of Judah and Israel. Jotham slept with his fathers and was buried in the City of David, and Ahaz his son reigned in his place.

2nd Paralipomenon: Chapter 28

Ahaz was twenty-five years old when he began to reign, and he reigned sixteen years in Jerusalem, and he did not do that which was right in the sight of the Lord, like David his father. He followed the ways of the kings of Israel, and he made engraved images. He sacrificed to their idols in the valley of Ben Hinnom, and passed his children through the fire, according to the abominations of the tribes that the Lord threw out from before the Israelites. He burnt incense on the bamahs, and the roofs, and under every shady tree. Lord the god delivered him into the hand of the king of Syria, and he struck him, and took captive of them a great band of prisoners, and carried him to Damascus.

Also, God delivered him into the hands of the king of Israel, who struck him with a great slaughter. Pekah the son of Remaliah king of Israel, killed in Judah in one day a hundred and twenty thousand mighty men, because they had forgotten Lord the god of their fathers. Zikri, a mighty man of Ephraim, killed Maaseiah the king's son, and Azrikam the chief of his house, and Elkanah the king's deputy. The Israelites took captive of their brothers three hundred thousand, women, and sons, and daughters, and they spoiled them of much property and brought the spoils to Samaria.

There was there a prophet of the Lord named Oded, and he went out to meet the army that was coming to Samaria, and said to them, "Look, the anger of Lord the god of your fathers is on Judah, and he has delivered them into your hands, and you have slain them in anger, and it has reached even to the sky. Now you talk of keeping the Judahites and Jerusalemites for servants and handmaidens. Look, am I not with you to testify for the Lord your god? Now listen to me, and free the prisoners of your brothers whom you have taken, for the fierce anger of the Lord is on you."

The chiefs of the sons of Ephraim rose up, Udias the son of Johanan, and Berechiah the son of Meshillemoth, and Hezekiah the son of Shallum, and Amasiah the son of Hadlai, against those that came from the war, and said to them, "You will not bring in here the prisoners to us, for sin against the Lord is on us, you mean to add to our sins, and our trespass. For our sin is great, and the fierce anger of the Lord is on Israel."

So the warriors left the prisoners and the spoils before the princes and all the congregation. The men who were called by name rose up, and took hold of the prisoners, and clothed all the naked from the plunder, and gave them garments and shoes. They gave them food to eat, and oil to anoint themselves with. They helped all those who were weak, with donkeys, and they took them to

Jericho, the city of palm-trees, with their brothers, and they returned to Samaria.

At that time king Ahaz sent to the king of Assyria to help him, and on this occasion, because the Edomites had attacked him, and struck Judah, and taken many prisoners. Also the Pelesets had made an attack on the cities of the plain country, and the cities of the south of Judah, and taken Bethshemesh, and the things in the Temple of the Lord, and the things in the house of the king, and of the princes, and they gave to the king: Ayalon, and Galero, and Sochoh, and Timnath, and Gimzo and their villages, and they lived there.

The Lord humiliated Judah because of King Ahaz of Judah because he grievously departed from the Lord. There came against him King Tiglath-Pileser[1] of Assyria, and he attacked him. Ahaz stole the things that were in the Temple of the Lord, and the things in the house of the king, and the princes, and gave them to the king of Assyria, but he was no help to him, but only troubled him in his affliction, and he departed yet more from the Lord, and King Ahaz said, "I will pray to the gods of Damascus that attack me."

He said, "In that as the gods of the king of Syria themselves strengthen them, I will sacrifice to them and they will help me." But they became a stumbling block to him, and all Israel.

Ahaz removed the vessels of the Temple of the Lord, and cut them in pieces, and shut the doors of the Temple of the Lord, and made to himself altars in every corner in Jerusalem, and in each of several cities in Judah he made bamahs to burn incense to foreign gods, and they provoked Lord the god of their fathers. The rest of his acts, and his deeds, the first and the last, look, they are written in the book of the kings of Judah and Israel. Ahaz slept with his fathers and was buried in the City of David, for they did not bring him into the sepulchers of the kings of Israel, and Hezekiah his son reigned in his place.

2nd Paralipomenon: Chapter 28 Notes

1 Codex Vaticanus: Thaglathphellasar
(ΘΑΓΛΑΘΦΕΛΛΑϹΑΡ)

- Aleppo Codex: Tlgt Plnåsr (תלגת פלנאסר)

- Leningrad Codex: Tillegat Pilne'eser (תִּלְגַת פִּלְנְאֶסֶר)

- Targum of Chronicles: Telegat Pilneser (תִּלְגַת פִּלְנְאֶסֶר)

Tiglath-Pileser III was the ruler of the Assyrian Empire between 745 and 727 BC, who forged the Neo-Assyrian Empire.

2nd Paralipomenon: Chapter 29

Hezekiah began to reign at the age of twenty-five years, and he reigned twenty-nine years in Jerusalem. His mother's name was Abiah, the daughter of Zachariah. He did that which was right in the sight of the Lord, like all that his forefather David had done. When he was established over his kingdom, in the first month, he opened the doors of the Temple of the Lord and repaired them.

He brought in the priests and the Levites, and put them on the east side, and said to them, "Hear, you Levites, now sanctify yourselves, and sanctify the Temple of Lord the god of your fathers, and throw out the impurity from the holy places. For our fathers have revolted, and done that which was evil before Lord the god, and have forgotten him, and have turned away their face from the tabernacle of the Lord, and have turned their back. They have shut up the doors of the temple, and put out the lamps, and have not burnt incense, and have not offered whole burnt offerings in the holy place to the god in Israel. The Lord was very angry with Judah and Jerusalem and made them an astonishment, and a desolation, and a hissing, as you see with your eyes. And, look, your fathers have been struck with the sword, and your sons and your daughters and your wives are in captivity in a land not their own, as it is even now. Therefore it is now in my heart to make a covenant, a covenant with Lord the god in Israel, that he may turn away his fierce anger from us. Now do not be lacking to your duty, for the Lord has chosen you to stand before him to minister, and to be ministers and burners of incense to him."

Then the Levites rose up, Mahath the son of Amasi, and Joel the son of Azariah, of the sons of Kohath.

Of the sons of Merari: Kish the son of Abdi, and Azariah the son of Jehallelel.

Of the sons of Gedsoni: Jodaad the son of Zimmah, and Joadam, these were the sons of Joah.

Of the sons of Elizaphan: Zabdi and Jehiel.

Of the sons of Asaph: Zachariah and Mattaniah.

Of the sons of Heman: Jehiel and Shimei.

Of the sons of Jeduthun: Shemaiah and Uzziel.

They gathered their brothers, and they purified themselves according to the king's command by the order of the Lord, to purify the Temple of the Lord. The priests entered into the Temple of the Lord, to purify it, and they threw out all the uncleanness that was found in the Temple of the Lord, even into the court of the Temple of the Lord, and the Levites received it to cast into the brook of Kidron. Hezekiah began on the first day, even on the new moon of the first month, to purify, and on the eighth day of the month they entered into the temple of the Lord: and they purified the Temple of the Lord in eight days, and on the thirteenth day of the first month they finished the work.

They went in to king Hezekiah, and said, "We have purified all the things in the Temple of the Lord, the altar of whole burnt offering, and its vessels, and the table of show-bread, and its vessels, and all the vessels which King Ahaz polluted in his reign, in his apostasy, we have prepared and purified. Look, they are before the altar of the Lord."

King Hezekiah rose early in the morning, and gathered the chief men of the city, and went up to the Temple of the Lord. He brought seven calves, and seven rams, and seven lambs, and seven goat kids for a sin-offering, for the kingdom, and the holy things, and for Israel. He told the priests the sons of Aaron to go up to the altar of the Lord. They killed the calves, and the priests received the blood and poured it on the altar, and they killed the rams and poured the blood on the altar, also they killed the lambs, and poured the blood round the altar. They brought the goats for a sin-offering before the king and the congregation and laid their hands on them. The priests killed them and offered their blood as a propitiation on the altar, and they made atonement for all Israel, for the king said, "The whole burnt offering and the sin-offering are for all Israel."

He stationed the Levites in the Temple of the Lord with cymbals, and lutes, and harps, according to the commandment of king David, and of Gad the king's seer, and Nathan the prophet, for by the commandment of the Lord the order was in the hand of the prophets. The Levites stood with the instruments of David, and the priests with the trumpets. Hezekiah told them to offer up the whole burnt offering on the altar, and when they began to offer the whole burnt offering, they began to sing to the Lord, and the trumpets accompanied the instruments of David king of Israel. All the congregation worshiped, and the psalm-singers were singing, and the trumpets sounding until the whole burnt sacrifice had been completely offered. When they had done offering it, the king and all that were present bowed, and worshiped.

King Hezekiah and the princes told the Levites to sing hymns to the Lord in the words of David, and Asaph the prophet, and they sang hymns with joy and fell and worshiped. Then Hezekiah answered and said, "Now you have consecrated yourselves to the Lord, bring near and offer sacrifices of praise in the Temple of the Lord."

The congregation brought sacrifices and thanksgiving offerings into the Temple of the Lord, and everyone ready in his heart brought whole burnt offerings. The number of the whole burnt offerings which the congregation brought, was seventy calves, a hundred rams, two hundred lambs, all these were for a whole burnt offering to the Lord. The consecrated calves were six hundred, and the sheep three thousand. But the priests were few, and could not flay the whole burnt offering, so their brothers the Levites helped them until the work was finished, and until the priests had purified themselves, for the Levites more zealously purified themselves than the priests. The whole burnt offering was abundant, with the fat of the complete peace-offering, and the drink-offerings of the whole burnt sacrifice. So the service was established in the Temple of the Lord. Hezekiah and all the people rejoiced because God had prepared the people, for the thing was done suddenly.

2nd Paralipomenon: Chapter 30

Hezekiah sent to all Israel and Judah, and wrote letters to Ephraim and Manasseh, that they should come into the Temple of the Lord in Jerusalem, to keep the Passover to Lord the god in Israel. For the king, and the princes and all the congregation in Jerusalem decided to keep the Passover in the second month. For they could not keep it at that time, because a sufficient number of priests had not purified themselves, and the people were not gathered to Jerusalem. The proposal pleased the king and the congregation. They established a decree that a proclamation should go through all Israel, from Beer-sheba to Dan, that they should come and keep the Passover to Lord the god in Israel at Jerusalem, for the multitude had not done it recently according to the scripture.

The posts went with the letters from the king and the princes to all Israel and Judah, according to the command of the king, saying, "Israelites, return to Lord the god of Abraham, and Isaac, and Israel, and bring back them that have escaped even those that were left of the hand of the king of Assyria. Do not be as your fathers, and your brothers, who revolted from Lord the god of their fathers, and he gave them up to desolation, as you see. Now don't harden your hearts, as your fathers did. Give glory to Lord the god, and enter into his sanctuary, which he has sanctified forever, and serve the Lord your god, and he will turn away his fierce anger from you. For when you turn to the Lord, your brothers and your children will be pitied before all that have carried them captives, and he will restore you to this land, for Lord the god is merciful and pitiful, and will not turn away his face from you if we return to him."

So the posts went from city to city in mount Ephraim, and Manasseh, and as far as Zebulun, and they were laughed at and scorned and mocked them. But the men of Asher, and some of Manasseh and of Zebulun, were ashamed and came to Jerusalem and Judah. The hand of the Lord was present to give them one heart to come, to do according to the commands of the king and the princes, by the word of the Lord. A great multitude was gathered to Jerusalem to keep the feast of unleavened bread in the second month, a great congregation. They arose and took away the altars that were in Jerusalem, and all of which they had burnt incense to false gods they tore down and cast into the brook of Kidron.

Then they killed the Passover sacrifice on the fourteenth day of the second month, and the priests and the Levites repented, and purified themselves, and brought whole burnt offerings into the Temple of the Lord. They stood at their post, according to their ordinance, according to the commandment of Moses the prophet, and the priests received the blood from the hand of the Levites.

For a great part of the congregation was not sanctified, and the Levites were ready to kill the Passover for everyone who could not sanctify himself to the Lord. For the greatest part of the people of Ephraim and Manasseh, and Issachar and Zebulun had not purified themselves, but ate the Passover contrary to the scripture.

On this account also Hezekiah prayed concerning them, "Lord the god be merciful concerning every heart that sincerely seeks Lord the god of their fathers, and is not purified according to the purification of the sanctuary."

The Lord listened to Hezekiah and healed the people. The Israelites who were present in Jerusalem kept the feast of unleavened bread seven days with great joy, and they continued to sing hymns to the Lord daily, and the priests and the Levites played on instruments to the Lord. Hezekiah encouraged all the Levites, and those that had a good understanding of the Lord, and they completely kept the feast of unleavened bread seven days, offering peace-offerings, and confessing to Lord the god of their fathers. The congregation purposed together to keep other seven days, and they kept seven days with gladness.

For Hezekiah set apart for Judah, even for the congregation, a thousand calves, and seven thousand sheep, and the princes set apart for the people a thousand calves and ten thousand sheep, and the holy things of the priests abundantly. All the congregation, the priests and the Levites, rejoiced, and all the congregation of Judah, and they who were present of Jerusalem, and the foreigners that came from the land of Israel, and the residents in Judah. There was great joy in Jerusalem, from the days of Solomon the son of David king of Israel there was not such a feast in Jerusalem. Then the priests the Levites rose up and blessed the people, and their voice was heard, and their prayer came into his sacred abode in the sky.

2nd Paralipomenon: Chapter 31

When all these things were finished, all Israel that were found in the cities of Judah went out, and broke in pieces the steles, and cut down Asherah, and tore down the bamahs and the altars out of all Judea and Benjamin, also of Ephraim and Manasseh, until they made an end, and all Israel returned, everyone to his inheritance, and to their cities.

Hezekiah appointed the courses of the priests and the Levites, and the courses of each one according to his ministry, to the priests and the Levites, for the whole burnt offering, and the peace-offering, and to praise, and to give thanks, and to minister in the gates, and in the courts of the Temple of the Lord. The king's proportion out of his property was appointed for the whole burnt offerings, the morning and the evening one, and the whole burnt offerings for the sabbaths, and the new moons, and for the feasts that were ordered in the law of the Lord. They told the people who lived in Jerusalem, to give the portion of the priests and the Levites, that they might be strong in the ministry of the Temple of the Lord. As he gave the command, Israel brought great amounts of first-fruits of grain, and wine, and oil, and honey, and every fruit of the field. The Israelites and Judah brought tithes of everything in great abundance.

They who lived in the cities of Judah themselves also brought tithes of calves and sheep, and tithes of goats, and consecrated them to Lord the god, and they brought them and laid them in heaps. In the third month, the heaps began to be piled, and in the seventh month, they were finished. Hezekiah and the princes came and saw the heaps, and blessed the Lord, and his people Israel. Then Hezekiah inquired of the priests and the Levites concerning the heaps. Azariah the priest, the chief over the house of Zadok, spoke to him, and said, "From the time that the first-fruits began to be brought into the Temple of the Lord, we have eaten and drunk, and left even more for the Lord has blessed his people, and we have left to this amount."

Hezekiah told them yet farther to prepare chambers for the Temple of the Lord, and they prepared them, and they brought there the first-fruits and the tithes faithfully, and Konaniah the Levite was superintendent over them, and Shimei his brother was next, and then Jehiel, Uzziah, Nahath, Asahel, Jerimoth, Jehozabad, Eliel, Ismakiah, Mahath, and Benaiah, and his sons were appointed by Konaniah and Shimei his brother, as Hezekiah the king, and Azariah who was in charge of the Temple of the Lord. Korah, the son of Imnah the Levite the eastern porter was over the gifts to distribute the first-fruits of the Lord, and the most holy things, by the hand of Eden, and Benjamin, and Jesou, and Shimei, and Omri, and Shekaniah, by the hand of the priests faithfully, to give to their brothers according to the courses, both great and small, besides the increase of males from three years old and upward, to everyone entering into the Temple of the Lord, a portion according to a daily rate, for service in the daily courses of their order.

This is the distribution of the priests according to the houses of their families, and the Levites in their daily courses from twenty years old and upward were in their order, to assign stations for all the increase of their sons and their daughters, for the whole number, for they faithfully sanctified the holy place. As for the sons of Aaron that executed the priests' office, even those from their cities the men in each of several cities who were named expressly were appointed to give a portion to every male among the priests, and everyone reckoned among the Levites. Hezekiah did so through all Judah and did that which was good and right before Lord the god. In every work which he began in service in the Temple of the Lord, and in the law, and the ordinances, he wanted his God with all his soul, and worked, and prospered.

2nd Paralipomenon: Chapter 32

After these things and this faithful dealing, King Sennacherib[1] of the Assyrians came to Judah and he laid siege to the fortified cities and intended to take them for himself. Hezekiah saw that Sennacherib came, and that his face was set to fight against Jerusalem. He took counsel with his elders and his mighty men to stop the wells of water which were outside of the city, and they helped him. He gathered many people, and stopped the wells of water, and the river that flowed through the city, saying, "In case the king of Assyria comes, and finds a lot of water, and strengthens himself."

Hezekiah strengthened himself, and rebuilt all the walls that had been pulled down, and the towers, and another wall in outside, and fortified the strong place of the City of David, and prepared arms in abundance. He appointed captains of war over the people, and they were gathered to meet him to the open place of the gate of the valley, and he encouraged them, saying, "Be strong and courageous, and don't be afraid, neither be dismayed before the King of Assyria, and before all the nation that is with him, for there are more with us than with him. With him are arms of flesh, but with us is Lord the god to save us, and to fight our battle."

The people were encouraged at the words of Hezekiah king of Judah. Afterward Sennacherib king of the Assyrians sent his servants to Jerusalem, and he went himself against Lachish, and all his army with him, and sent to Hezekiah king of Judah, and to all Judah that was in Jerusalem, saying, "Sennacherib king of the Assyrians says, 'In what do you trust, that you will remain in the siege of Jerusalem? Does not Hezekiah deceive you, to deliver you to death and famine and thirst, saying, 'Lord the god will deliver us out of the hand of the king of Assyria?'"

"Is this not Hezekiah, who has taken down his altars and his bamahs, and has spoken to Judah and the residents in Jerusalem, saying, 'You will worship before this altar and burn incense on it?' Don't you know what I and my fathers have done to all the nations of the countries? Could the gods of the nations of all the earth at all rescue their people out of my hand? Who is there among all the gods of those nations whom my fathers destroyed, worthy of trust? Could they deliver their people out of my hand, that your god should deliver you out of my hand? Now then, don't let Hezekiah deceive you, and don't let him make you so confident, and don't believe him, as no god of any kingdom or nation is able to save his people out of my hand, or the hands of my fathers, therefore your god will not deliver you out of my hand.'"

His servants continued to speak against Lord the god, and his servant Hezekiah. He wrote a letter to insult

Lord the god in Israel, and spoke concerning him, saying, "As the gods of the nations of the earth have not
saved their people out of my hand, so the god of
Hezekiah will not save his people out of my hand."

He cried with a loud voice in Judahite[2] to the people
of Jerusalem on the wall, calling them to assist them, and
pull down the walls, so that they might take the city. He
spoke against the god of Jerusalem, like against the gods
of the nations of the earth, the creations of the hands of
men. King Hezekiah and Isaiah the prophet, the son of
Amos, prayed concerning these things, and they cried to
the sky. The Lord sent a messenger, and he destroyed
every mighty man and warrior, and leader and captain
in the camp of the king of Assyria, and he returned with
shame of face to his land and came into the house of his
god, and some of them that came out of his bowels killed
him with the sword. So the Lord delivered Hezekiah
and the residents in Jerusalem out of the hand of Sennacherib king of Assyria, and out of the hand of all his
enemies, and gave them rest around it. Many brought
gifts to the Lord to Jerusalem and gifts for Hezekiah king
of Judah, and he was exalted in the eyes of all the nations
after these things.

In those days Hezekiah was sick even to death and
prayed to the Lord, and he listened to him and gave him
a sign. But Hezekiah did not repay the Lord according to

353

the return which he made him, but his heart was lifted, and so anger came against him, and Judah and Jerusalem. Hezekiah humiliated himself after the exaltation of his heart, he and the residents in Jerusalem, and the anger of the Lord did not come on them in the days of Hezekiah. Hezekiah had wealth and great fame. He built for himself treasuries of gold, and silver, and precious stones, also for spices, and stores for arms, and for precious vessels, and cities for the produce of grain, and wine, and oil, and stalls and mangers for every kind of livestock, and folds for flocks, and cities which he built for himself to store sheep and oxen in great abundance, for the Lord gave him a very great store.

The same Hezekiah dammed up the course of the water of Gion above, and brought the water down straight south of the City of David. Hezekiah prospered in all his works. Notwithstanding, in regard to the ambassadors of the princes of Babylon, who were sent to him to inquire of him concerning the prodigy which came on the land, the Lord left him, to try him, to know what was in his heart. The rest of the acts of Hezekiah, and his kindness, see, they are written in the prophecy of Isaiah the son of Amos the prophet, and the Book of the Kings of Judah and Israel. Hezekiah slept with his fathers, and they buried him in a bamah among the sepulchers of the sons of David, and all Judah and the residents in Jerusalem gave him glory and honor at his death, and then Manasseh his son reigned in his place.

2nd Paralipomenon: Chapter 32 Notes

1 Codex Vaticanus: Sennachêrim (ⲤⲉⲚⲚⲀⲬⲎⲢⲒⲘ)

- Aleppo Codex: Snḥryb (סַנְחֵרִיב)

- Leningrad Codex: Sancheriv (סַנְחֵרִיב)

- Targum of Chronicles: Sancheriv (סַנְחֵרִיב)

Sennacherib was the king of the Assyrian Empire between 705 and 681 BC.

2 Codex Vaticanus: Ioudaesti (ⲒⲞⲨⲆⲀⲒⲤⲦⲒ). Translation: Judahite

- Aleppo Codex: Yhwdyt (יְהוּדִית). Translation: Judahite

- Leningrad Codex: Yehudit (יְהוּדִית). Translation: Judahite

- Targum of Chronicles: lishan beit kudesha (לִישָׁן בֵּית קוּדְשָׁא). Translation: language of sacred temple

2nd Paralipomenon: Chapter 33

Manasseh was twelve years old when he began to reign, and he reigned fifty-five years in Jerusalem. He did that which was evil in the sight of the Lord, following all the abominations of the tribes that the Lord destroyed before the Israelites. He rebuilt the bamahs that his father Hezekiah had pulled down, and set up statues to the Ba'als and Asherah, and worshiped all the army of the sky, and served them.

He built altars in the Temple of the Lord, concerning which the Lord said, "In Jerusalem will be my name forever."

He built altars to all the army of the sky in the two courts of the Temple of the Lord. He also passed his children through the fire in the valley of sons of Hinns,[1] and he divined, and used auspices, and sorcery, and appointed those who had divining spirits, and enchanters, and worked abundant wickedness before the Lord, to provoke him. He set the engraved idol, the molten statue, the idol which he made, in the Temple of God, of which God had said to David and Solomon his son, "In this house, and Jerusalem, which I have chosen out of all the tribes of Israel, I will put my name forever, and I will not again remove the foot of Israel from the land which I gave to their fathers, if only they will pay attention to do all things which I have commanded them, according to all the law and the ordinances and the judgments given by the hand of Moses."

So Manasseh led astray Judah and the inhabitants of Jerusalem, to do evil beyond all the nations which the Lord drove out from before the Israelites. The Lord spoke to Manasseh, and his people, but they did not listen. The Lord brought on them the captains of the army of the king of Assyria, and they took Manasseh in bonds, and bound him in shackles, and brought him to Babylon. When he was afflicted, he searched for the face of Lord the god and was greatly humiliated before the face of the god of his fathers, and he prayed to him, and he listened to him, and listened to his cry, and brought him back to Jerusalem to his kingdom, and Manasseh knew Lord the god.

Afterward he built a wall outside the City of David, from the southwest southward in the valleys and at the entrance through the fish-gate, as men go out by the gate around, even as far as Ophel, and he raised it much, and set captains of the army in all the fortified cities in Judah. He removed the strange gods, and the engraved idols out of the Temple of the Lord, and all the altars which he had built in the mount of the Temple of the Lord, and in Jerusalem, and outside the city. He repaired the altar of the Lord and offered on it a sacrifice of peace-offering and thank-offering, and he told Judah to serve Lord the god in Israel.

Nevertheless, the people still sacrificed on the bamahs to Lord the god. The rest of the acts of Manasseh, and his prayer to God, and the words of the seers that spoke to him in the name of the god in Israel, look, they are in the account of his prayer, and God listened to him. All his sins, and his travels, and the places where he built the bamahs, and set up their Asherah and engraved idols, before he repented, look, they are written in the books of the seers. Manasseh slept with his fathers, and they buried him in the garden of his house, and Amon his son reigned in his place.

Amon was twenty-two years old when he began to reign, and he reigned two years in Jerusalem. He did that which was evil in the sight of the Lord, as his father Manasseh did, and Amon sacrificed to all the idols which his father Manasseh had made and served them. He was not humiliated before the Lord as his father Manasseh was humiliated, for his son Amon abounded in transgression. His servants conspired against him and killed him in his house. The people of the land killed the men who had conspired against king Amon, and the people of the land made Josiah his son king in his place.

2ⁿᵈ Paralipomenon: Chapter 33 Notes

1 Codex Vaticanus: Gae - banae - ennom (ΓΑΙ-ΒΑΝΑΙ-ΕΝΝΟΜ)

• Aleppo Codex: gy bn hnm (גי בן הנס). Translation: valley of the son of Hinns

• Leningrad Codex: gei ven-hinnom (גֵּי בֶן־הִנֹּם). Translation: valley of the son of Hinnom

• Targum of Chronicles: becheilat bar hinom (בְּחֵילַת בַּר הִנוֹם). Translation: sacred service (or strength, might) of sons of Hinom

The Greeks also translated this name in other books, including the 'abyss of Onom' (φαραγγα Ονομ) in Joshua chapter 15, and 'grove of Sonnam' (ναπης Σοννομ) in Joshua chapter 18. The Masoretic version of Joshua also included the scribal note that clarified that this was known as 'valley of the Raphites to the northerners' (אֲשֶׁר בְּעֵמֶק רְפָאִים צָפוֹנָה).

The difference between in the names Sonnam and Hinnom in Joshua chapter 18 likely originated when the Aramaic translation was created, as the Canaanite's script, which was used for Samaritan and Judahite in the early iron age, had similar shapes for the H ($\mathbf{\lambda}$) and the Ś ($\mathbf{\mp}$). While the Aramaic script did not have a similar H (η) and Ś ($\mathbf{y}$), the early Greek alphabet did have a similar H (ϵ) and Š ($\mathbf{c}$), and therefore, the error could be interpreted as a Greek copying error. However, a virtually identical error is found in the Judahite Apocalypse of Ezra, which rendered the Sea of Edom as the Sea of Sodom. In that case, it was the word 'the/of' in between 'sea' and 'Edom' that was misread as an S, indicating the error took place in the Canaanite script.

The origin of the name Hnm (הנם) is likely a plural of hinn (حنّ), a reference to an ancient extinct type of being that once lived on the Earth in Semitic folklore. The hinns continue to be part of the Islamic and Druze religions, although their roles in the religions vary. It is agreed that they are extinct, however, it isn't clear what they were. Many sources describe the hinns and binns as powerful, gigantic primordial creatures, suggesting they were influenced by finding the bones of extinct animals. Conversely, the Revelations of ‘Abdullah Al-Sayid Muhammad Habib claims the hinns were air creatures, and the binns were water creatures, while the medieval Islamic historian al-Tabari claimed they were created from poisonous fire (سموم). In most versions of the stories, they fought in part of a series of wars for control of the earth before the creation of humanity, and most of the ancient species became extinct, including the hinns.

The substitution of 'forest' or 'woodland' for 'valley of the sons...' is clearly not a translation error. The combination of 'valley/abyss' and 'forest/woodland' suggests it is a reference to a gravesite, and not a physical valley. At the time, Canaanites marked gravesites by planting trees, usually oak, which was known as the 'Asherah' tree, because it could self-pollinate, and was therefore seen as a 'virgin' tree. In the context of a gravesite, it is likely that the term 'sons of hinns' did not refer to some known people, but an ancient gravesite of a by then unknown people. Oak trees are known to live over 1000 years, and reproduce, so the gravesite in question could have already been thousands of years old. Later during the reforms of King Josiah, ancient graves and Asherah groves near Jerusalem were destroyed, and he was specifically recorded as destroying a statue in the valley of the sons of Hinns, implying that this was the gravesite he destroyed.

2nd Paralipomenon: Chapter 34

Josiah was eight years old when he began to reign, and he reigned thirty-one years in Jerusalem. He did that which was right in the sight of the Lord, and followed the ways of his father David, and did not turn to the right or the left. In the eighth year of his reign, when he was still a youth, he began to seek Lord the god of his father David, and in the twelfth year of his reign he began to purge Judah and Jerusalem from the bamahs, and Asherah, and the ornaments for the altars, and the molten images. He pulled down the altars of Ba'als that were before his face and the bamahs that were above them, and he cut down Asherah, and the engraved idols, and broke in pieces the molten images, and reduced them to powder, and cast it on the surface of the tombs of those who had sacrificed to them. He burnt the bones of the priests on the altars and purged Judah and Jerusalem.

He did so in the cities of Manasseh, Ephraim, Simeon, Naphtali, and the places around them. He pulled down the altars and Asherah, and he cut the idols in small pieces, and cut off all the bamahs from all the land of Israel, and returned to Jerusalem. In the eighteenth year of his reign, after having cleansed the land, and the house, he sent Shaphan the son of Azaliah, and Maaseiah ruler of the city, and Joah son of Joahaz his recorder, to repair the Temple of Lord the god. They came to

Hilkiah the high priest, and gave the money that was brought into the Temple of God, which the Levites who kept the gate collected of the hand of Manasseh and Ephraim, and the princes, and of everyone that was left in Israel, and of the children of Judah and Benjamin, and of the residents in Jerusalem.

They gave it into the hand of the workmen, who were appointed in the Temple of the Lord, and they gave it to the workmen who worked in the Temple of the Lord, to repair and strengthen the house. They gave it also to the carpenters and builders, to buy squared stones, and timber for beams to cover the houses which the kings of Judah had destroyed. The men were faithfully engaged in the works, and over them were superintendents, Jahath and Obadiah, Levites of the sons of Merari, and Zachariah and Meshullam, of the sons of Kohath, appointed to oversee, and every Levite, and everyone that understood how to play on musical instruments. Overseers were over the laborers, and overall the workmen in the respective works, and of the Levites have appointed scribes, and judges, and porters.

When they brought out the money that had been brought into the Temple of the Lord, Hilkiah the priest found a book of the law of the Lord given by the hand of Moses. Hilkiah answered and said to Shaphan the scribe,

"I have found a book of the law in the Temple of the Lord," and Hilkiah gave the book to Shaphan.

Shaphan brought in the book to the king and also gave an account to the king, saying, "This is all the money given into the hand of your servants that work. They have collected the money that was found in the Temple of the Lord, and given it into the hand of the overseers, and into the hands of those who do the work."

Shaphan the scribe brought word to the king, saying, "Hilkiah the priest has given me a book."

Shaphan read it before the king. It came to pass, when the king heard the words of the law, that he tore his garments. The king commanded Hilkiah, and Ahikam the son of Shaphan, and Abdon the son of Micah, and Shaphan the scribe, and Asaiah the servant of the king, saying, "Go, inquire of the Lord for me, and for everyone that is left in Israel and Judah, concerning the words of the book that is found, for great is the anger of the Lord which has been started among us, because our fathers have not listened to the words of the Lord, to do according to all the things written in this book."

Hilkiah went, and the others who the king told, to Huldah the prophetess, the wife of Shallum son of Tekoah, son of Hasrah, who kept the commandments, and she lived in Jerusalem in the second quarter, and they spoke to her accordingly. She said to them, "Lord the god in Israel said this, 'Tell the man who sent you to me, the Lord says, Look, I bring evil on this place, even all the words that are written in the book that was read before the king of Judah, because they have forgotten me, and burnt incense to foreign gods, that they might provoke me by all the works of their hands, and my anger is started against this place, and it will not be quenched. Concerning the king of Judah, who sent you to seek the Lord, this you will say to him, Lord the god in Israel says, "As for the words which you have heard, in that your heart was ashamed, and you were humiliated before me when you heard my words against this place, and the inhabitants of it, and you were humiliated before me, and ripped your clothing, and cried before me, I also have heard, says the Lord. Look, I will gather you to your fathers, and you will be gathered to your grave in peace. Your eyes will not look on all the evils which I am bringing on this place, and on the inhabitants of it."

They brought back word to the king. The king sent and gathered the elders of Judah and Jerusalem. The king went up to the Temple of the Lord, he and all Judah, and the inhabitants of Jerusalem, and the priests, and the Levites, and all the people great and small, and he read in their ears all the words of the Book of the

Covenant that was found in the Temple of the Lord. The king stood at a pillar, and made a covenant before the Lord, to walk before the Lord, to keep his commandments and testimonies, and his ordinances, with all his heart and with all his soul, to perform the words of the covenant that were written in this book. He caused all that were found in Jerusalem and Benjamin to stand, and the inhabitants of Jerusalem made a covenant in the Temple of Lord the god of their fathers. Josiah removed all the abominations out of the whole land which belonged to the Israelites, and caused all that were found in Jerusalem and in Israel, to serve Lord the god all his days, he did not stop from following Lord the god of his fathers.

2nd Paralipomenon: Chapter 35

Josiah kept a passover to Lord the god and sacrificed the passover on the fourteenth day of the first month. He appointed the priests at their charges and encouraged them for the services of the Temple of the Lord. He told the Levites that were able to act in all Israel, that they should consecrate themselves to the Lord, and they put the holy box in the house which Solomon the son of David king of Israel built, and the king said, "You must not carry anything on your shoulders, now then minister to the Lord your god, and his people Israel. Prepare yourselves according to the houses of your families, and according to your daily courses, according to the writing of David king of Israel, and the order by the hand of his son Solomon. You stand in the house according to the divisions of the houses of your families for your brothers the sons of the people, so let there also be a division of the house of the Levites of their family. Kill the Passover victim, and prepare it for your brothers, to do according to the word of the Lord, by the hand of Moses."

Josiah gave as an offering to the children of the people, sheep, and lambs, and goat kids, all for the passover, even for all that were found, in number amounting to thirty thousand, and three thousand calves, these were from the property of the king. His princes gave an offering to the people, and the priests, and the Levites, and

Hilkiah and Zachariah and Jehiel the chief men gave to the priests of the Temple of God, they even gave for the passover sheep, lambs, and kids, amounting to 2600, and 300 calves. Konaniah, and Benaiah, and Ishmaiah, and Nethanel his brother, and Hashabiah, and Jehiel, and Jehozabad, heads of the Levites, gave an offering to the Levites for the passover, 5000 sheep and 500 calves.

The service was duly ordered, and the priests stood in their place, and the Levites in their divisions, according to the command of the king. They killed the passover victims, and the priests sprinkled the blood from their hand, and the Levites flayed the victims. They prepared the whole burnt offering to give to them, according to the division by the houses of families, even to the sons of the people, to offer to the Lord, as it is written in the book of Moses. Thus they did until the morning. They roasted the passover victim with fire according to the ordinance and boiled the holy pieces in copper vessels and cauldrons, and the feast went on well, and they quickly served all the children of the people. After they had prepared for themselves and the priests, for the priests were engaged in offering the whole burnt offerings and the fat until night, then the Levites prepared for themselves, and their brothers the sons of Aaron.

The sons of Asaph the psalm-singers were at their post according to the commands of David, Asaph, Heman, and

Jeduthun, the prophets of the king, also, the chiefs and the porters of the several gates, it was not for them to stir from the service of the holy things, for their brothers the Levites prepared for them. So all the service of the Lord was duly ordered and prepared on that day, for keeping the Passover and offering the whole burnt sacrifices on the altar of the Lord, according to the command of King Josiah. The Israelites that were present kept the passover at that time, and the feast of unleavened bread seven days. There was no passover like it in Israel from the days of Samuel the prophet, or any king of Israel. They have never held a passover like Josiah, and the priests. The Levites, and all Judah and Israel who were present, and the residents in Jerusalem, kept to the Lord.

In the eighteenth year of the reign of Josiah, this passover was kept, after all these things that Josiah did in the house. King Josiah burnt the ventriloquists,[1] and those with knowledge,[2] and the engravings, and the idols, and the hooks[3] which were in the land of Judah and in Jerusalem, that he might confirm the words of the law that were written in the book which Hilkiah the priest found in the Temple of the Lord.

There was no king like him before him, who turned to the Lord with all his heart, and all his soul, and all his strength, according to all the law of Moses, and after him there rose up none like him. Nevertheless, the Lord did not turn from his fierce anger and the Lord was greatly angry against Judah, for all the provocations where Manasseh provoked him, and the Lord said, "I will even remove Judah also from my presence, as I have removed Israel, and I have rejected the city which I chose, even Jerusalem, and the temple of which I said, 'My name will be there.'"

Pharaoh Necho[4] king of Egypt went up against the king of the Assyrians to the river Euphrates, and king Josiah went to meet him. He sent messengers to him, saying, "What have I to do with you, king of Judah? I have not come today to war against you, and God has told me to hurry. Beware of the god that is with me, in case he destroys you."

However, Josiah did not turned from him, but prepared to fight against him, and did not listen to the words of Necho by the mouth of God, and he came to fight in the plain of Megiddo. The archers shot at king Josiah, and the king said to his servants, "Take me away, for I am severely wounded."

His servants lifted him out of the chariot, and put him in the second chariot which he had, and brought him to Jerusalem, and he died and was buried with his fathers, and all Judah and Jerusalem lamented over Josiah. Jeremiah mourned over Josiah, and all the chief men and chief women uttered a lamentation over Josiah until this day, and they made it an ordinance for Israel, and, look, it is written in the lamentations. The rest of the acts of Josiah and his hope are written in the law of the Lord. His acts, the first and the last, look, they are written in the book of the Kings of Israel and Judah.

2nd Paralipomenon: Chapter 35 Notes

1 Codex Vaticanus: engastrimythous (ЄΓΓΛCΤΡΙΜΥѲΟΥC).
Translation: ventriloquists

This verse is missing from the Masoretic text and Targum of Chronicles.

2 Codex Vaticanus: tous gnôstas (ΤΟΥCΓΝѠϹΤΛϹ).
Translation: those with knowledge

This verse is missing from the Masoretic text and Targum of Chronicles

3 Codex Vaticanus: carasim (ΚΛΡΛϹΙΜ)

This verse is missing from the Masoretic Text and Targum of Chronicles. This appears to be a Greek transliteration of the Hebrew word kerosim (קְרָסִים), meaning 'hooks,' or 'clasps.' This may be a reference to the meat-hooks that were used in the temple, in chapter 4, and in any event, proves there was a Semitic language source-text to this section of text, which is missing from the Masoretic Texts.

4 Codex Vaticanus: Pharaô Nechaô (ΦΛΡΛѠΝЄΧΛѠ).
Translation: Pharaoh Necho

- Aleppo Codex: Nkw (נכו)

- Leningrad Codex: Necho (נְכוֹ)

- Targum of Chronicles: Chagira (חֲגִירָא)

The name in the Septuagint and Masoretic text is accepted as a reference to Pharaoh Necho II, king of Egypt between 610 and 595 BC. Under Necho II the Egyptians fought a series of wars to help the Neo-Assyrian Empire, and stop the rising power of the Neo-Babylonian Empire. Necho II also commissioned the first known circum-navigation of the African Continent, which left from a Red Sea port, and returned to the Nile after three years.

2nd Paralipomenon: Chapter 36

The people of the land took Joahaz the son of Josiah, and anointed him, and made him king over Jerusalem in the room of his father. Joahaz was twenty-three years old when he began to reign, and he reigned three months in Jerusalem. His mother's name was Amital, daughter of Jeremiah of Libnah. He did that which was evil in the sight of the Lord, according to all that his forefathers had done.

Pharaoh Necho II surrounded him in Deblatha in the land of Hama, that he might not reign in Jerusalem. The king brought him over to Egypt, and imposed a tribute on the land, a hundred talents of silver and a talent of gold. Pharaoh Necho II made Eliakim the son of Josiah king over Judah in the room of his father Josiah and changed his name to Jehoiakim. Pharaoh Necho II took his brother Joahaz and brought him into Egypt, and he died there, but he had given the silver and gold to Pharaoh. At that time the land began to be taxed to give the silver at the command of Pharaoh, and everyone as he could borrow the silver and the gold of the people of the land, to give to Pharaoh Necho II. Jehoiakim was twenty-five years old when he began to reign, and he reigned eleven years in Jerusalem. His mother's name was Zechora, daughter of Nerias of Ramah. He did that which was evil in the sight of the Lord, according to all that his forefathers did.

In his days came King Nebuchadnezzar II[1] of Babylon into the land and he served him three years, and then revolted from him. The Lord sent against them the Chaldeans, and plundering parties of Syrians, and plundering parties of the Moabites, and of the Ammonites, and of Samaria, but after this, they departed, according to the word of the Lord by the hand of his servants the prophets. Nevertheless, the anger of the Lord was on Judah so that they should be removed from his presence, because of the sins of Manasseh in all that he did, and for the innocent blood which Jehoiakim shed, for he had filled Jerusalem with innocent blood, yet the Lord would not completely destroy them.

King Nebuchadnezzar of Babylon came up against him, and bound him with bronze shackles, and carried him away to Babylon. He carried away a part of the vessels of the Temple of the Lord to Babylon and put them in his temple in Babylon. The rest of the acts of Jehoiakim, and all that he did, look, are not these things written in the book of the Chronicles of the Kings of Judah? Jehoiakim slept with his fathers and was buried with his fathers in Ganozae, and Jehoiachin his son reigned in his place.

Jehoiachin was eight years old when he began to reign, and he reigned three months and ten days in Jerusalem and did that which was evil in the sight of the

Lord. At the turn of the year, king Nebuchadnezzar II sent, and brought him to Babylon, with the precious vessels of the Temple of the Lord, and made Zedekiah his father's brother king over Judah and Jerusalem.

Zedekiah was twenty-one years old when he began to reign, and he reigned eleven years in Jerusalem. He did that which was evil in the sight of Lord the god, he was not ashamed before the prophet Jeremiah, nor because of the word of the Lord, in that he rebelled against King Nebuchadnezzar II, which he adjured him by god not to do, but he stiffened his neck and hardened his heart so as not to return to Lord the god in Israel. All the great men of Judah, and the priests, and the people of the land transgressed greatly in the abominations of the heathen and polluted the Temple of the Lord which was in Jerusalem.

The Lord the god of their fathers sent by the hand of his prophets, rising early and sending his messengers, for he spared his people, and his sanctuary. Nevertheless, they sneered at his messengers, and set at nothing his words, and mocked his prophets, until the anger of the Lord rose up against his people, till there was no remedy. He brought against them the king of the Chaldeans, and killed their young men with the sword in the house of his sanctuary, and did not spare Zedekiah, and had no mercy on their virgins, and they led away their old men, he delivered all things into their hands.

All the vessels of the Temple of God, the great and the small, and the treasures of the Temple of the Lord, and all the treasures of the king and the great men, he brought all to Babylon. He burnt the Temple of the Lord, and broke down the wall of Jerusalem, and burnt its palaces with fire, and completely destroyed every beautiful vessel. He carried away the remnant to Babylon, and they were servants to him and to his sons until the establishment of the kingdom of the Medes.

That the word of the Lord by the mouth of Jeremiah might be fulfilled, until the land should enjoy its sabbaths in resting and sabbath keeping all the days of its desolation, till the accomplishment of seventy years. In the first year of King Cyrus[2] of the Persians, after the fulfillment of the word of the Lord by the mouth of Jeremiah, the Lord stirred up the spirit of Cyrus king of the Persians, and told him to make proclamation in writing throughout all his kingdom, saying, "King Cyrus of the Persians says to all the kingdoms of the earth, Lord the god of the sky has given me power, and he has commanded me to build a temple to him in Jerusalem, in Judea. Who is there of you of all his people? His god will be with him, and let him return."

2nd Paralipomenon: Chapter 36 Notes

1 Codex Vaticanus: Nabouchodonosor
(ΝΑΒΟΥΧΟΔΟΝΟϹΟΡ)

- Aleppo Codex: Nbwkdnåṣr (**נבוכדנאצר**)

- Leningrad Codex: Nevuchadnetzar (נְבוּכַדְנָאצַּר)

- Targum of Chronicles: Nevuchadnetzar (נְבוּכַדְנֶאצַּר)

This is accepted as a reference to Nebuchadnezzar II, king of the Neo-Babylonian Empire between 605 and 562 BC. Nebuchadnezzar II was the son of Nabopolassar, an Assyrian official who rebelled against Assyria in 626 BC. Nebuchadnezzar II was the chief architect of the Neo-Babylonian Empire, who in 605 BC, after taking the throne, launched an invasion of Assyria and Syria with his Median allies, and defeated the Assyrians and Egyptians, and incorporated Syria and Phoenicia into his Empire.

2 Codex Vaticanus: Cyros (ΚΥΡΟϹ)

- Aleppo Codex: Kwrš (**כורש**)

- Leningrad Codex: Kovresh (כּוֹרֶשׁ)

- Targum of Chronicles: Kovresh (כּוֹרֶשׁ)

Cyrus II, also called Cyrus the Great, established the Achaemenid Dynasty, and the first Persian Empire. Between 559 and 530 he conquered an empire stretching from the Aegean Sea to the Indus River.

Septuagint Manuscripts

The following is a list of the Septuagint manuscripts referenced in the notes for this book.

LXX A (Codex Alexandrinus) is dated to the 5th century. It is currently located at the British Library (Royal 1 D. VIII) in London.

LXX B (Codex Vaticanus) is dated to the 4th century. It is currently located at the Vatican Library (Gr. 1209 in Vatican City.

Alternative Translations

The following is a list of alternative translations that were used for comparative analysis.

The Aleppo Codex is dated to circa 920 AD. For centuries it was housed at the Central Synagogue of Aleppo, from which its name is derived. It was the oldest known complete copy of the Hebrew scriptures used within Judaism until 1947, when it was seized and divided among Jewish families during anti-Jewish riots in Aleppo. The sections that have resurfaced are currently at the Israel Museum in Jerusalem. Approximately 40% is still missing.

The Leningrad Codex is dated to 1008 (or 1009 AD. It is currently located at the National Library of Russia (Firkovich B 19 A) in St. Petersburg. The Leningrad Codex is the oldest complete copy of the Hebrew scriptures used within Judaism.

Targum of Chronicles is ascribed to the Talmudic sage, Rabbi Joseph. Based on the Aramaic dialect, the targum was likely make in Babylonia, sometime between 350 and 1150 AD.

Also Available

Also Available

- Octateuch: The Original Orit

Enoch and Metatron Series:
- Books of Enoch Collection

- Books of Enoch and Metatron Collection

- Books of Metatron Collection

- Secrets of Enoch

Other Translations:
- Apocalypses of Ezra

- Arabic Maccabees

- Life of Adam and Eve

- Memories of the New Kingdom

- Septuagint's Esther and the Vetus Latina Esther

- Septuagint's Ezekiel and the Ba'al Cycle

- Septuagint's Job and the Testament of Job

- Septuagint's Proverbs and the Wisdom of Amenemope

- The Amarna Letters

- Testaments of the Patriarchs Collection

- Tobit and Ahikar

- Ugaritic Texts: Ba'al Cycle

- Wisdom of Ahikar